ART-CENTERED EDUCATION
AND THERAPY FOR
CHILDREN WITH DISABILITIES

ART-CENTERED EDUCATION AND THERAPY FOR CHILDREN WITH DISABILITIES

FRANCES E. ANDERSON, Ed.D., A.T.R., H.L.M.

Distinguished Professor of Art
Art Department
College of Fine Arts
Illinois State University

CHARLES C THOMAS • PUBLISHER
Springfield • Illinois • U.S.A.

Published and Distributed Throughout the World by

CHARLES C THOMAS • PUBLISHER
2600 South First Street
Springfield, Illinois 62794-9265

© *1994 by* CHARLES C THOMAS • PUBLISHER
ISBN 0-398-05896-2 (cloth)
ISBN 0-398-06006-1 (paper)
Library of Congress Catalog Card Number: 93-33203

With THOMAS BOOKS *careful attention is given to all details of manufacturing
and design. It is the Publisher's desire to present books that are satisfactory as to
their physical qualities and artistic possibilities and appropriate for their particular
use.* THOMAS BOOKS *will be true to those laws of quality that assure a good
name and good will.*

*Printed in the United States of America
SC-R-3*

Library of Congress Cataloging-in-Publication Data

Anderson, Frances E. (Frances Elisabeth), 1941–
    Art-centered education and therapy for children with disabilities
/ by Frances E. Anderson.
        p.   cm.
    Includes indexes.
    ISBN 0-398-05896-2.— ISBN 0-398-06006-1 (pbk.)
    1. Handicapped children—Education—United States—Art.   2. Art
therapy for children—United States.   3. Handicapped children—
Education—United States.   I. Title.
LC4025.A53   1994
371.9'0445—dc20   93-33203
                                                                          CIP

This book is dedicated to all past, present, and future members of the Dead Bug Society. May we always acknowledge God's Creative Spirit that is the foundation for our Inner Wonder Child and all artistic endeavors. (I Chronicles, xxix: 11–14)

F.E.A.
President, DBS!

FOREWORD

It is a pleasure to write the foreword to this excellent work by Dr. Frances Anderson. *Art-Centered Education and Therapy for Children with Disabilities* is an extremely well-written and comprehensive text that addresses the needs of regular education, special education, art teachers, and art therapists who will be working with exceptional children in the classroom. Throughout the text, Dr. Anderson presents a very compelling case that "Art is fundamental to the core of the curriculum of any school." Her work affirms that art clearly serves as both a conduit and stimulant for the social, physical, emotional, and academic growth of children.

In addition to her knowledge and expertise in art and children with disabilities, I was continually impressed with the underlying values and sensitivity that Dr. Anderson conveys toward the uniqueness of the exceptional child.

As one reflects on the educational philosophy that Dr. Anderson espouses in the text, one is reminded of the aphorism "All fruit do not ripen at the same time." The effective teacher does not hold an "absolute standard against which to judge a child's art work...." It is clear that Dr. Anderson views each child as an individual and as having unique adaptive needs. As she states, "... the concept of individualization is *crucial* in adapting art for a child with a specific disability."

The information presented was well researched and is rich with practical examples. Chapter Three provides many methods of adaptability in art, especially in the use of the computer. Chapter Four reaffirms the need for a comprehensive individualized assessment of the child, which includes a clear statement about the importance of art. Chapters Five through Nine provide a plethora of examples and strategies for integrating art into learning language arts, mathematics, reading, social studies, and science within the curriculum. Implicit in the strategies presented in the text is the strong belief that "Did Not does not equal Cannot." Teachers are provided with a wealth of practical techniques that enable them to effectively teach the exceptional child to learn and grow both academically and socially.

A cornerstone of the book can be found in the saying "Give me a fish, and I eat for a day. Teach me to fish, and I eat for a lifetime." Closely embroidered among the myriad of strategies and techniques is the fundamental belief of the author that it is crucial to teach skills and strategies that enable students to develop the competencies that result in self-sufficiency.

In this time of increased public scrutiny of the role that faculty research and scholarship plays in higher education, one is reassured by the work of Dr. Anderson. This text reaffirms one of the major benefits of scholarship. By translating theory into practice, Dr. Anderson has succeeded in weaving into a single fabric the abstract and the applied and does so with a clarity and force that will benefit many teachers and students. Classroom teachers will become more effective, and the educational experiences of the exceptional child will be greatly enriched as a result of her work.

Through her scholarly writings and pioneering efforts, Frances Anderson has made many significant contributions in the areas of art therapy and art education for exceptional children. *Art-Centered Education and Therapy for Children with Disabilities* is another example of an important addition to the fields of exceptionality and art made by this Distinguished Professor.

GREGORY F. ALOIA, PH.D.
Associate Vice President and Dean of Graduate Studies
Illinois State University

INTRODUCTION

Two years ago the second edition of *Art for All the Children: Approaches to Art Therapy for Children with Disabilities* was published. In the 14 years since the first edition of this book was published, the field of art for children with disabilities has mushroomed from less than a handful of books to over fifty. I found it impossible to do justice to this greatly expanded field with only one book. Therefore, I decided to develop two books: one for graduate students in art therapy and one for pre-service undergraduate art and special education teachers, and art therapy students. *Art-Centered Education and Therapy for Children with Disabilities* is the second of these two books.

If the trend in special education continues, there will be few if any self-contained classrooms for children with disabilities. This inclusion of all children into the regular education program will stretch the educational and moral resources of our teachers, and may work at odds with the very philosophy that is behind inclusion. This book has been written to help both the regular education, and art and special education teachers, both pre- and in-service, better understand some of the issues and realities of providing education and remediation to children with disabilities.

The book is also offered as a model of a concept that has governed my personal and professional career of over 30 years—the concept that we must live, learn and develop through art—that art belongs at the core of the public school curriculum. Additionally, I strongly feel that art offers one of the most powerful ways to grow and develop socially, physically and emotionally as well as academically. The power of art to heal, motivate, teach, and empower needs to be realized and utilized. I hope this book demonstrates art power and inspires many art therapists and teachers to try an art-centered approach.

The first chapter provides a brief overview of the main characteristics of the six major disabilities which adults are likely to encounter in children (and for which there are monies available for education and remediation via Public Law 101-476, the Individuals with Disabilities Education Act (1990), Public Law 101-336, the Americans with Disabilities Act (1990), and other related federal legislation).

The second chapter provides an overview of how all children develop in art, and Chapter 3 addresses ways art can be adapted for children with mental retardation, learning disabilities, behavioral disorders/emotional disturbance, physical disabilities, deafness and visual impairments. This information has been provided to help the art and special education teacher/consultant and art therapist plan art-centered educational and therapeutic experiences appropriate for all children—especially those with disabilities.

The next five chapters address art-centered approaches to reading, language arts, mathematics, science and social studies to demonstrate and illustrate the reality behind education through art.

The final chapter addresses issues related to health, safety, and quality of art materials, and how to obtain art supplies so that children can experience art-centered education and therapy.

ACKNOWLEDGMENTS

This book would not have been completed without the help of many persons. First, I would like to acknowledge and thank Dr. Lynne Raiser, Associate Professor of Special Education, University of North Florida, for her willingness to contribute a chapter on art and language arts.

Thanks also go to Dr. Richard A. Salome, Professor of Art, Illinois State University, for his critical review of Chapter 2 on children's art development. I also want to thank him for permitting me to include examples of children's artwork from his personal collection and his Children's Development in Art Checklist (1991) which appears in Chapter 2. He is a consummate researcher and scholar and I have enormous respect and appreciation for his work.

I wish to thank the following publishers and professional organizations for permitting the reprinting of materials: Davis Publications, Worcester, MA; The International Collection of Child Art, The University Museum, Illinois State University, and Dr. Barry E. Moore, Curator; The National Art Education Association, Reston, Virginia; and Charles C Thomas, Publisher, Springfield, Illinois.

Thanks are also due to Dr. Tom Anderson, Chairperson of the Art Education Department, The Florida State University, Tallahassee, for assistance in photographing artwork. I also want to credit Eileen Callan for some of her art adaptation ideas and illustrations which appear in Chapter 3. Victoria Foster and Robert Mechtly need to be acknowledged for their help in creating many of the illustrations in this book.

As someone with learning disabilities, I have needed special help in copy editing and want to acknowledge the excellent work of Susan Swartwout in this capacity. Roxann Moss was a patient and dedicated word processor and thanks also go to her.

I must also thank Dr. Lanny Morreau and Dr. Mack Bowen of the Department of Specialized Educational Development, Dr. Carol Thornton of the Mathematics Department, and Dr. Maria De Gammarino of the Music Department at Illinois State University for providing timely material, information and for being important sounding boards for my ideas.

This book could not have been complete without examples of artwork from children with disabilities. I want to thank the children and their parents who so willingly permitted me to include case material and artwork in this book. I especially wanted to thank the students from the Chattahoochee Publishing Company (Chattahoochee Elementary School, Chattahoochee Florida) for permitting me to include excerpts from their books in Chapter 5.

Finally, I wish to thank my friends who have become my family for their prayers, encouragement and support during the six years that I have labored on this book. Now it is time for rejoicing, and for the sea (Psalm 139: 9 and 10).

"If I take on wings and fly to the sea, there will Thy hand guide me."

F.E.A.

CONTENTS

ART-CENTERED EDUCATION
AND THERAPY FOR
CHILDREN WITH DISABILITIES

Chapter 1

A BRIEF DISCUSSION OF
CHILDREN WITH DISABILITIES

Children who have a disability are first of all CHILDREN. Describing these children as persons first and then as having a disability under-scores a focus on the person and not a focus on the disabling condition (Anderson, 1992). Throughout this book, therefore, handicapped, impaired, and mentally and physically challenged children will be described as children with a specific disability.

While Public Law (PL) 94-142 (1975) and PL 101-476 (the reauthorization of PL 94-142 passed in 1990) remain the major legislation affecting the education of children with disabilities (and mandating placements in the least restrictive environment), there has been a philosophical movement toward advocating the elimination of special educational placements in favor of complete integration of all children into regular education programs. This philosophy has been influenced by both the ecological, the normaliz-ing and the Regular Education Initiative (REI) approaches to educating children with disabilities. The ecological approach advocates viewing chil-dren with disabilities in terms of their *abilities* and how they interact with their subculture, their surroundings and the significant people in the imme-diate environment. In the ecological approach the child's education is achieved via a team of educators, therapists and counselors.

Normalization is governed by the principle that it is essential to set up and maintain the child and his behaviors so that they are as "culturally normative as possible" (Wolfensberger, 1979, p. 28; cited by Blandy, 1989, p. 7). Art activities in a normalizing context would be those that are as age appropriate as possible—that is, they would be the same ones normally used by nondisabled age-mates, and the art experiences would occur (as much as possible) in a typical regular education art class (Blandy, 1989).

In the late 1980s the Regular Education Initiative (REI) emerged. The REI has been an effort "to move beyond the narrow bounds of special education... and explore new and exciting alternatives for educating *all* students in our schools" (Lilly, 1988, p. 256). The REI encourages schools

---

Note: Some material in this chapter is based on Frances Anderson's *Art for All the Children: Approaches to Art Therapy for Children with Disabilities* (Springfield, IL: Charles C Thomas, Publisher, 1992), pp. 1-102.

and school districts to consider a re-examination and "restructuring of their services to all children including those with special needs" (Lilly, 1988, p. 256).

Out of the REI emerged the inclusion concept for the education of children with disabilities. Inclusion means that learners with disabilities attend their neighborhood/home school (the school that they would normally attend if they had no disabilities). Learners with disabilities are placed in regular classes and participate in the regular extracurricular events alongside their same-aged peers. In the inclusion approach educational support services are viewed as a process that occurs in the regular classroom. This process concept is in contrast to the way most support educational services have been provided, that is, they have been provided in a *specific place* (a segregated/self-contained special education classroom or resource room [Peters, n.d., p. 3]). In the inclusion approach, a child with disabilities is

> educated with supports and aids as necessary with his/her age appropriate peers who do not have disabilities. Inclusion is a belief that all children and youth have the same needs for acceptance, friendships and connectedness. It is a belief that we need one educational system for *all* students, that all students can benefit by inclusion in the general education classroom. (Peters, n.d., p. 2)

While *philosophically* in agreement with the basic tenets of these normalizing, ecological, REI, and inclusive approaches to working with children with disabilities, this author believes that there is a *reality principle* that must be considered. For example, how appropriate is it to include children with severe disabilities in regular education classes when there are already too many students in the class (i.e. 35 to 40) and the teacher has no support staff (and may have limited training to deal with children with severe disabilities)? Additionally, inclusion relies on consultants that provide support services to the children in the regular classroom. The issues of who will provide these consultants and who will fund them have not yet been clarified.

We are still legally bound by PL 94-142 and PL 101-476 which mandate *a continuum of support services.* Under the regulations of these laws the *least restrictive environment* (LRE) into which a child with disabilities will be placed may mean a special education class or resource room as well as a regular education classroom (Bruinicks & Larkin, 1985).

While there has been one recent report of successful inclusion in regular education art classrooms by seven art teachers (Guay, 1993), this issue warrants much more scrutiny. Until experience and research on a larger scale affirms the total feasibility of inclusive approaches (that include children with the most severe disabilities), and until the economy permits the kinds of consultants and support staff enabling all children, with or without disabilities, to be educated in the regular classroom, we must continue to be bound by the legal mandates of PL 94-142 and PL 101-476 and be committed to special placements when *they are most appropriate and indeed are the least restrictive environment.*

While some educators advocate interactions with children with disabilities *without* prior knowledge of the precise nature of those disabilities because this knowledge may cause "labeling" and "prejudging," this author strongly believes that educational decisions must be made with informed knowledge of the specific disability that a child may have. Some disabling conditions necessitate special interventions and special working conditions. This knowledge would be especially important in working with children with epilepsy, with allergies, with physical disabilities and with children who are on medication.

Keeping these issues in mind we begin with a brief overview of the characteristics of children with the following six categories of disabilities: children with mental retardation; children with learning disabilities; children with behavioral disorders and emotional disturbances; children with physical impairments; children with deafness and children with visual impairments. These six categories are covered because they are those identified by the Individuals with Disabilities Education Act (IDEA) of 1990 (PL 101-476) (which is the reauthorization of PL 94-142). Our brief discussion of the major categories of disabilities will be presented beginning with the most frequently occurring disabilities (mental retardation) and proceed to those children with the lowest incidence of disabilities (children with visual impairments). Implications for the art program and the teacher and/or art therapist are included in this discussion. A more detailed discussion of art adaptations may be found in Chapter 3. Also, Chapters 5, 6, 7, 8, and 9 are devoted to discussing how art can become a central means of educating across the rest of the school curriculum. As a part of the discussion of art activities, specific art adaptations are included to demonstrate that no matter what type of disability a child may have, art adaptations can be developed to insure that that child can partake of the art experience and be included as much as possible in the regular education program.

Prior to each listing of characteristics the legal definition from PL 101-476 of the disability will be included.

CHILDREN WITH MENTAL RETARDATION

Definition Issues

The regulations governing the IDEA PL 101-476, 1990 (formerly PL 94-142) state that the term "mentally retarded" is defined as "significantly subaverage general intellectual functioning existing concurrently with deficits in adaptive behavior and manifested during the developmental period, which adversely affects a child's educational performance" (IDEA, Reg. 300.7 *Federal Register 57* (189) September 29, 1992, p. 44801).

The following intelligence test scores are one means of describing degrees of mental retardation: Mild, 50–55 to 70; Moderate, 35–40 to 50–55; Severe, 20–25 to 35–40; and Profound, below 20–25. Social adaptability should be considered in determining intelligence.

In 1992, the American Association of Mental Retardation redefined mental retardation as referring to:

> substantial limitations in present functioning. It is characterized by significantly subaverage intellectual functioning, existing concurrently with related limitations in two or more of the following applicable adaptive skill areas: communication, self-care, home living, social skills, community use, self-direction, health and safety, functional academics, leisure and work. Mental retardation manifests before age 18. (*AAMR*, 1992, p. iii)

This definition includes a focus on adaptive skills and is based on the following four assumptions:

1. an appraisal that includes differences in linguistic, cultural, behavioral and communication factors,
2. adaptability is related to the environmental and community context of the individual's age-mates and the individual's specific support needs,
3. there are both limitations and strengths in an individual's adaptabilities and capabilities, and
4. there will be an improved ability to function with additional appropriate support over a prolonged period.

The AAMR's definition includes diagnosis, classification and types of support. First, mental retardation is diagnosed to indicate the person's qualifying for support services. Second, the person's strengths and weakness and necessity for support are appraised in the following areas: emotional, psychological, and physical health. This assessment includes these areas: communication, self-care, home living, social skills, community use, self-direction, health and safety, functional academics, leisure, work, emotional and psychological, and environmental (living, working and educational areas) (*AAMR*, 1992).

Characteristics of Children with Mental Retardation

Children With Mild Mental Retardation (Intelligence test scores ranging from 50–55 to 70)

- A lessened learning ability shows up in memory, language, attention span and academics
- Harder to focus on tasks (thus it takes more energy to focus, leaving less energy for other tasks such as attention to minutia; limited ability to block out irrelevant stimuli while focusing on a task)
- Lacks the learning methods others use such as grouping items to recall numbers, etc., and lacks the ability to rehearse. The learning modes used by these children are not automatic (as with most normal children)
- Low self-concept
- Cannot select, self-monitor, and evaluate the way he chooses to try to solve a learning task
- Development is at one-half to three-fourths the rate of average children (it takes almost twice as many repetitions for a child with mild mental retardation to learn something as it does for normal children [25 to 30 versus 17])
- Schooling may go only as far as the second to the sixth grade
- Difficulty abstracting and generalizing, so he needs to be taught everything directly
- Does not learn incidentally
- Often does not carry-over information from one situation to another
- Behavior problems
- Is disruptive
- Predisposed to fail
- Often does not choose to engage in challenging tasks
- Lacks persistence and perseverance
- Short attention span
- Lower tolerance for frustration
- Poor social interactions due to delayed language development (social skills have to be specifically taught)
- Stutters
- Poor articulation in language, and language skills are below the mental age of the child

Art Implications

- Choose activities that have a high success factor.
- Provide frequent feedback.
- Provide for continuous reinforcement and encouragement.

- Repeat vocabulary and skills through the same/several art lessons.
- Sequence art experiences to move from simpler to more and more difficult tasks and concepts, and include repetition.
- Team with classroom teachers and focus on the same key concepts via integrating them with art experiences.
- Recognize that art can help develop/reinforce motor skills, language development, perceptual training and social skills.
- Be prepared to use task analysis and cognitive behavior modification methodologies. (These are the major approaches used by special educators.) (Anderson, 1978, 1992)

Children with Moderate Mental Retardation (Intelligence test scores 35–40 to 50–55)

- Develops at one-half to one-fourth the rate of the average child
- Most develop a final mental age that ranges between three to seven years
- Cannot read but may recognize key words
- Can count up to 10
- Can write numbers
- May tell time, remember some phone numbers
- May understand money concepts
- Has delayed and poor motor skills
- Lacks general coordination
- Lacks social adaptability
- Tends to be impulsive
- Tends to emotionally regress when confronted with stressful situation
- May have fewer life experiences than average children

Art Implications

- Use limited palette to reduce the frustration of being confronted with too many choices.
- Focus the program on basic art skills. (Specifically teach basic cutting, pasting, painting skills, etc.)
- Focus on sensory awareness and manipulation of art tools and media.
- Consider simple activities that include repetition of words, artistic process and ideas.
- Incorporate vocabulary throughout art experiences to help build language skills.
- Be prepared to use task analysis and cognitive behavior modification methodologies. (These are the major approaches used by special educators.) (Anderson, 1978, 1992)

Children with Severe and Profound Mental Retardation (Intelligence test scores: Severe, 20-25 to 35-40; Profound, below 20-25)

- May not develop beyond the Scribbling stage of artistic development (some do move into Preschematic stage)
- Have delayed language
- Have problems with fine and gross motor skills
- Exhibit passivity

(These children have many of the traits described under moderate mental retardation—only in a larger degree.)

Art Implications

- Focus on gross motor development before fine motor.
- Help build social skills.
- Utilize task analysis to teach art skills (may have to focus on teaching the child to hold and use paintbrushes, pencils and scissors).
- Behavior modification and token economies may need to be used by the teacher and art therapist.
- Age-appropriate activities are needed (teacher and art therapist need to consider both mental age and chronological age in planning art experiences).
- Some of the activities in the art program may just be manipulating media for kinesthetic pleasure and emotional release (Shectman, 1992).
- Color and shape drills may be needed to help with identification of shapes.
- A multisensory approach will be most effective.
- Maintain consistency in art sessions (same routine, putting on smocks, listening to adult, working period, clean up, sharing of what was created).
- Be prepared to use task analysis and cognitive behavior modification methodologies. (These are the major approaches used by special educators.) (Anderson, 1978, 1992)

CHILDREN WITH LEARNING DISABILITIES

Definition Issues

The federal definition under the regulations governing PL 101-476, (1990) (the IDEA) states:

"Specific learning disability" means a disorder in one or more of the basic psychological processes involved in understanding or in using language, spoken or written, which may manifest itself in an imperfect ability to listen, think, speak, read, write, spell, or to do mathematical calculations. Such disorders include such conditions as perceptual disabilities, brain injury, minimal brain dysfunction, dyslexia, and developmental aphasia. Such term does not include children who have learning problems which are primarily the result of visual, hearing, or motor disabilities, of mental retardation, of emotional disturbance, or of environmental, cultural, or economic disadvantage (Public Law 101-476, Individuals with Disabilities Education Act, 20 U.S.C. Chapter 33 section 1401, 15, October 30, 1990).

Characteristics of Children with Learning Disabilities

Most Often Cited Characteristics

According to a review of the literature by Hallahan and Kaufman (1989) the most frequently cited characteristics are:

1. hyperactivity
2. perceptual motor skills
3. emotional liability (frequent shifts in emotional mood)
4. disorders of attention (short attention span, distractibility)
5. perseveration
6. disorders of memory and thinking
7. specific academic problems in reading, arithmetic, writing and spelling
8. disorders of speech and hearing
9. equivocal neurological signs
10. electroencephalographic irregularity (Hallahan & Kaufman, 1989, p. 113)

Other Characteristics

• Fine and gross motor skills problems
• Perceptual problems
• Problems interpreting and organizing visual stimuli
• Problems with attention and hyperactivity
• Problems with ability to problem solve
• Problems with ability to conceptualize
• Problems with social skills
• Negative self-concept related to inability to do academic tasks
• Problems with communicating feelings and thoughts
• Problems with motivation (most children tend to be passive)
• A tendency to have an overall attitude of learned helplessness
• A tendency to give up on challenges and tasks too quickly
• Problems with solving story mathematical problems
• Problems with using correct problem-solving methods

Adaptations and Suggestions for Teachers and Art Therapists
Who Work with Children with Learning Disabilities

- Apply self-instruction, self-monitoring and reciprocal teaching. (Self-instruction is modeled by an adult. First one talks out loud and the child repeats this same behavior. Next the child repeats, but whispers. Next he talks to himself. The child self-monitors to check if he is staying on task.)
- Incorporate token economies.
- Utilize direct instruction. (Focus on the material to be taught, not on the learning problem of the child.)
- Incorporate microcomputers.
- Use game strategies.
- Use structured approaches for hyperactivity.
- Incorporate movement in the art experience.
- Reduce extraneous stimuli in the art room.
- Match tasks to the learning level of the child.
- Clearly state directions.
- Check for understanding by having the child tell you in different words what he is supposed to do.
- Put the easily distractible child in low stimulus areas (carrels).
- Poor motor skills may require extra adult help.
- Art helps with perceptual learning in providing practice seeing gestalts and part-whole relationships.
- Art helps with visualization.
- Art enables multisensory approaches. (Anderson, 1978, 1992)

CHILDREN WITH BEHAVIORAL DISORDERS/
EMOTIONAL DISTURBANCE

Definition Issues

There are several ways that this disability has been described and defined. This lack of agreement is due to the varied treatment approaches utilized and to the lack of agreement as to the causes of behavioral disorders and emotional disturbance. To further complicate the situation, there is a lack of an economical, precise and easy-to-use means of assessing children who have behavior problems. Finally sociocultural and environmental factors have different impacts on children.

Given these complications, the definition included in the regulations governing PL 101-476 (the 1990 reauthorization of PL 94-142) will be our guideline.

(i) The term ("Seriously emotionally disturbed") means a condition exhibiting one or more of the following characteristics over a long period of time and to a marked degree which adversely affects a child's educational performance—

(A) An inability to learn which cannot be explained by intellectual, sensory, or health factors;

(B) An inability to build or maintain satisfactory interpersonal relationships with peers and teachers;

(C) Inappropriate types of behavior or feelings under normal circumstances;

(D) A general pervasive mood of unhappiness or depression; or

(E) A tendency to develop physical symptoms or fears associated with personal or school problems.

(ii) The term includes schizophrenia. The term does not apply to children who are socially maladjusted unless it is determined that there is an emotional disturbance. (*Federal Register 57*(189), September 29, 1992, p. 44802)

In the 1990 IDEA the term "autism" was removed and is now considered a separate category of disability. However, we will include its definition later in this segment.

Characteristics of Children with Behavioral Disorders/Emotional Disturbance

Four Clusters of Problem Behaviors

1. Conduct Disorders

- problems with authority figures
- mistrustful of others
- selfish
- tough
- impulsive
- antisocial

2. Anxious/Withdrawn

- inferiority complex
- self-conscious
- anxious
- depressed
- sad
- dependent
- sensitive, excessively shy, and timid
- highly controlled feelings and other behaviors
- inflexible
- rigid
- lack spontaneity

- have learned helplessness/victim stance
- low self-esteem contributes to poor academic performance and poor interpersonal skills/relationships
- stressful home environs, lack of warmth in the family (these combine and may result in a tendency to be self-destructive)

3. Immature

- clumsy
- passive
- short attention span
- slow
- lacking interest in school
- relate to children younger than they are
- some of their behaviors are similar to children with autism

4. Socially Aggressive

- active in gangs
- aggressive
- belligerent
- frequently exhibit destructive and lawbreaking behaviors

Other Issues

Subcultures influence a child's behavior especially when the subculture of his family differs with the values and culture of school and the community. Behaviors can interfere with one's ability to fit into the rules and mores expected at school. Some students' behaviors are censured by classmates and result in isolation for the child with the behavior problems.

Adaptations include the need to specifically teach social skills, teach children to think before acting on impulses, and role-playing to develop empathy for others' reactions.

Children who are immature and anxious/withdrawn have internalizing characteristics. Children who have conduct disorders and are socially aggressive are characterized as having externalizing traits.

Children with Severe and Profound Emotional Disturbance

Schizophrenia

- Loss of connection with the real world
- Bizarre thinking processes; many, many inappropriate behaviors
- Appears after the child is five years of age and older—usually during adolescence

Autism*

Autism has been defined in the regulations governing PL 101-476 as:

... a developmental disability significantly affecting verbal and nonverbal communication and social interaction, generally evident before age 3, that adversely affects a child's educational performance. Other characteristics often associated with autism are engagement in repetitive activities and stereotyped movements, resistance to environmental change or change in daily routines, and unusual responses to sensory experiences. The term does not apply if a child's educational performance is adversely affected primarily because the child has a serious emotional disturbance, as defined in paragraph (b) (9) of this section (see definition of "seriously emotionally disturbed"). (*Federal Register* 57 (189), Tuesday, September 29, 1992, p. 44802)

- These children are profoundly socially withdrawn, have language problems, self-stimulatory behaviors and thinking disorders. All these problems appear before two and one-half years of age.
- All children with autism and/or childhood schizophrenia lack basic self-help skills (feeding, toileting, dressing).
- These children may seem deaf/blind because they appear to be totally unaware of what is happening around them (do not respond to sounds or lights in a typical way).
- They cannot be tested in normal ways . . . some are idiot savants.
- Some may not be able to talk and seem not to understand spoken words.
- Some parrot what others say (echolalia).
- Others speak in a gibberish.
- These children cannot express or receive physical affection.
- Other people including significant others are treated more like objects and not real persons.
- Self-stimulating behaviors include sucking the thumb, beating or banging the head, patting part of the body and twirling objects.
- Some hit and scratch themselves and may have to be put into restraints (more self-destructive than self-stimulating).
- These children show a lot of aggression and have severe temper tantrums.
- About half of those who receive intensive treatment of over 40 hours a week prior to reaching age three and one-half may recover completely.
- Children who are not treated before three and one-half will likely become psychotic adults.

---

*Note: "Autism" is now a separate category in the IDEA 1990 legislation but will be discussed here along with schizophrenia.

Adaptations and Suggestions for Teachers and Art Therapists Who Work With Children with Behavioral Disorders/Emotional Disturbance

Educational Considerations

- Behavior modification for children with severe and profound emotional disturbance at a very intense and individual level is necessary for educational programming.
- For children with moderate and mild behavioral disorders/emotional disturbance, the educational focus is on developing communication skills and social skills. These skills need to be specifically taught.
- Educational programs for children with moderate and mild behavioral disorders/emotional disorders must focus on specifically teaching basic academic skills.

Art Implications

- Be consistent with classroom management (discipline) in terms of the approaches used in the rest of the school program.
- Praise/encourage desirable/appropriate behaviors.
- Withhold rewards or ignore undesirable behaviors.
- Set realistic expectations.
- Explain appropriate behaviors and what happens when behaviors are inappropriate.
- Have a consistent routine (set up, explain art experiences, working time, sharing, closure and cleanup).
- Provide choices as often as possible (even very small choices such as where child wants to sit, what size brush he wants to use).
- Set limits before any art is begun so that it is clear which are appropriate behaviors and which are not.
- Avoid rewarding negative behaviors.
- Keep in mind the low frustration tolerance of the child (plan high success experiences and experiences that are not very long timewise).
- Keep in mind the short attention span of the child and plan art accordingly. Plan for a second, third, and fourth backup art experience.
- Consider group projects and work (but carefully choose which child goes in what group).
- Encourage cooperation and sharing. (Anderson, 1978, 1992)

CHILDREN WITH PHYSICAL DISABILITIES

Definition Issues

Children with physical disabilities are a large heterogeneous group who have physical problems (excluding primary visual or auditory disabilities) that interfere with learning or participation in regular school classes and whose disabilities require special equipment, training, or materials. Because of the medical and health problems of these children, a team approach is used that includes medical personnel and special educators (Hallahan & Kauffman, 1988).

Again we turn to the *Federal Register* for the legal definition of physical disabilities and health impairments.

> "Orthopedically Impaired" means a severe orthopedic impairment that adversely affects a child's educational performance. The term includes impairments caused by congenital anomaly (e.g., clubfoot, absence of some member, etc.), impairments caused by disease (e.g., poliomyelitis, bone tuberculosis, etc.), and impairments from other causes (e.g., cerebral palsy, amputations, and fractures or burns which cause contractures). (*Federal Register, 57* September 29, 1992, p. 44802)

In the general category of physical disabilities we will also include the *Federal Register* definition of "other health impaired."

> Limited strength, vitality or alertness, due to chronic or acute health problems such as a heart condition, tuberculosis, rheumatic fever, nephritis, asthma, sickle cell anemia, hemophilia, epilepsy, lead poisoning, leukemia, or diabetes that adversely affects a child's educational performance. (*Federal Register, 57*(189) September 29, 1992, p. 44802)

The term "traumatic brain injury" has been made a separate disability category in the IDEA of 1990 (PL 101–476) and it is defined as:

> . . . an acquired injury to the brain caused by an external physical force, resulting in total or partial functional disability or psychosocial impairment, or both that adversely affects a child's educational performance. The term applies to open or closed head injuries resulting in impairments in one or more areas, such as cognition; language; memory; attention; reasoning; abstract thinking; judgment; problem-solving; sensory, perceptual and motor abilities; psychosocial behavior; physical functions; information processing; and speech. The term does not apply to brain injuries that are congenital or degenerative, or brain injuries induced by birth trauma. (*Federal Register, 57*(189) September 29, 1992, p. 44802)

Characteristics of Children with Physical Disabilities

Five Major Groupings

1. Children with Neurological Impairments

- Children with brain damage
- Problems with learning

- Problems with speech and language
- Problems with motor coordination
- Attention deficits
- Paralysis
- Seizures
- Emotional problems

a) Cerebral Palsy

- Muscles that are stiff and tense
- Inaccurate voluntary movement
- Involuntary movements
- Floppy muscle tone
- Rigid muscles
- Spasticity in arms, and leg rigidity (or vice versa)
- Some may also have hearing, visual, perceptual speech and mental processing impairments
- Drooling
- Facial contortions
- Generally below average intelligence scores

b) Seizure Disorders

- May be generalized or partial
- May occur every few seconds or once a year
- May be only a small twitch in the face or major convulsions

c) Epilepsy

- About half have average intelligence
- Those who are not mentally retarded have above-normal number of learning problems, as well as behavior and emotional problems

d) Spina Bifida

- Paralysis or loss of sensation and/or function below the spinal defect site
- Lack of bladder control
- Lack of bowel control

e) Multiple Sclerosis

- Appears in adolescence and adulthood
- Muscle weakness
- Vision problems
- Speech problems
- Emotional problems

- Walking problems
- Weak muscles
- Spastic movements

2. Children with Musculoskeletal Conditions

Included in this grouping are children with burns, amputations, muscle disease (arthritis, muscular dystrophy and scoliosis).

- Mobility problems
- Problems with motor control that also cause problems with standing, sitting, walking and with fine motor (hand) use
- Problems accepting disability
- Physical appearance causes acceptance problems of child's condition as well as the acceptance of other people (rejection and shame factors)
- Lack of family acceptance and support

a) Muscular Dystrophy

Duchenne Form

- Muscle fibers become weaker and weaker (muscles replaced by fat tissue. Only males have Duchenne form. They rarely live beyond childhood.)
- Verbal abilities are below average

Dejerine Form

- Onset in adolescence. Males and females can contract the disease. Muscle weakness is in upper body (arms, shoulders and face)
- Disease moves at a slower rate and many children live a normal life span

b) Arthritis

- Range from mild to major joint swelling and deformed joints
- Many movements are painful or impossible

c) Other Musculoskeletal Conditions (Legg-Calve-Perthes, osteogenesis imperfecta, scoliosis, clubfoot, arthogyposis)

Osteogenesis imperfecta

- Spontaneous bone breakage
- Frequent school absences

Arthogyposis

- Small or missing muscles in limbs
- Weakened muscles in limbs

3. Children with Congenital Malformations

- Defects of heart and lungs and extremities
- Fetal alcohol syndrome, crack babies, tertogen drug use

   Characteristics

   - Hyperactivity
   - Brain damage
   - Retardation
   - Lack of limbs
   - Web feet
   - Head and facial defects/facial deformities
   - Mental disabilities
   - Speech disabilities
   - Auditory disabilities
   - Visual disabilities

4. Children with Disabilities Caused by Accidents and Other Physical Conditions

a) Accidents

   - Poisoning, auto/vehicle accidents, burns, falls

b) Other Physical Conditions (AIDS, allergies, cancer, hemophilia, rheumatic fever, sickle cell anemia, kidney diseases, cystic fibrosis, asthma)

   - Problems with mobility
   - Require more time to complete tasks
   - Tire easily
   - Have breathing problems
   - May be especially sensitive to chemicals and types of art materials
   - Need frequent rest
   - May have emotional problems due to physical appearance or peer isolation/rejection (as in AIDS)

AIDS may require isolation if child is aggressive (bites and/or scratches uncontrollably). Drooling may require special attention.

5. Children who are Neglected and/or Abused

Physical disabilities can be the result of neglect, physical abuse and sexual abuse. Children with physical disabilities are at greater risk for neglect and other forms of abuse from their family members. Medical neglect and physical neglect can result in brain damage, emotional trauma, internal injuries, deformed skeletons and faces, and sensory impairments.

These children may have many unmet emotional and physical needs, may need lots of emotional nurturance, positive attention, many success experiences, opportunities to feel and be independent, and many opportunities to feel accepted.

Adaptations and Suggestions for Teachers and Art Therapists Who Work with Children with Physical Disabilities

Psychological Issues

- Need acceptance
- Need many life-broadening experiences
- Need to be free to succeed
- Need to be free to fail
- Need to feel safe and not self-conscious
- Tend to be shy, introverted
- Need help in accepting physical limitations
- May regress when frustrated
- May show frustration with aggressive verbal behaviors
- May need help in setting realistic goals
- Need help in building positive self-concepts
- May be infantile
- May be dependent
- Degree of family acceptance is directly related to degree of self-acceptance of child of his disability

Educational Considerations

- Normalize school experience.
- Assist with mobility.
- Plan activities that are short term. (Frequent school absences may prevent completion of many activities that are long term [more than a few days in duration]).
- Provide for instruction in home or hospital setting.
- Encourage child to make use of remaining abilities whenever possible.
- Provide as many real-life experiences as possible to counter limited ones that child may have had.
- Provide many field trips.
- Encourage the child to work with instructional team (physical therapists, speech pathologists and other medical personnel).
- Some children with physical disabilities have shorter lifespans. (Teachers and other staff need to be personally prepared for this, and the staff need to help classmates deal with this issue.)

- School staff need to know how to lift and move children with physical disabilities.
- The child should do as much of his own work as possible.
- The child needs to build mastery in as many areas (art and other areas) as possible.
- The child may need speech remediation.

Art Implications

- Use computer-assisted art to perform fine motor skills.
- Empower child through successful art experiences.
- Provide opportunities for lots of practice/work on gross motor functions (painting, tearing, pounding clay, etc.).
- Select art experiences that fully utilize child's existing fine motor skills.
- Consider the child as the best source of ways to adapt his art tools, activities and work spaces.
- Carefully select appropriate art experiences that will empower child, not frustrate him.
- Use spill-proof paint and water containers in work areas.
- Securely tape paint and drawing papers to tables or easels.
- Thicken handles of art tools if necessary.
- Adapt feet, mouth or helmet pointers to hold art tools.
- Avoid art experiences that require pounding or sharp edges if child has limited fine motor control or strength, or if child is a hemophiliac or has osteogenesis imperfecta.
- Plan art experiences that can be completed in one or two periods so that children who are absent often can have a sense of completion about their artwork. (Anderson, 1978, 1992)

Note: Be cautious with art media and check on health and safety hazards of chemicals that are in art materials.

CHILDREN WHO ARE DEAF OR HARD-OF-HEARING

Definition Issues

In the provisions of the IDEA (PL 101–476, 1990, which is the reauthorization bill for PL 94–142) there are two categories listed under the definitions of children with hearing impairments. These two categories are deafness and hard-of-hearing.

"Deafness" means a hearing impairment that is so severe that the child is disabled in processing linguistic information through hearing, with or without amplification, that adversely affects a child's educational performance.

"Hearing impairment" means an impairment in hearing, whether permanent or fluctuating, that adversely affects a child's educational performance but that is not included under the definition of "deafness" in this section. (*Federal Register, 57,* September 29, 1992, p. 44801)

Recent developments among communities of persons with hearing impairments have resulted in a special awareness and pride. Those persons who have hearing impairments now prefer to be referred to as persons who are deaf or hard-of-hearing.

Characteristics of Children Who Are Deaf or Hard-of-Hearing

- Socially isolated
- Limited language ability and communication adds to isolation
- If family has accepted the deafness of the child, then that child is more accepting of the disability
- Often families will ignore the child who is deaf if he is the only one with this disability
- Children tend to stay in the close-knit deaf community
- Lack socialization skills such as ability to use small talk, to give and receive compliments, or to accept and give criticism
- May lack many ordinary growing-up experiences
- Tend to understand concrete ideas, concepts, but have difficulty dealing with abstractions
- Usually have the full range of intellectual functions that other children have, but the language barrier seriously impairs academic performance (third grade reading level is average for most persons who are deaf)
- Generally are better at math and spelling than reading
- Have art abilities typical of nonimpaired age-mates
- Have heightened visual awareness—especially peripheral vision
- Tend to learn by using models (copying)
- Need constant language practice/reinforcement
- Need opportunities to interact with non-deaf peers

Adaptations and Suggestions for Teachers and Art Therapists Who Work with Children Who Are Deaf or Hard-of-Hearing

- Seat child about six feet from the adult.
- Severely limit or eliminate environmental noise.
- Be aware that visual stimuli can be distracting.

- Be aware that adults need to talk slowly.
- Use gestures, facial expressions, visual aids and actual demonstrations.
- Always speak facing the child who is deaf.
- Be sensitive to the "self-conscious" issues in asking children who are deaf to answer questions and recite in front of the class or group.
- Repeat information using different words. (Some words can be easier to speechread than others.)
- Write out questions and/or instructions that are given to students. (It may be easier for children who are deaf to respond to information that is both spoken and written out.)
- Use only partially completed art examples to prevent exact copying.
- Provide many examples of concepts covered.
- Use every art experience as a potential means to reinforce vocabulary or to learn new words.
- Combine art with drama activities.
- Use more three-dimensional art media. (There is some evidence that three-dimensional media are preferred over two-dimensional art media.)
- Use round tables.
- Wait to ask questions/discuss work until the child is finished. (Anderson, 1978, 1992)

CHILDREN WITH VISUAL IMPAIRMENTS

Definition Issues

Special education and special adaptations will be needed for the one out of every thousand school children who have visual impairments. Visual impairments are generally defined in three ways: legally, educationally, and in terms of the federal regulations governing PL 101–476, the IDEA of 1990.

This legal definition is the one used to determine if someone can qualify for special benefits.

> ...a legally blind person has visual acuity of 20/200 or less in the eye that is better even when glasses are used. Additionally the term *legally blind* is used when a person has a narrow field of vision that is not greater than 20 degrees. (This is a sort of tunnel vision.) Those persons whose vision in the better eye with correction is between 20/70 and 20/200 are termed partially blind or partially sighted. (Anderson, 1992, p. 78)

A person who has to rely on Braille or aural reading methods is considered educationally blind. Those students who can read only using magnification or must rely on large-print books are also considered educationally blind.

The federal definition under the regulations of the IDEA states that

"Visual impairment" means a visual impairment that, even with correction, adversely affects a child's educational performance. This term includes both partial sight and blindness. (*Federal Register 57*(189), September 1992, p. 44802)

Characteristics of Children with Visual Impairments

- Language development is similar to that of sighted peers
- Intellectual performance is similar to that of sighted peers
- Conceptual ability is somewhat less developed than that of sighted peers
- Abstract thinking is also somewhat less developed than that of sighted peers (especially true for those blind from birth)
- Spatial concepts are the hardest for children who are blind to understand (most can only do this by their tactile and kinesthetic senses; analogy and extrapolation must be used to communicate many concepts)
- Lack integrative function that sight provides in understanding objects in the world: must use synthetic touch (direct tactile experience with objects small enough to hold) and analytic touch (direct tactile experiences with only parts of objects). Is done linearly, not simultaneously (as with our sighted perceptual gestalts)
- Are able to focus on tasks with ease
- Have highly developed listening abilities
- Academic achievement is not affected by visual impairments
- Mobility is a major concern/potential problem
- Lack visual feedback to help learn social skills (nonverbal gestures, expressions)
- May rock, rub the eyes (tends to put off sighted people)

Adaptations and Suggestions for Teachers and Art Therapists Who Work with Children with Visual Impairments

- Methods will be similar to those used with sighted peers.
- Available sight needs to be maximized.
- Listening skills need to be taught specifically.
- Auditory learning is much more efficient than using Braille and large print to get information.
- Mobility needs to be maximized in the child in order to build independence.
  Hands-on learning is essential.

- Provide more time for grasping information and learning concepts.
- Permit whenever possible the use of other senses for learning.
- Expectations should be similar to those of sighted peers.
- Maximize light in the classroom.
- Seat the child near the front, close to chalkboards, etc.
- Provide frequent rest periods.
- Allow 1½ times as long as sighted peers for task completion.
- Individualize art experiences.
- Textured and three-dimensional media will be the art media of choice.
- Rely on all senses to explain art.
- Have consistent setups for work areas.
- Have consistent storage areas for art media.
- Provide orientation points.
- Use a drawing screen.
- Use scented markers and paint colors.
- Use completed examples of art activities to convey concepts. (Anderson, 1978, 1992)

REFERENCES

American Association on Mental Retardation. (1992). *Mental Retardation: Definition, classification, systems of supports: Workbook.* Washington, DC: AAMR.

Anderson, F. E. (1992). *Art for all the children: Approaches to art therapy for children with disabilities.* Springfield, IL: Charles C Thomas.

Anderson, F. E. (1978). *Art for all the children: A creative sourcebook for the impaired child.* Springfield, IL: Charles C Thomas.

Blandy, D. (1989). Ecological and normalizing approaches to disabled students and art education. *Art Education, 42*(3), 7–11.

Bruininks, R. H., & Lakin, C. H. (Eds.). (1985). *Living and learning in the least restrictive environment.* Baltimore: Brooks.

Council for Exceptional Children. (1976). Official action of the delegate assembly. Reston, VA: Author.

Federal Register, 57(189) September 29, 1992.

Guay, D. M. P. (1993). Cross-site analysis of teaching practices: Visual art education with students experiencing disabilities. *Studies in Art Education, 34*(4), 222–232.

Hallahan, D. P., & Kauffman, J. M. (1988). *Exceptional children: Introduction to special education.* Englewood Cliffs, NJ: Prentice-Hall.

Lilly, M. S. (1988). The regular education initiative: A force for change in general and special education. *Education and Training in Mental Retardation, 26*(12), 253–260.

Minnesota Inclusive Education Technical Assistance Program. (n.d.). *Inclusive school communities.* Minneapolis, MN: University of Minnesota.

Peters, B. (n.d.). Definitions of mainstreaming, integration and inclusion. Unpublished manuscript.

Public Law 94–142, 1975. The education for all children act.

Public Law 101–476, 1990. The individuals with disabilities education act.

Shectman, A. E. (Ed.). (1992). *Insights: Art in special education. Educating the handicapped through art.* Trenton, NJ: Art Educators of New Jersey.

Chapter 2

HOW CHILDREN DEVELOP IN ART

A review of the research on children's artistic development indicates general agreement that children begin to explore visual art media by first making random marks or scribbles with a drawing tool on a piece of paper or any available surfaces such as walls, floors, etc. Scribbling is followed by a Schematic phase which merges with a Transitional period characterized by increasingly realistic artwork (Lowenfeld & Brittain, 1987; McFee, 1970; Salome & Moore, 1979a, 1979b; Salome, 1991, 1993).

Research on children's stages of artistic development (McFee, 1970; Salome & Moore, 1979a, 1976b; Salome, 1991, 1993) suggests that children's art development is on a continuum and that movement from one stage of development to another is as much a function of culture, environment, and schooling as it is a function of maturation. Table 2.8 illustrates how these scholars have charted children's artistic development (McFee, 1970; Salome & Moore, 1979a, 1976b; Salome, 1991, 1993).

It is important to be aware of children's development in art because this knowledge will greatly facilitate the planning of appropriate art experiences. One should also be aware of the child's mental and chronological age, fine motor strengths (and weaknesses) and have some information about the subculture within which the child lives.

Children's drawings may reflect a number of circumstances including emotional state, perceptual or learning problems, as well as chronological age and physical limitations. Some generalization can be made about the ages at which children begin to scribble, draw representative symbols or a baseline and skyline. Thus, a child who is in the first or second grade who continues to scribble may be doing so for a number of reasons. If the child does not move to drawing schemata for persons or other objects, it may suggest several problems including mental retardation, physical abuse, sexual abuse, and/or perceptual or learning problems (Anderson, 1992).

SCRIBBLING STAGE

Lowenfeld (1987)	McFee (1970)	Salome/Moore (1979)
18 mos to 4 yrs	2 yrs to 7 yrs	2 yrs to 4 yrs

26

At about two years of age the child develops the eye/hand coordination necessary to pick up a drawing instrument and make a mark on a page. These initial marks are made at random and will be relatively disordered sweeps across the paper. These random scribbles are records of kinesthetic actions which may be pleasurable to the child. The child does not make the connection between the marks on the page, her moving the drawing tool across the page, and objects in the environs.

Next the child will begin to exercise some control over these marks. This controlled-scribble substage occurs typically six months after the child first makes random marks on a page (Lowenfeld & Brittain, 1987). Now the child realizes that there is a connection between these scribbles and the moves she makes with the drawing tool in her hand.

At around three and one-half years, the child begins to give names to her scribbles. The marks still look just like any controlled scribbles — but the child has begun to think symbolically and identifies these marks with names.

PRESCHEMATIC STAGE

Lowenfeld	McFee	Salome & Moore
4 yrs to 7 yrs	(combines with Schematic stage), 3.5 yrs to adult	4 yrs to 7 yrs

A graphic symbol for a human begins to develop. This early graphic symbol is usually a circular shape with straight lines coming out of it to symbolize legs/feet or arms, depending on where these lines are placed.

Then at around five years (according to Lowenfeld and Brittain, 1987), other symbols for objects are drawn. These graphic symbols often are shapes for houses, trees, suns and birds. These shapes will fluctuate in much the same way that a child alters sounds. Her graphic symbols continue to fluctuate until around age seven when they become fairly stable. When the child's schemata are similar within drawings and across drawings of similar subject matter, the child moves into the next stage: the Schematic stage.

During the Preschematic stage, children can identify words and learn simple counting skills. However, reading sentences does not occur until the child adds a baseline and orders objects on that baseline. Baselines are indicative of the Schematic stage of artistic development (Lowenfeld & Brittain, 1987).

Initially children select colors for their drawings and paintings because of the personal appeal colors have. Correct color/object choice occurs during the Schematic stage of artistic development.

Often the art materials themselves may be all the motivation a child needs. Art materials and experiences that involve several senses at once are even stronger motivators for the child. One of the most inherently motivat-

TABLE 2.1
GROWING CHART/SCRIBBLING STAGE
(Lowenfeld 1.5 - 4 yrs) (McFee 2 - 7 yrs) (Salome/Moore 2-4 yrs)

	Yes	Sometimes	Not Yet
Random Scribbles			
1. Makes disordered marks			
2. Pounds clay randomly			
Controlled Scribbles			
1. Repeats marks after discovering controlled movement			
A. Horizontal			
B. Vertical			
C. Circular			
2. Uses various methods of grasping,drawing, or painting with tool			
3. Makes coils and balls in clay			
Named Scribbles			
1. Gives names to scribbles and lumps of clay			
2. Distinguishes one color from another			
3. May be able to name five colors			
4. May be able to name two geometric shapes			
5. Matches shapes on the basis of color			
6. May be able to trace a square			
7. Randomly picks colors for painting			
Other			
1. May follow cleanup procedures			
2. Shares sometimes			
Comments:			

Note. From Art for All the Children: Approaches to Art Therapy for Children with Disabilities (pg. 102) by F. E. Anderson, 1992, Springfield, IL: Charles C Thomas. Copyright 1992 by Charles C Thomas. Adapted by permission.

ing art media is clay because it so powerfully engages the sense of touch and is so easily manipulated by a child's hands.

Other methods of motivating the child in art are effectual if they relate directly to the child's own experiences (Henley, 1992). For example, having the child draw a picture of the school children on the playground right after she has been outside playing will result in a more highly motivated art experience. Thus direct experience is one of the most powerful ways to motivate a child in art—or in any other subject.

Even with direct experiences, asking the child specific questions about the subject for a drawing or painting can help the child focus and become aware of details. For example, having the child draw a picture of playing on the playground will be more vivid if the adult asks about the colors of the swings, seesaws and jungle gym equipment, or asks the child which activity

Figure 2.1. This marker drawing is by a three-year-old male. Note that there is some control evident in the lines and there appears to be a configuration of a face. This artwork is typical of a child who is naming scribbles and just beginning to form recognizable symbols. This artwork would be placed in the early Preschematic stage of artistic development (c. 33 × 48 cm from the collection of R. A. Salome).

she likes best, or who plays with her, and what colors are the coats of the children on the playground.

The role of the teacher will be one of facilitator. The art program should provide a multisensory approach, and it should relate as much as possible to the child's world. The art program should also include basic information about artistic processes, art vocabulary, information about artists and basic design elements. The child cannot be expected to learn artistic process and content on her own—this information needs to be transmitted and instruction needs to be planned for this information to be included.

In fact, an art-centered curriculum approach is the most efficient way for the child to learn about all aspects of her world and the basic school subjects. Chapters 5–9 of this book provide many examples of how an art-centered approach can be used in the best sense to teach the child language arts, reading, science, math and social studies.

There are also some excellent commercially available art curricula. These curricula begin in the first grade teaching the child basic art production skills, concepts about the history of art, art criticism and aesthetics, for example, *Discover Art* (Chapman, 1980), *Art: Meaning, Method & Material* (Hubbard & Rouse, 1972), or Navigator Art (Dunn & Berekley Co. Art Teachers, 1993). Table 2.9 summarizes children's development in responding to art.

Children also need time to practice art skills and repeated opportunities to use paint, clay, crayons, markers and other art media. Repeated experiences help develop skills and mastery and self-confidence in using art materials. The child will be most involved with the process of making art and will not be concerned with the completed product. Adults need to understand this fact and not expect children to create pictorially representative artwork. It is not until the child moves into the second or third grade that the art outcome—the product—will be as important as the creating of that artwork. This concern with the process and not the end product is one of the hardest things for adults—both parents and classroom teachers—to understand. And indeed if one visits an elementary school and sees artwork displayed that is (very realistic) adult-looking—i.e., Halloween pictures with witches and pumpkins from a first or second grade room—it may be more reflective of the teacher's art than that of the children's honest artistic statements.

> Drawings of objects that are very detailed may reflect children's informational level about these items. Generally children (beginning at around five years of age) who fail to include items from their surroundings, or who rather consistently draw stereotypic images, may have some degree of mental retardation; or physical, emotional or cultural deprivation; or physical, sexual or emotional abuse (Lowenfeld & Brittain, 1987; Manning, 1987; Oster & Gould, 1987; Malchiodi, 1990). (Anderson, 1992, p. 104)

Children with Disabilities Whose Art is Preschematic

According to Henley (1992) some children with disabilities depict a figure as the central form in a drawing. This figure is egocentric with little or no attention to realism. There is a style in the schemata that is greatly abstracted. Developmentally delayed learners bring a life experience to their artwork that is three or four times that of typical children. These life experiences appear as styles that are idiosyncratic. These strange design devices and abstractions are naive. Additionally, there is an impoverishment of form and a lack of details in artwork by children with developmental delays.

TABLE 2.2
GROWING CHART/PRESCHEMATIC STAGE
(Lowenfeld 4-7 yrs) (Salome/Moore 3-7 yrs) (McFee includes this
stage with the Schematic stage 3.5-16 yrs)

	Yes	Sometimes	Not Yet
Two-Dimensional Work 　1. Form for person emerges--usually a representation of self or some family member 　　a.　Head, feet depicted (c. five years) 　　b.　Details of arms, face, included in figure drawings (c. six years) 　　c.　Body parts drawn with greater accuracy than ability to name or recognize them 　　d.　Names all parts of face and rest of body 　2. Representative symbols for trees, persons, houses, etc., constantly being altered as concepts are being built 　3. Colors picked for their intrinsic, subjectiveappeal. Rarely relate to actual color of object in world 　4. Spatial Representation 　　a.　Objects float in space 　　b.　Objects appear randomly placed 　　c.　Placement reflects egocentricity of child **Three-Dimensional Work** 　1. May be able to make a ball of clay 　2. May be able to make a flat clay form 　3. May be able to join two pieces of clay 　4. May be able to make a construction that stands on its own **Art Skills Achieved (c. five years)** 　1. May be able to hold crayon correctly 　2. May be able to hold brush correctly 　3. May be able to hold scissors correctly 　4. Tears paper in straight line 　5. Mixes two colors correctly 　6. Glues objects but may: 　　a.　Have trouble using right amount 　　b.　Have trouble applying even coat 　　c.　Place glue on wrong side of object 　7. Identifies most colors except 　　a.　Grey 　　b.　Bright and dull colors 　8. Has trouble identifying smooth textures, thick/thin, and light lines **Other** 　1. Will work side by side and share art media but cannot really cooperate with other children 　2. May be able to identify own work 　3. May be able to follow directions in sequence 　4. May be able to clean up without prodding 　5. May be able to cut paper with scissors 　6. May be able to cut some cloth with scissors **Comments**			

Note: From Art for All the Children: Approaches to Art Therapy for Children with Disabilities (pg. 107) by F. E. Anderson, 1992, Springfield, IL: Charles C Thomas. Copyright 1992 by Charles C Thomas. Adapted by permission.

Figure 2.2. This drawing, by a four-year-old male, has several versions of a car and a figure that float in space. There is no ground or skyline. The differences in the two figures and the variations of details in the cars are all characteristic of artwork from the Preschematic stage of art development (36 × 22.5 cm. © International Collection of Child Art. Ewing Museum of Nations, Illinois State University, Normal, Illinois. Reproduced by permission).

Figure 2.3. This marker drawing is by a five-year-old girl. Here we see five different versions of schemata for human figures. Each figure is varied in terms of hair, hands (or lack of arms and fingers) and legs length. The child is experimenting with the human form symbol which is typical of Preschematic artwork. Note that the figures are not all ordered along a drawn or paper baseline. This lack of a baseline, and objects that float, are also characteristic of the Preschematic stage of artistic development (c. 33 × 48 cm from the collection of R. A. Salome).

Figure 2.4. This picture was created by a five-year-old boy. The figure has very large fingers and arms, and very long legs and a small head and body. Note the small sun and small tree and the six round shapes in the upper left-hand corner. The floating figure and round shapes as well as the disproportioned figure (with inaccurate numbers of fingers) are characteristic of the Preschematic stage of art development (22.9 × 34.5 cm. © International Collection of Child Art. Ewing Museum of Nations, Illinois State University, Normal, Illinois. Reproduced by permission).

SCHEMATIC STAGE

Lowenfeld	McFee	Salome/Moore
7 yrs to 9 yrs	3.5 yrs to *c.* 16 yrs (adult)	6 yrs to 10 yrs

In the Schematic stage the child begins to develop a personalized symbol or schema for the sun, a house, a person and other objects. These graphic symbols are both universal and also may have some feature that is unique to each child. They also are consistently drawn by that child. (A child's repeated visual symbol for objects such as a person, tree, house, sun, or flower is termed a "schema.") Once the child establishes these visual symbols, she will continue to draw them in a consistent manner. The child's schemata will not change unless there are specifically planned art experiences or some event that might cause the artist to enlarge or change her symbol. These images are not stereotypic but are the learner's visual language and reflect the information that she has about the object (schema) she draws.

Skyline and Baseline Emerge

Children typically include a baseline by the time they are eight years old (according to Lowenfeld and Brittain, 1987), and a line of sky appears along the top of the page. When the child places objects in an organized way along her baseline, it usually means that the child is ready to read words in sentences. The child is interested in drawing objects in two dimensions. It is not until several years later that the child begins to realize that objects she sees should be drawn with some attempt to show them as objects that have three dimensions. Pictures that have two baselines may be an attempt by the artist to provide some illusion of depth in the picture.

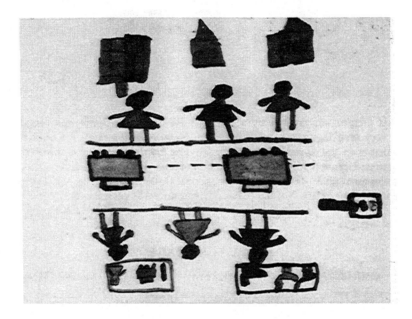

Figure 2.5. This depiction of a street with one side drawn upside down is one of the ways that children in the Schematic stage of development organize the space in the picture plane. This depiction is called a fold-over because if one folded the picture along the street, the objects in the lower half would be right side up. Note the schemata for cars and people. The cars have all four wheels showing on one side, because the 10-year-old female artist was drawing what she knows about cars and not what one sees when one looks at a car from its side (21 × 28 cm. © International Collection of Child Art. Ewing Museum of Nations, Illinois State University, Normal, Illinois. Reproduced by permission).

Fold-over/Fold-up and X–Ray Pictures Appear

The child represents space by using fold-overs and x-ray pictures as well as baselines. A fold-over or fold-up object in a drawing appears sideways or upside down (see Figs. 2.5 & 2.6). For example, a child may draw both sides of a street with houses, and the houses along the bottom of the page will be upside down. However, if one folds the picture along the street, these same houses will be right side up (Fig. 2.5). Figure 2.6 shows Native Americans sitting around the campfire. Native Americans are placed like the spokes of a wheel and some appear to be lying down. If the picture were folded, those Native Americans would appear sitting right side up.

Figure 2.6. Another way of folding-over or folding-up is illustrated in this picture of "Indian Friends" around a campfire by an eight-year-old female. Here just part of the painting is folded down—the left and right parts of the circle of Native Americans. The Native Americans themselves are examples of this artist's schema for a Native American—they all look the same. These schemata are very characteristic of artwork from the Schematic stage of development (48.3 × 63.5 cm. © International Collection of Child Art. Ewing Museum of Nations, Illinois State University, Normal, Illinois. Reproduced by permission).

Sometimes the child will fold-up only one item in her artwork. This might be a dinner table or ironing board. The artist is doing this to show what is on the table or board and does not understand how to draw items in perspective nor how to foreshorten items. The child is including in her drawing those things that are important to her.

X-ray pictures are typical at this stage. (When one encounters x-rays in the artwork of adults, it is considered unusual and often may indicate pathology.)

The child may want to include the inside and outside of an item. The cutaway (i.e., x-ray) is done to accomplish this task. Examples of x-ray depictions may be found in Figures 2.7 and 2.9.

Figure 2.7. In "Jonah and the Whale," by a seven-year-old girl, we see an x-ray of the ocean which reveals the fish and person. Note the skyline at the top of the picture and the unfilled space between the sky and the ocean. The x-ray and the skyline are typical of the Schematic stage of art development (17⅞ × 25⅜ cm. © International Collection of Child Art. Ewing Museum of Nations, Illinois State University, Normal, Illinois. Reproduced by permission).

A child may enlarge a schema or omit some part of the symbol depending on its importance. For example, in Figure 2.8 we see children skiing. The artist has enlarged one of the girls for special emphasis. This larger figure is probably the artist. A child with physical disabilities may omit feet in her drawing because they are not useful to her. Or she may be denying her inability to use her feet.

Children also have a schema for the colors of items they draw. This color schema is very consistent. Usually graphic symbols are depicted with correct color/object relationship. There are few, if any, variations in the colors, so for example flowers are red, suns are yellow, trees are green.

At the end of the Schematic stage the child begins to include more of what she sees of objects and less of what she knows about items in her pictures.

Figure 2.8. In Figure 2.8 by a six-year-old girl from Japan, titled "When I Went Skiing," we see elements of Schematic work in the double baseline and the schemata for the figures. The figures themselves have been made smaller in the background to suggest some depth, but note the car placed at the top of the picture which indicates that the artist does not yet fully understand perspective techniques. All the figures appear stiff and flat, and all but two of the figures are depicted facing forward. Two of the figures appear to be drawn from the side. The figure in the center is probably that of the artist. Note that this figure is larger than the others indicating the artist has enlarged the figure for special emphasis or that this person is more important than others in the picture. The houses are typical of Schematic drawings and there appears to be an x-ray view of the house in the lower right. This work is very typical of Schematic stage artwork. The picture plane is filled and organized, but the artist does not yet fully understand overlapping shapes or other ways to depict depth in the picture. Also, the figures are fairly flat and stiff and no legs or arms are bent, even though the subject of skiing would imply lots of action (17⅞ × 25⅜ cm. © International Collection of Child Art. Ewing Museum of Nations, Illinois State University, Normal, Illinois. Reproduced by permission).

Thus one would probably see cars with only two wheels (as opposed to those with four wheels). The sky meets the ground, and this space is organized and filled with objects. The artistic process is still of primary importance to the child.

Some children have mental ages that are different from their chronological ages. Thus, a child who is chronologically twelve but whose mental age is nine, probably will create artwork that is more typical of children whose mental and chronological ages are nine years.

Figure 2.9. In this crayon drawing, titled "Woodmar Shopping Center in Hammond" by a seven-year-old girl, every part of the picture is organized and filled with objects. This filling of the page is a characteristic of artists that occurs late in the Schematic stage. The objects in the space appear flat even though the artist has attempted to show the illusion of depth by attempting one-point perspective in the aisles in the shoe store. The artist has also included x-rays of many of the stores so that she can draw what is inside. There is a schemata for cars and for the figures, but some of the figures are drawn sideways and are varied in terms of the types of clothing that they wear. These side views and variations in the schemata are also characteristics of late Schematic/early Gang Age stage according to Lowenfeld and Brittain (1987) (Transitional stage according to Salome, 1993) artwork. Note the way that the cars fill the space, but they do not overlap each other. Overlapping is also more characteristic of later Schematic/early Gang Age (Transitional stage) artwork (45.7 × 61 cm. © International Collection of Child Art. Ewing Museum of Nations, Illinois State University, Normal, Illinois. Reproduced by permission).

Children with Disabilities Whose Art is Schematic

Some children with mental retardation or emotional disorders may not choose to have a figure as the major theme in their drawings. Domestic animals may be preferred. Also children with mental retardation and visual impairments or who are deaf or hard-of-hearing may create art that has schemata typical of Schematic stage art, but there may be other elements in their artwork that are typical of later artistic developmental levels (Henley, 1992).

DAWNING REALISM/(GANG AGE) STAGE	or	CULTURAL REALISM STAGE	or	TRANSITIONAL STAGE
Lowenfeld		McFee		Salome/Moore
9 yrs to 12 yrs		6.5 yrs to 16 yrs (adult)		9 yrs to 15 yrs

The next stage that a child typically goes through is called the Transitional stage by Salome and Moore (1979a, 1979b, 1992), the Dawning Realism/Gang Age (Lowenfeld & Brittain, 1987) or Cultural Realism (McFee, 1970). A composite checklist (Table 2.5) developed by Salome (1991) has been included along with the Summary Chart for the Gang Age (Table 2.4), so the reader can compare these two stages.

This is the period of a child's growth when same-sex groups become very important. These all-male and all-female cliques have different interests that show up in artwork. Boys' artwork will include sports, space and trendy themes (such as Rambo or the Ninja Turtles). Boys' choice of heroes and superheroes are allusions to male sexuality, but are expressed in these safer subjects. Girls' artwork will have subjects dealing with horses/unicorns, parties and organizations (only for girls). Girls often avoid drawing figures with sexual characteristics, preferring horses, unicorns and dog faces as safer subjects of their artwork (Henley 1992). Additionally, vocational roles are important subjects that appear in artwork for both boys and girls.

Figure drawings have more details included, such as dress details and patterns. There are attempts to show action, but the child has not learned how to use shading and foreshortening. Arms and legs bend at joints, but the figures look very stiff on the page. There is a tendency for figures to contain fewer geometric shapes and more accurately depicted forms for body parts and other items than those done in the Schematic stage. These drawings will have some characteristics of both the Schematic stage and subsequent Realism stages. The child does include a continuous contour line around figures (as opposed to each part outlined separately in the Schematic stage). There is some differentiation in figures to show waists, hair and hips, but still these efforts are not totally representational.

Color also becomes more representational, and shades and tints of colors will be used. The child is now aware of her environs and is more observant. These observations will be reflected in the way she uses color. Now the child uses shades and tints of color. Also, spatial representation is shown using overlapping objects, diminishing size, ground plane and even linear perspective. The entire picture (the ground plane) is organized and filled, and

TABLE 2.3
GROWING CHART/SCHEMATIC STAGE
(Lowenfeld 7-9 yrs) (McFee 3.5-15 yrs) (Salome/Moore 6-10 yrs)

	Yes	Sometimes	Not Yet
Human Schema (two-dimensional work)			
1. Child develops her <u>own</u> human schema			
2. Includes body, arms, legs (or clothing)			
a. Head and facial parts			
b. Other details			
3. Frontal view (sometimes side view or combination), mostly frontal but figures rarely shown directly interacting with each other			
4. Ovals heads, circles for eyes			
5. Figures have geometric-shaped parts			
6. Parts outlined separately			
7. Arms and legs lack joints			
8. Figures appear still & flat, little body action depicted			
9. Figure proportions incorrect			
Spatial Representation (two-dimensional work)			
1. Objects set along a baseline			
2. Sometimes two baselines in same picture			
3. Shapes are flat			
4. Skyline appears (strip at top of picture)			
5. Fold-over or fold-up pictures			
6. Top and side views of items combined			
7. Different events or time sequences in same picture			
8. X-ray presentations			
9. Generally shallow depth			
Color			
1. Schema for colors develops			
2. More accurate relationship of colors to objects			
Schemata vary at times			
1. Significant parts enlarged			
2. Unimportant items omitted			
3. Suppressed objects (ideas) may be left out			
4. Child draws from memory unless motivated to do otherwise			
Art Skills			
1. Has ability to use:			
a. Painting tools			
b. Drawing tools			
c. Scissors			
2. Can sculpt with clay using the additive method			
3. Better able to share work			
4. Can cooperate with others on group projects			
Comments:			

TABLE 2.4
GROWING CHART: GANG AGE/THE DAWNING REALISM (Lowenfeld 9-12 yrs)
Or CULTURAL REALISM (McFee 6.5-16 yrs [adult])
Or TRANSITIONAL (Salome/Moore 9-15 yrs)

	Yes	Sometimes	Not Yet
Human Schema (two-dimensional work)			
1. Many more details appear			
2. Fewer geometric shapes and more natural forms and shapes included for body parts			
3. Many more details in the figure			
4. Many more details in clothing (patterns, decoration)			
5. Hemlines straight			
6. Folds omitted			
7. Figures stiff, little action portrayed			
8. Schema appears in three-dimensional media as well			
Spatial Representation (two-dimensional work)			
1. Space between sky and ground filled and ordered			
2. Baseline disappears			
3. Overlapping of objects			
4. Still some exaggeration of objects due to emotional importance			
Color			
1. Less generalized schema			
2. Variations in the object/color relationship (shades and tints of colors used)			
Topics differ for artwork by boys and girls			
1. Girl's work tends to have			
a. More smiling people			
b. More clothing details			
c. More objects depicting the environs			
d. Fewer sports themes			
e. Music/parties			
f. Horses			
2. Boy's work tends to have			
a. Cars			
b. Sports themes			
c. Space/rocket themes			
Art Skills			
1. Can mix own colors			
2. Can use wood tools appropriately			
3. Can work three-dimensionally with paper			
4. Still uses additive method in clay			
5. Works well with others (in same-sex groupings)			
Comments			

Note: From Art for All the Children: Approaches to Art Therapy for Children with Disabilities (pg. 121) by F. E. Anderson, 1992, Springfield, IL: Charles C. Thomas. Copyright 1992 by Charles C. Thomas. Adapted by permission.

TABLE 2.5
DEVELOPMENTAL STAGE CHECKLIST
(SALOME, 1991)

Culture/Country _____ ID# _____

Developmental stage _____ Sex _____ Age _____

Title _____

Preschematic (3 to 7 years)
_____ Primitive representative symbols have minimal resemblance to objects.
_____ One symbol may represent several objects.
_____ Shapes/lines lose meaning when separated from the whole
_____ No organization in picture, right/left, or vertical organization
_____ No baseline; figures float in space
_____ Pictures developed item by item, parts often unrelated
_____ Color used subjectively
_____ Head/leg and global figures change to figures of assembled, outlined parts
_____ Little or no action shown
_____ Few details in figures and objects; parts may be missing
_____ Little or no environmental detail

Schematic (6 to 10 years)
_____ Color relates more to nature and environment
_____ Paper basing and baseline appears. Deviations may include:
　　　_____ X-ray
　　　_____ Double or elevated baseline
　　　_____ Top/side view combinations (fold-ups)
_____ Human figure drawings may include:
　　　_____ Oval-shaped heads, circles for eyes
　　　_____ Frontal position
　　　_____ Separately outlined parts
　　　_____ Geometric shapes
　　　_____ No joints, little action, figures appear stiff
　　　_____ Incorrect proportion
　　　_____ Assembled appearance
_____ Schema for objects are recognizable
_____ Schema may be repeated with little variation in a work
_____ Objects and shapes related in the picture

Transitional (9 to 12 years)
_____ Symbols are more realistic, but picture includes both schematic and realistic
　　　　characteristics
_____ Color is used objectively
_____ Spatial organization includes:
　　　_____ Overlapping
　　　_____ Diminishing size
　　　_____ Ground plane
　　　_____ Position in space
　　　_____ Linear perspective sometimes used
_____ Different perspective devices may be used in one art work
_____ Much more detail and differentiation of objects and figures

TABLE 2.5 (Continued)
DEVELOPMENTAL STAGE CHECKLIST

Transitional (9 to 12 years)
_____ Human figure drawings may include:
        _____ More descriptive detail in body and clothing
        _____ Stiffness due to problems in depicting joints and proportions
        _____ No foreshortening or shading (figures appear flat)
        _____ Parts retain meaning when separated from whole
        _____ Continuous contour line used rather than separately outlined parts
        _____ Vocational roles and some gender differences (hair, waist, hips, muscles)
        _____ Clothing emphasized
Realism (11 years onward)
_____ Objects and figures represented as they appear
_____ Changing optical conditions portrayed:
        _____ Motion
        _____ Light
        _____ Distance
        _____ Atmosphere
_____ Human figures
        _____ Shown in a variety of positions
        _____ Action and situations portrayed
        _____ Facial expressions
        _____ Portraits include characteristics of subject
        _____ Rounding of limbs due to shading/foreshortening
_____ Drawings may include:
        _____ All perspective devices
        _____ Social criticism
        _____ Good compositional organization; movement, expression, and drama
        _____ Skilled use of media and procedures
        _____ Appearance of individual styles

Note. From Developmental Stage Checklist. by R. A. Salome, 1991, Unpublished manuscript. copyright 1991 by R. A. Salome, Illinois State University, Normal, IL. Reprinted by permission.

there is no longer a strip of sky at the top of the page nor a baseline at the bottom with empty space in between. The child no longer uses x-ray, fold-up or folded-over objects to depict spatial relationships.

PSEUDO-NATURALISM STAGE	or CULTURAL REALISM or STAGE	REALISM STAGE
Lowenfeld	McFee	Salome/Moore
12 yrs to 14 yrs	6.5 yrs to 16 yrs (adult)	11 yrs on

Children at this stage fluctuate between the values of their peer culture and the values of their families. Artwork is more realistic and some, but not all students, can successfully produce realistic pictures. Most learners are very critically aware of discrepancies between what they see and how they are able (or unable) to create realistic artwork. Students' artwork is a combi-

Figure 2.10. This is by a nine-year-old boy. The painting is titled "My Friends." This early Gang Age work shows repeated figures that are in front of a fence. The overlapped items and the placement of the fence higher and behind the boys is an attempt to create some depth in the painting. While the boys are depicted doing active things (flying a plane and bouncing a ball), the arms and knees are stiff and appear frozen. The figures are shown in profile which is a characteristic of the Gang Age. The dark contour line around the items and figures is a characteristic noted by Salome (1991) in his Transitional stage. The belt tabs and cuffs are clothing details which are typical of the Gang Age and the Transitional stages (48 × 64 cm. © International Collection of Child Art. Ewing Museum of Nations, Illinois State University, Normal, Illinois. Reproduced by permission).

Figure 2.11. This is by a twelve-year-old American boy and is titled "Snowball Battles with my Friends." The figures in this artwork are overlapping and there is some attempt at the use of perspective to depict the building in the lower left. Again, the space of the picture is carefully organized and filled. However, we now see figures that are less geometric. Careful attention has been given to the clothing details. The artist has attempted to indicate much action, but the figures are still stiff and still very flat. These stiff figures with a black outline around body and clothing parts, the filled and ordered picture plane, attention to clothing details, more accurate depiction of body shapes (i.e., little or no use of geometric shapes for body parts) and the overlapping figures all put this artwork in Salome's (1993) Transitional phase of artistic development (or Gang Age according to Lowenfeld & Brittain, 1987) (48.3 × 63.5 cm. © International Collection of Child Art. Ewing Museum of Nations, Illinois State University, Normal, Illinois. Reproduced by permission).

nation of what they see and know. Children are pulled toward a peer culture and will either join this group or become more of a "loner" and withdraw into a fantasy world. Now the learner understands abstraction and symbolism. The artistic outcome, the product, is much more important to students than the process of creating art.

Motion, as well as the changes of light and atmosphere on objects, are now understood. Objects and figures are now proportionally related to each other and the environment. Isometric, linear, aerial perspective devices and foreshortening are understood and used.

Human figures now show sexual differences. Age and differing facial expressions are also depicted. Figures are shown in different positions and situations. Lines are used expressively and to depict depth in drawings. Clothing details, including folds and wrinkles, now appear.

Artwork is also used to make social and political statements. Action, as well as exaggeration for dramatic and humorous effects, are other characteristics of the artwork of the Realism stage.

Artwork of Learners with Disabilities/Whose Art Is Pseudo-Naturalistic

Henley (1992) notes that there is a large self-conscious factor that learners with disabilities have about their artwork. These learners may revert to rigid and stereotypic form and figures. There are often combinations of Schematic and Preschematic elements along with more realistic depictions in the same drawing. Learners with disabilities may have greater mood shifts that may be initiated by their greater self-consciousness in terms of their artwork. If these learners are in a regular art education class, they may be ridiculed for drawing stick figures (which may occur from age 11 to adulthood).

A learner with emotional disturbance may be capable of drawing in a realistic style similar to her nondisabled peers, but will quickly regress to a style reflective of her emotional level, which is most likely that of a child in the Schematic stage (Henley, 1992).

BEYOND THE PSEUDO-NATURALISTIC STAGE— LOWENFELD'S ADOLESCENT ART/AGE OF DECISION STAGE

Table 2.7 summarizes Lowenfeld's Adolescent Art/Age of Decision stage. It is very similar to his Pseudo-Naturalistic stage, and it is understandable why McFee, and Salome and Moore, have grouped artwork from these two Lowenfeldian stages into a Cultural Realism/Realism stage. Because art therapists still look to Lowenfeld's stages as their benchmarks for normal children's development, a summary chart of the Adolescent Art stage is included in Table 2.7.

Figure 2.12. Titled "Buildings," it is by a fourteen-year-old Japanese girl. The artist has used overlap and isometrics to depict the buildings. However, the artist has not totally mastered this technique. Note the sidewalk, which does not totally reflect mastery of one-point perspective. This partially realistic rendering of buildings is reflective of the Transitional phase (Salome, 1993) of artistic development (Pseudo-Naturalistic stage according to Lowenfeld & Brittain, 1987) (48.3 × 63.5 cm. © International Collection of Child Art. Ewing Museum of Nations, Illinois State University, Normal, Illinois. Reproduced by permission).

Figure 2.13. Titled "The Bookie," it is by a seventeen-year-old American male. This picture demonstrates mastery of the woodcutting technique. The artist also has correctly used one-point perspective in rendering the buildings. Caricature has been used in the depiction of the figure. This personalized style is a feature of adolescent art. This print is typical of Cultural Realism (McFee, 1970)/ Realism (Salome, 1993) (Adolescent Art according to Lowenfeld & Brittain, 1987)) (22.9 × 15.2 cm. © International Collection of Child Art. Ewing Museum of Nations, Illinois State University, Normal, Illinois. Reproduced by permission).

SUMMARY OF VARIOUS DEVELOPMENTAL APPROACHES

The chart in Table 2.8 illustrates how the stages identified by Lowenfeld (1987), Piaget (as a reference point) (1956), McFee (1970), Gardner (1990), and Salome and Moore (1979a, 1979b;) relate to each other and to ages of

Figure 2.14 is by an eleven-year-old Japanese girl and is titled "Playing in the Snow." This picture shows figures that are much more realistic. The body proportions are more accurate and it is obvious that there are elbows and bent knees in the figures. We see attention to details of clothing, especially the hats. Both body parts and other objects in the picture are no longer outlined. Also, some figures are rendered facing the viewer, others are placed sideways and there is even a figure with a three-quarter back view. Both the sled and the shovel are rendered using perspective conventions. All these character-istics put this artwork in the Cultural Realism (McFee, 1970) period (or the Pseudo-Naturalistic phase according to Lowenfeld & Brittain, 1987) (38.1 × 54 cm. © International Collection of Child Art. Ewing Museum of Nations, Illinois State University, Normal, Illinois. Reproduced by permission)

Figure 2.15 is titled "View of St. Albans" and is by a fifteen-year-old Welsh girl. The drawing is clearly a realistic depiction of a cityscape and illustrates artistic mastery which places it in the Cultural Realism stage of development (McFee, 1970)/Realism (Salome, 1993)/Adolescent Art—Age of Decision (Lowenfeld & Brittain, 1987) (14 inches × 18⅝ inches. © International Collection of Child Art. Ewing Museum of Nations, Illinois State University, Normal, Illinois. Reproduced by permission).

TABLE 2.6
GROWING CHART/PSEUDO-NATURALISTIC STAGE: (Lowenfeld 12-14 yrs)
or CULTURAL REALISM (McFee 6.5-16 yrs [adult])
or REALISM (Salome/Moore 11 yrs on)

	Yes	Sometimes	Not Yet
Human Figure (two-dimensional work)			
1. Joints indicated, figures active			
2. Color variations including tints and tones and shades indicated			
3. Sexual characteristics <u>sometimes</u> exaggerated			
4. Figures of different ages			
6. Cartoons/caricatures			
7. The above reflected in three-dimensional media as well			
Spatial Representation (two-dimensional work)			
1. Baseline disappears			
2. Horizon line included			
3. Discovery of perspective methods			
a. One-point and two-point			
b. Aerial atmospheric effects			
Three-Dimensional Work			
1. Interest in making functional clay work			
2. Interest in making representational figures in clay, plaster, and wire			
Other General Concerns			
1. Focus on decorative qualities in work			
2. Interest in fantasy topics			
3. Concern for various artistic techniques			
4. Concern for end-product			
5. Heightened criticism of own work			
Comments:			

<u>Note</u>. From <u>Art for All the Children: Approaches to Art Therapy for Children with Disabilities</u> (pg. 126) by F. E. Anderson, 1992, Springfield, IL: Charles C Thomas. Copyright 1992 by Charles C Thomas. Adapted by permission.

typical children. Table 2.9 illustrates the developmental stages children go through in responding to art.

USEFULNESS OF ARTISTIC DEVELOPMENTAL STAGE THEORIES

Child art has been studied in terms of the connection between the personality traits and color choice (Altschuler & Hattwick, 1969), in terms of the relationship between details included and intelligence (Goodenough, 1926; Harris, 1963), what children have included in artwork based on their memories of these topics (Lowenfeld & Brittain, 1987), in terms of universal developmental traits (Lansing, 1972; Piaget & Inhelder, 1956), or the lack of these universals (Feldman, 1980; Hess-Behrens, 1970).

Wilson and Wilson (1983) have even advocated the uselessness of children's artistic developmental stages. However, some recent research by Salome has

Figure 2.16 is titled "A Royal Marine Funeral" and is by a sixteen-year-old male. This painting clearly shows mastery of the artform. The art exemplifies the Cultural Realism stage (McFee, 1970)/Realism (Salome, 1993) of artistic development according to Salome (1993) (Adolescent Art—Age of Decision according to Lowenfeld & Brittain, 1987). Note that the artist has purposely selected a closeup of the pallbearers and the casket to heighten the drama of the funeral. Further, the artist has used one-point and aerial perspective, and foreshortening. He has also carefully rendered the uniforms and faces to capture the soldiers' different expressions (13½ inches × 14⅜ inches. © International Collection of Child Art. Ewing Museum of Nations, Illinois State University, Normal, Illinois. Reproduced by permission).

further documented (based on a large cross-national sample of artwork) "the existence of stages or levels of achievement in representational skills for children's artworks across different countries and cultures, with a wide range of skills for the older children" (Salome, 1993, p. 4). Further, both Salome (1993) and Perez (1993) confirm the relationship between age and developmental level. Perez examined over 8,000 examples of artwork by children from 12 different countries and reported that as children's chronological ages increased, there was an increase in representational aspects of their artwork.

It is apparent that no one theory or approach can account for the influences on children's art of culture, education, environment, and family as well as the influence of abilities and opportunities to learn (McFee & Degge, 1980). Therefore, children's art must be studied from several perspectives.

This author continues to find artistic developmental stages useful. They

TABLE 2.7
ADOLESCENT ART: THE PERIOD OF DECISION (Lowenfeld 14-17 Yrs)
or CULTURAL REALISM (McFee 6.5 yrs - 16 yrs [adult])
or REALISM (Salome/Moore, 11 yrs on)

	Yes	Sometimes	Not Yet
Two-Dimensional Work 1. Drawings similar to 12 year-old work 2. Concern for acquiring art skills 3. Visually-oriented learner (Lowenfeld & Brittain, 1987) concerned about including details in work, including light and shadow 4. Haptic-oriented learner (Lowenfeld & Brittain, 1987) has much greater focus on subjective impressions of subject matter 5. Increased attention-span 6. Mastery of a variety of art media **Spacial Representation (two-dimensional work)** 1. Visually oriented learner (Lowenfeld & Brittain, 1987) have interest in learning one, two and three pt., and atmospheric perspective 2. Haptic-oriented learner (Lowenfeld & Brittain, 1987) will include subjective impressions based on mood, will distort representation to serve subjective purpose **Human Figure (two-dimensional work)** 1. Some learners will attempt naturalistic representations including proportion and visual detail and action 2. Some will exaggerate details for specific purpose 3. Some learners will cartoon and caricature to make a point **Other**			

Note: From <u>Art for All the Children: Approaches to Art Therapy for Children with Disabilities</u> (pg. 121) by F. E. Anderson, 1992, Springfield, IL: Charles C. Thomas. Copyright 1992 by Charles C. Thomas. Adapted by permission.

provide general benchmarks and a context within which to place a child's artistic efforts, skills and abilities. These stages do inform the ways one plans art experiences that will be age appropriate. However, to make comparisons between artwork by several different children or to hold the developmental characteristics of one stage as an absolute standard against which to judge a child's artwork may be harmful. The best evaluative approach would be to compare the artwork of one child against her own artwork over time while keeping the general artistic developmental context in mind. Thus, one would need to be aware of what all children do in art as well as what is effected by culture, subcultural learning, and teaching.

TABLE 2.8

SUMMARY CHART OF CHILD ART DEVELOPMENT ACCORDING TO: LOWENFELD, PIAGET, MCFEE, CHAPMAN, SALOME & MOORE, GARDNER

LOWENFELD (1987)

AGE   0 .... 1.5yrs..... 2 yrs.... 4 yrs.... 7 yrs.... 9 yrs.... 12 yrs..... 14 yrs
      SCRIBBLING
               (1.5 ....   4 yrs)
     a. uncontrolled
       b. controlled
         c. named
            PRESCHEMATIC
                   (4 ......   7yrs)
              SCHEMATIC
                      (7 ......   9 yrs)
                 GANG AGE
                        (9 ......   12 yrs)
                PSEUDO-NATURALISTIC
                          (12 ......   14 yrs)
                  HIGH SCHOOL-ADOLESCENT ART
                            (14 ..... 17yrs)

PIAGET (1956)

AGE   0 .... 2 yrs ..... 4 yrs ..... 7 yrs .... 11 yrs . 12 yrs ..... 14 yrs
      SENSORIMOTOR
        (0 ....   2 yrs)
      CONCRETE OPERATIONS
               (2 .... 11 yrs)
        PREOPERATIONAL
            (2 ......   4 yrs)
        INTUITIVE THOUGHT
               (4 ......   7 yrs)
               CONCRETE OPERATIONS
                    (7 .... 11 yrs)
                 FORMAL OPERATIONS
                      (12 yrs)

(See following page for continuation of Table 2.8.)

TABLE 2.8 (Continued)

**SUMMARY CHART OF CHILD ART DEVELOPMENT ACCORDING TO:
LOWENFELD, PIAGET, MCFEE, CHAPMAN,
SALOME & MOORE, GARDNER**

MCFEE (1970)

AGE..   2yrs..... 3yrs..... 4yrs..... 5yrs..... 6yrs..... 7yrs..... 9yrs..... 10yrs..... 11yrs..... 12yrs..... 15yrs
        SCRIBBLING
        (2 . . . . 7 yrs)
                SCHEMATIC
                (3.5 . . . . .around 16 yrs)
                        CULTURAL REALISM
                        (6.5 16
                                                                                            (adult)

SALOME & MOORE (1979)

AGE..   2yrs..... 3yrs..... 4yrs..... 5yrs..... 6yrs..... 7yrs..... 9yrs..... 10yrs..... 11yrs..... 12yrs..... 15yrs
        SCRIBBLING
        (2 . . . . 4 yrs)
                PRESCHEMATIC
                (3 . . . . 7 yrs)
                        SCHEMATIC
                        (6 . . . . 10 yrs)
                                TRANSITIONAL
                                (9 . . . . 15 yrs)
                                        REALISM
                                        (11 . . . . .on)

GARDNER (1990)

AGE..   2yrs..... 3yrs..... 4yrs..... 5yrs..... 6yrs..... 7yrs..... 9yrs..... 10yrs..... 11yrs..... 12yrs..... 15yrs
        SCRIBBLING
        (age not specified)
                CONVENTIONAL
                        (7 . . . 8 yrs)
                CULTURAL INFLUENCE
                        (9 years . . . . on)
                ARTISTIC PROWESS
                (Adolescence up)
                (not all reach this stage)
                        (13 . . . . . on)

TABLE 2.9

SUMMARY OF CHILDREN'S DEVELOPMENT IN RESPONDING TO ART

PARSONS (1987)

AGE   0 . . . . 2 yrs . . . . 10 yrs . . . . 13 yrs . . . . Adult

Stage 1   (2 yrs - ?)
  FAVORITISM
    (color appeal, subject matter
      are major influences)
        Stage 2 (age unspecified)
          REALISM AND BEAUTY
            (Representational quality
              of art work is major influence)
              Stage 3 (age unspecified)
                EXPRESSIVENESS
                  (Intensity of emotions
                    conveyed to viewer by
                      artist is major influence)
                    Stage 4 (age unspecified)
                      STYLE AND USE OF MEDIA AND ART ELEMENTS
                        (Differing opinions about art work considered)
                      Stage 5 (age unspecified)
                        AUTONOMY (Viewers own judgements
                      about art work considered in
                        conjunction with Stage 4 components).

GARDNER (1990)

AGE   0 . . . . 2 yrs . . . . 10 yrs . . . . 13 yrs . . . . Adult

Stage 1 (age unspecified - young children)
  COST OF WORK, SUBJECT MATTER, SIZE OF PICTURE
    (Similar to Parsons' Stage 1 FAVORITISM)
        Stage 2   (2 . . . . 10 yrs of age)
          STRONG REPRESENTATIONAL WORKS ARE BEST
            Stage 3   (adolescents . . . . .adulthood)
            RELATIVISTIC
              (Similar to Parsons' Stage 5 Autonomy.
                No one right way to judge art work).

REFERENCES

Altschuler, R., & Hattwick, L. (1969). *Painting and personality.* Chicago: University of Chicago Press. (Original work published 1947.)

Anderson, F. E. (1992). *Art for all the children: Approaches to art therapy for children with disabilities.* Springfield, IL: Charles C Thomas.

Chapman, L. (1978). *Approaches to art in education.* New York: Harcourt Brace Jovanovich.

Chapman, L. (1980). *Discover art: One through six.* Worcester, MA: Davis.

Dunn, P., & Berkley County S.C. Art Teachers. (1993). Navigator Art. The University of South Carolina, Columbia, SC.

Feldman, D. H. (1980). *Beyond universals in cognitive development.* Norwood, NJ: Ablex.

Feldman, D. H. (1987). Developmental psychology and art education. *Art Education, 36*(2), 19–21.

Feldman, D. H. (1987). Developmental psychology and art education; two fields at the crossroads. *Journal of Aesthetic Education, 21*(2), 243–254.

Gardner, H. (1990). *Art education and human development.* (Occasional Paper number 3). Los Angeles, CA: The Getty Center for Education in the Arts.

Goodenough, F. (1924). *The intellectual factor in children's drawings.* Unpublished doctoral dissertation, Stanford University, Palo Alto, CA.

Harris, D. B. (1963). *Children's drawings as measures of intellectual maturity.* New York: Harcourt Brace Jovanovich.

Henley, D. (1992). *Exceptional children, exceptional art.* Worchester, MA: Davis.

Hess-Behrens, N. N. (1973). The development of the concept of space as observed in children's drawings: A cross-nation/cross-cultural study. National Center for Educational Research and Development (H.E.W. R02-0611).

Lowenfeld, V., & Brittain, L. (1987). *Creative and mental growth* (8th ed). New York: Macmillan.

Malchiodi, C. (1990). *Breaking the silence: Art therapy with children from violent homes.* New York: Brunner/Mazel.

Manning, T. (1987). Aggression depicted in abused children's drawings. *The Arts in Psychotherapy, 14,* 15–24.

McFee, J. (1970). *Preparation for art.* Belmont, CA: Wadsworth.

McFee, J. K., & Degge, R. (1980). *Art, culture, and environment: A catalyst for teaching.* Dubuque, IA: Kendall/Hunt.

Oster, G. D., & Gould, P. (1987). *Using drawings in assessment and therapy.* New York: Brunner/Mazel.

Parsons, M. J. (1987). *How we understand art.* Cambridge, Great Britain: Cambridge University Press.

Perez, J. (1993). A cross-national study of child art: Comparing for universal and culturally influenced characteristics. Unpublished doctoral dissertation, Illinois State University, Normal, IL.

Piaget, J., & Inhelder, B. C. (1956). *The child's concept of space.* New York: Humanities Press.

Salome, R. A. (1993). Development of children's graphic representational abilities. Unpublished manuscript, Illinois State University, Normal, IL.

Salome, R. A. (1991). Developmental Stage Checklist. Unpublished manuscript, Illinois State University, Normal, IL.

Salome, R. A., & Moore, B. (1979). *Development of figure concepts in the graphic artwork by children from different countries.* Chicago, IL: International Film Bureau.

Salome, R. A., & Moore, B. (1979). *Development of spatial relations in the graphic artwork by children from different countries.* Chicago, IL: International Film Bureau.

Wilson, B., & Wilson, M. (1983). The use and uselessness of developmental stages. *Art Education, 36*(2), 4–5.

Chapter 3

ART ADAPTATIONS FOR
CHILDREN WITH DISABILITIES

In planning appropriate art experiences for children with disabilities, it may be necessary to adapt the situation, the art materials and tools and the instructional sequence. One of the creative challenges of working with children with disabilities is being able to solve the adaptation problems that occur.

It is important to learn the principles behind adaptation planning because each child is different and may require a totally novel art adaptation. Additionally, with the current focus on inclusion and integration of all (or nearly all) children with disabilities into regular education classrooms, the need to know how to adapt art experiences takes on more urgency—especially for the regular classroom and art teacher. This chapter provides many examples of art adaptations to demonstrate these principles (Anderson, 1992, 1979).

THE TEAM APPROACH TO ADAPTATIONS

One important principle is the team approach to adaptations. The teacher, physical therapist, occupational therapist, medical staff, and/or art therapist must TEAM up with the child in devising adaptations. The child may be one of the best sources of information and feedback about the usefulness of a specific adaptation. Do not hesitate to involve the child in the team (see Figs. 3.1 & 3.2). Be willing to try many different solutions, positions, etc., and do not be afraid to make mistakes. Finally, in devising adaptations be aware that a child's file should be consulted. All staff, including medical staff that know the child's strengths and limitations, should also be consulted. Medical limitations should *always* be considered.

The team approach emphasizes another key principle. Each child is unique and has unique adaptative needs. Therefore, the concept of individualization is *crucial* in adapting art for a child with a specific disability.

Additionally, in developing adaptations one should be aware of the characteristics of each child's disability. In Chapter 1 of this book some of the characteristics of disabilities are covered along with implications for planning art experiences. The reader may wish to review this material as preparation for developing adaptations and as a supplement to the information covered in this chapter.

Finally, art materials and media may have some safety and health hazards that MUST be considered. The last chapter in this book covers health and safety issues of art media, materials and tools. Everyone planning art activities or children with disabilities is *URGED* to read Chapter 10 and become informed about these art health and safety issues (Anderson, 1992).

PLEASE NOTE: The reader is asked to examine the illustrations and photographs and the accompanying captions before reading further.

Note: Some of the illustrations in this section are adapted from Frances E. Anderson's, *ART FOR ALL THE CHILDREN: Approaches to Art Therapy for Children with Disabilities* (Springfield, IL: Charles C Thomas, Publisher), 1992.

Figure 3.1. Planning art adaptations takes creativity, patience and teamwork. The child is the central member of that team. Often, finding the best working conditions or best adaptation for a paintbrush or drawing tool is a trial-and-error process in which the child has the final say. Here, a girl who is 10 years old has chosen to draw with markers. She prefers markers because they are easier to control than paint, which is a much more fluid media. She has determined her best working setup. In this instance because of her limited range of movement (mostly left to right), the adaptations team has decided to rotate the paper as she completes various parts of the drawing.

Figure 3.2. This is the finished drawing which depicts a girl playing ball outside. Unless the viewer knew about the age and disability of the artist, he might think that the figures were executed by a student who had developmental delays or some other disability. Knowing that the drawing was completed by a 10-year-old girl with cerebral palsy heightens one's appreciation for the controlled line that the artist was able to achieve.

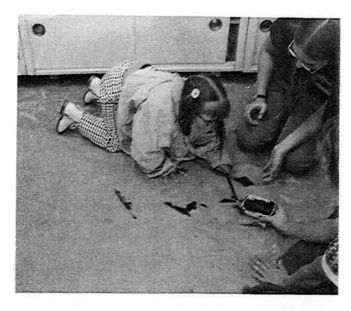

Figure 3.3. Sometimes it is much easier to work on the floor—especially in completing a life-size portrait. Here a girl who has both visual impairments and physical disabilities is doing just that. Before deciding to permit a child with disabilities to work on the floor or to be moved from her wheelchair to sit in a chair, *check with medical personnel and check the child's medical files.* It might also be wise to have written clearance prior to moving any child.

Figure 3.4. In another instance, a child may work best sitting down using a table easel. Here a 10-year-old girl with physical disabilities is painting sitting down. The paper is securely taped to a strong (yet fairly light) cardboard back which is secured to the easel. The easel should also be anchored from behind by a sandbag.

Figure 3.5. These illustrations are examples of some ways a table can be adapted to fit the needs of a child in a wheelchair. The illustration at the lower left shows how a work surface can be adapted so that it can be adjusted to fit the best working angle for a child. Concept taken from Callan (1987) by permission. Illustration credit: R. Mechtly.

Figure 3.6. Wheelchairs come in all heights and sizes and many have arms that do not fit under the art table. When this happens and the child cannot be moved from his wheelchair to sit in a chair, a lapboard can be used. The board should not be too heavy, but should be sturdy. Strong, recycled cardboard can be trimmed to fit any wheelchair. The lapboard should be securely fastened to the arms of the wheelchair using strong tape. Illustration credit: V. Foster and R. Mechtly.

Figure 3.7. Children who have been taught to learn by modeling or copying will tend to do the same thing during an art experience. Other children may need assistance in focusing on an art task. These children may benefit from working in individual carrels. Cardboard can make a simple private work space as is illustrated here. When a child is to work in this kind of isolated work place, it will be important to have all the children in the group also work in individual carrels. Otherwise, the child might think this isolation is a punishment. This is especially true with the child who is deaf or hard-of-hearing. When asking the child to work in isolation, it may help to explain that everyone will be working *in secret* until their artwork is completed, and then their work will be shown/shared with the rest of the group. Illustration credit: V. Foster and R. Mechtly.

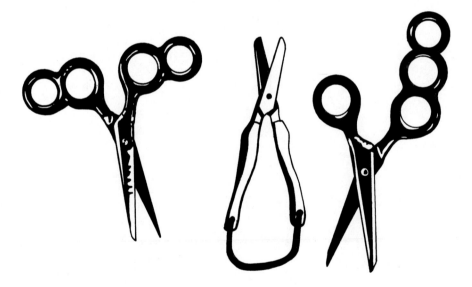

Figure 3.8. Lack of scissors skills are the most frequently cited problem children with disabilities have (Anderson, 1980). Here are three types of scissors that can help children with their cutting skills. The scissors in the center are called "Easy Grip" scissors. Because they stay open to the maximum position and always return to this spot when used, a child can easily learn this step in cutting. Also, the Easy Grip scissors require very little effort to make a cut, which would be very helpful for children who have very limited strength in their hands. The scissors on the left are four-holed scissors. These scissors are meant to be used in a hand-over-hand motion with the adult's fingers in the outer holes on each side. When using these scissors with a child, the adult can demonstrate the exact way to hold the hand and to rotate the wrist. The scissors on the right have been modified by welding two more holes on one side. These "fist grip" scissors were made especially for a child who could not open his hand to hold other scissors. Illustration credit: R. Mechtly.

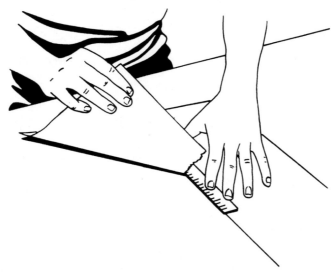

Figure 3.9. Some children cannot handle scissors at all. They still can cut paper by using a tearing board or ruler/straight edge. The straight edge is placed along the line to be cut or torn. One hand holds down the straight edge and the index finger and thumb of the other hand holds the paper and pulls the paper against the straight edge. Illustration credit: R. Mechtly.

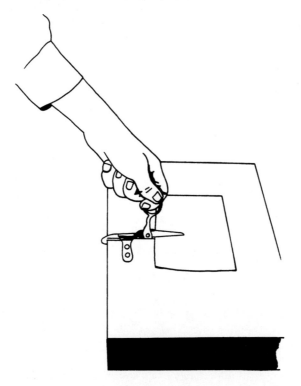

Figure 3.10. This modification illustrates how a pair of scissors can be mounted on a board. One blade is stationary. The paper, after it is placed on the board, can be cut with a one-handed stroke. Between cuts the paper must be moved. Illustration credit: V. Foster and R. Mechtly.

Figure 3.11. Handles of brushes, markers and pencils can be thickened by adding recycled foam rubber to them. Here a piece of foam rubber has been rubberbanded to a brush enabling a child to more easily grasp the tool. Observe how the drawing paper has been secured to the work surface with tape. Illustration credit: R. Mechtly.

Figure 3.12. A favorite activity is to go on a texture safari and collect and later "record" these textures by making crayon rubbings of them. Children (both with and without disabilities) often have difficulty in making an even rubbing because they are not using the side of the crayon. By holding the crayon (with label peeled off) in a large bulldog clip, the problem is eliminated. The bulldog clip can also be helpful in holding other art tools so the reader is encouraged to experiment. Illustration credit: V. Foster and R. Mechtly.

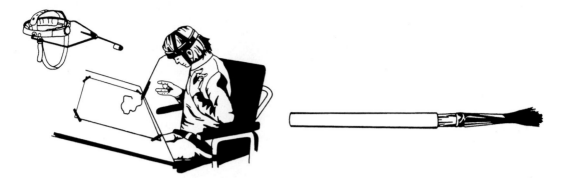

Figure 3.13. Children who have limited or no use of their hands, but can move their heads, can fully participate in drawing and painting activities if the pencil or brush is attached to a head pointer. If this is not possible, then it may be possible to use a foot- or a mouth-held art tool (see Fig. 3.14). Illustration credit: R. Mechtly.

Figure 3.14. If the head pointer does not work, and the child can hold things in his mouth, a paintbrush or pencil can be adapted for mouth use. A length of plastic tubing that is wide enough to fit over the tool can be obtained from a pharmacy or hardware store. It can be cut to the desired length and slipped over the handle of the art tool. Be sure to check with medical records and personnel before fitting a child with a mouth holder for art tools. Also, be sure the plastic material is safe to use in the mouth, and always sterilize the holder and brush before use. Illustration credit: R. Mechtly.

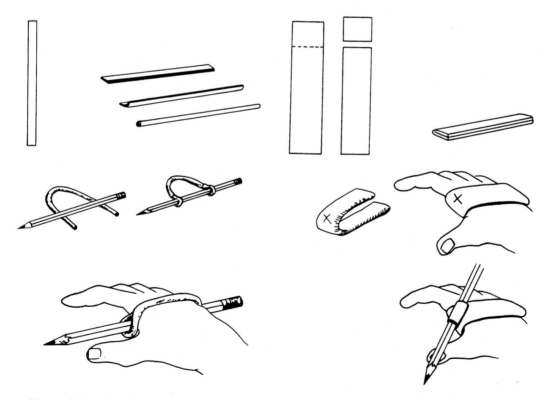

Figures 3.15 and 3.16. Orthoplast is a special material used by occupational and physical therapists to construct adaptive equipment. It is available from hospital suppliers. When orthoplast is heated to 200 degrees F (in water or a warm oven), it can be easily molded. These two figures illustrate two ways orthoplast can be used to assist a child with physical disabilities to easily hold a drawing (or painting) tool. Adapted from Callan (1987) by permission. Illustration credit: R. Mechtly.

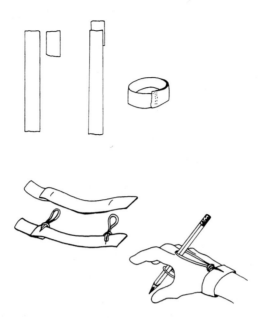

Figure 3.17. Velcro can be used to help hold and fasten a variety of art media and tools. In this illustration, rubber bands have been added to velcro wrist bands to provide a tension that also is springy, making it easier to grasp and manipulate the drawing or painting tool. Note that there are slits in the wrist bands through which the rubber bands are attached. Illustration credit: R. Mechtly.

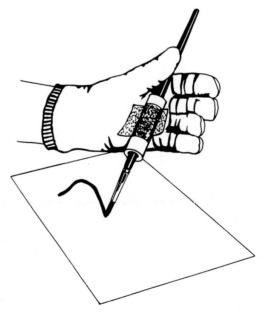

Figure 3.18. Velcro can also be used to help hold a brush or pencil. In this illustration the velcro is glued to the palm of an old glove and to the dowel holding a brush or pencil. Adapted from Callan (1987) by permission. Illustration credit: R. Mechtly.

TOP VIEW

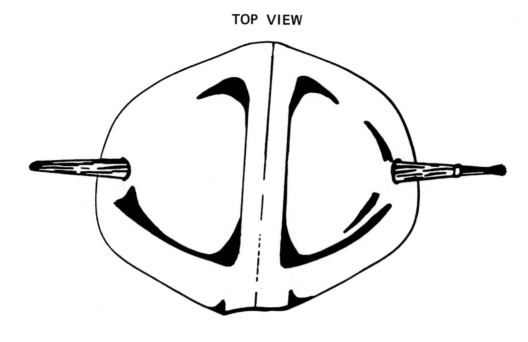

SIDE VIEW

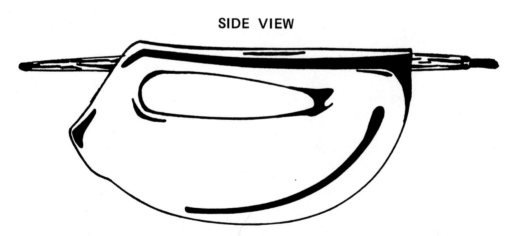

Figure 3.19. The handle from a recycled plastic gallon jug can be used to create a special handle, enabling a child with hands that cannot be opened (i.e., are in a fist configuration) to draw or paint. Sufficient space should be left around the jug handle so that holes for the pencil or brush handle can be punched into the plastic. Note that there are two ways of holding and using this special plastic handle. The art tool may need to be taped to the plastic so that it does not slip when weight is applied to it. Adapted from Callan (1987) by permission. Illustration credit: R. Mechtly.

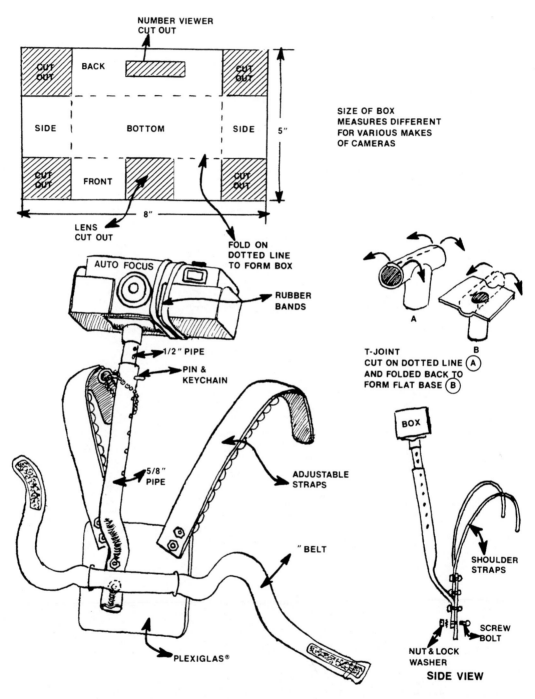

Figure 3.20. If a child has limited use of his hands, a special holder can be constructed to hold an instamatic autofocus camera. The camera permits the child to make his own design decisions and has eliminated the need for fine motor skills.

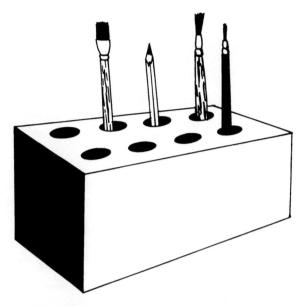

Figure 3.21. A simple holder can be made to store and distribute drawing and painting tools. Here holes have been drilled in a sturdy block of wood. Note that the holes are deep enough (about half the length of the brushes and markers and pencils) to securely hold the tools. Also note that the holes are far enough apart to permit ease of selection and replacement by children with limited fine motor control. Illustration credit: R. Mechtly.

Figure 3.22. Providing a reference or orientation point will be very helpful for children with visual impairments. There are several ways to accomplish this task. The child's paper can be placed in a cookie sheet that has a raised edge on all sides. The paper should be cut just a bit smaller than the inner parameter of the cookie sheet. Both the paper and the cookie sheet should be anchored. Children with limited motor control, difficulty with boundaries or perseveration may also benefit by drawing or painting on paper secured to this kind of cookie sheet. A lot of cleanup problems can be prevented when using fingerpaint if the child can paint on paper placed in a raised-edge cookie sheet. Illustration credit: R. Mechtly.

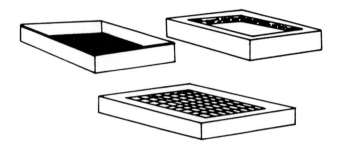

Figure 3.23. A screen board can be made to provide a special textured surface on which children with visual impairments can draw. First a piece of screen is cut to standard paper size (either 9 by 12 inches or 12 by 18 inches). The rough edges need to be taped over with masking tape. Next, the screen is taped to a piece of cardboard that is about 11 by 14 inches (or 14 by 20 inches for the larger size screen). A frame of 1¾ inch thick cardboard is added as a parameter. A piece of paper can be secured on top of the screen. Now a texture pattern will be left as the child draws on the paper with a crayon. Adapted from Callan (1987) by permission. Illustration credit: R. Mechtly.

Figure 3.24. Note how this eight-year-old child who is blind places his nondominant hand on the lower right-hand corner of the drawing paper. This corner placement provides an orientation point for the artist. His hand remained over the corner of the paper the entire time he was working on his marker drawing. Before he began his drawing, the art therapist verbally and tactually oriented him to the drawing paper by saying, "B, this is the lower right hand of your drawing paper" (while she placed his right hand on the corner of the paper).

Figure 3.25. Children with limited motor control may tend to knock over water and paint containers. Velcro can be used to anchor containers. Gravel can be placed in the water and paint containers to provide added stability. Illustration credit: V. Foster and R. Mechtly.

Figure 3.26. Sometimes it is easier for a child to approach a water container from the side instead of from the top. Here a girl with physical disabilities paints her wood sculpture. The water container is a recycled plastic jug with a window cut into its side. Rocks have been placed in the bottom of the jug for added stability and to minimize tipping. Larry S. Barnfield designed this adaptive water container.

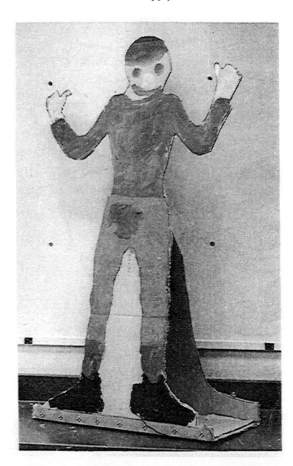

Figure 3.27. An eight-year-old boy who was deaf decided to accept the additional challenge of constructing a life-size portrait of one of his favorite television characters, the Fonze. He worked on a recycled bicycle box and used his own body trace as the outline. He left additional cardboard at the bottom of the figure and when he finished painting the portrait, he folded this cardboard up behind the figure to create a freestanding figure.

FOUR CATEGORIES OF ADAPTATIONS

Our discussion of art adaptations shall include four categories: adaptations in the physical space, adaptations in the art media and tools, adaptations in the instructional sequence, and technological adaptations. Each category is discussed in relation to issues in working with children with the six major disabling conditions.

Adaptations in the Physical Space

Physical space can have a profound influence on a child's behavior. Attention to the space in which the art experiences are to occur can help the child stay on task, focus, create unique art solutions, and prevent disruptive behavior and other frustrations (Anderson, 1992, 1979; Susi, 1989).

CHILDREN WITH MENTAL RETARDATION. Limit visual stimuli by eliminating distracting items on walls and bulletin boards. Use dividers/cardboard carrells to separate children while working so they will not be able to copy each other's work (Fig. 3.7). Be sure students understand that being separated/isolated is not a punishment. Use a game format in which each child is asked to keep his work a secret until it is completed. Reconvene the class after completion of the artwork so all can share and discuss what each has done.

CHILDREN WITH LEARNING DISABILITIES. Same as above. Have individualized work spaces that are perceived as a reward (a privilege) rather than a punishment. Keep art materials stored (out of child's reach and view) until the group understands what they are to do in class.

CHILDREN WITH BEHAVIORAL DISORDERS/EMOTIONAL DISTURBANCE. Same as above. A child that works in a smaller room/space will be less likely to be hyperactive—the space will help control the behavior. Avoid working in a very large space with a very hyperactive child, as the space will stimulate lots of movement (unless that is one of your goals).

CHILDREN WITH PHYSICAL DISABILITIES. If medically possible, have the child work on the floor or work sitting in a chair instead of staying in his wheelchair (Fig. 3.3). (See Figures 3.4 and 3.5 for table modifications.) If it is medically or logistically inappropriate to remove the child from his wheelchair, use a lap board made from heavy cardboard that is secured to the arms of the wheelchair with very strong tape (Fig. 3.6). Be sure the art room is a barrier-free environs. Use tape to secure paper to the worktable. Use sandbags, water jugs or C-clamps to help secure other art materials to the work surface.

CHILDREN WHO ARE DEAF/HARD-OF-HEARING. Seat the children at a round table so all can see the signs and understand everything that is being said during the introductory and ending "show-and-tell" parts of the art session. Also, try to position those children who can speechread near the teacher. After the children understand the art experience in which they are to engage, explain that each child will work independently and keep his work a secret. Use cardboard carrels during the working period to encourage unique (uncopied) artwork (Fig. 3.7). Be sure to reconvene the class as a group after individual, "secret" art-making.

CHILDREN WITH VISUAL IMPAIRMENTS. Have the art room organized so that there is a consistent storage place for all art materials. This enables the child to be able to move around the room and get his own art materials. This encourages independence. Seat the child near the best light to maximize whatever vision he still may have.

Adaptations in Art Media and Tools

Perhaps the largest category of art adaptations is in media and tools. It is also the most challenging for the teacher and therapist. Teamwork with the child will be essential as well as a willingness to engage in "trial and error" in designing appropriate art media and tool adaptations. The emphasis has to be on individual children in specific situations (Anderson, 1992, 1979; Callan, 1987).

Two-Dimensional Media and Tools

Scissors/Cutting Skills

CHILDREN WITH MENTAL RETARDATION AND CHILDREN WITH LEARNING DISABILITIES. Use task analysis (discussed later in this chapter), four-hole scissors for hand/over/hand teaching, or preparation of materials by precutting shapes (Fig. 3.8).

CHILDREN WITH BEHAVIORAL DISORDERS/EMOTIONAL DISTURBANCE. Use scissors with rounded points to prevent injury. Provide specific guidelines for use, and specify consequences for misuse prior to letting students use scissors.

CHILDREN WITH PHYSICAL DISABILITIES. Use preparation of materials by precutting shapes. Use a straight edge or board to tear (Fig. 3.9). The child may be able to use either fist-grip scissors, or specially mounted electric scissors (Fig. 3.10). Team up the child with a peer who has the ability to use scissors, or provide adult assistance. Be sure the child makes the design decisions even though he cannot manipulate scissors. Have a box of cloth scraps that can be easily torn, and help by putting a one-inch cut in the cloth to help the child get started in tearing the cloth.

CHILDREN WHO ARE DEAF/HARD-OF-HEARING. No specific adaptations.

CHILDREN WITH VISUAL IMPAIRMENTS. Provide pre-cut art materials. If using scissors, ones with rounded points may prevent injuries.

Cut and Paste/Glue Artwork

CHILDREN WITH MENTAL RETARDATION. Precut shapes. Use task analysis to teach appropriate pasting skills. Consider using several types of paste and glue containers/dispensers, and individualizing the pasting tasks. Glue sticks may be preferred over glue bottles from which glue can flow uncontrollably. See adaptations for cutting/scissors above.

CHILDREN WITH LEARNING DISABILITIES. See above. The art experience may provide opportunities to practice sequencing and to teach basic geometric shapes. Math problems can be given with the answer being the number of shapes the child gets to paste down and use in his artwork.

CHILDREN WITH BEHAVIORAL DISORDERS/EMOTIONAL DISTURBANCE. See adaptation section on cutting and the use of scissors. Assess the situation to determine whether the child might use scissors to cut himself or to hurt someone else. Use precut shapes if you feel the child will get frustrated in trying to cut out shapes or will hurt himself or someone else with the scissors.

CHILDREN WITH PHYSICAL DISABILITIES. Use precut shapes. Adapt gluing by creating a special sticky surface by mounting contact paper *sticky side* out on a piece of cardboard. The child then can place shapes on the sticky surface without the frustration of having to apply glue. Or team children up to maximize fine motor strengths.

CHILDREN WHO ARE DEAF/HARD–OF–HEARING. Utilize the art experience to reinforce vocabulary.

CHILDREN WITH VISUAL IMPAIRMENTS. Use different textured papers from which to precut different shapes. A glue stick might work better than a glue bottle.

Markers, Pencils and Other Drawing Tools

CHILDREN WITH MENTAL RETARDATION. Thicken handles using foam rubber or dowels with a hole drilled into them into which the drawing tool is placed (Fig. 3.11). Check to insure materials are nontoxic. Use a crayon held sideways in a bulldog clip to facilitate texture rubbings (Fig. 3.12).

CHILDREN WITH LEARNING DISABILITIES AND CHILDREN WITH BEHAVIORAL DISORDERS/EMOTIONAL DISTURBANCE. Use scented markers occasionally for added multisensory experiences and for increased motivation. Have enough paper and topics so the child does not get bored or finish early, and/or have a second art experience planned in case the child finishes early. Check to insure materials are nontoxic.

CHILDREN WITH PHYSICAL DISABILITIES. Use a special holder for pencils/drawing tools. This can be a helmet holder, a mouth holder or a foot/shoe holder (Figs. 3.13 & 3.14). Orthoplast can be molded to fit individual hand needs (Figs. 3.15–3.17). Velcro can be sewn to a glove and glued to a drawing tool (Fig. 3.18). Adapt brushes using the handle from a plastic gallon jug (Fig. 3.19). Secure drawing paper with tape. Move the paper as needed according to the individual child's range of movement (Fig. 3.1 & 3.2). Check to insure materials are nontoxic. Keep mouthpiece holders sanitized and limit use to only the same child. Use weighted water and paint containers to prevent the child from tipping them. Store brushes and drawing tools in special wood holders that enable the child to actually select art tools himself (Fig. 3.21). Use a crayon held sideways in a bulldog clip to facilitate texture rubbings (Fig. 3.12). Use preparation of materials if necessary, or avoid using drawing/painting activities and adapt the art activity by having the child use an autofocus camera (Fig. 3.20).

CHILDREN WHO ARE DEAF/HARD–OF–HEARING. Demonstrate what the child is being asked to do. Provide a partially completed example. Use the "secret game" to encourage children to work independently and at specially shielded work areas (as in using carrells) (Fig. 3.7). Students are asked to keep their artwork hidden or "secret" from others until it is completed. In keeping work a secret, children will not be tempted to copy. The "secret game" format motivates the children to do their work. Be sure the child understands why he is being separated from the others during the working part of the art session. If children are not working in carrells, have the group work at a round table. This enables the children to see everyone, thus making it easier to communicate. Have the children discuss, answer questions, etc., *AFTER* work is finished because deaf children who use total communication or sign language have to put down art tools so they can use their hands in signing. Analyze the art activity to identify new vocabulary, and provide clear definitions for new words.

CHILDREN WITH VISUAL IMPAIRMENTS. Use an orientation/reference point or method: (a) Tape paper down and tear off lower right-hand corner, or put a piece of tape over the lower right-hand corner so the child can orient himself to the page. Or (b) have the child work on a paper that is placed (and taped) in a cookie sheet that has sides to it. These edges also provide orientation points/areas. (c) The child can draw on a screen board with a crayon. The crayon leaves a textured trail. (d) A raised edge can be created by "drawing" with a white glue bottle that has a small opening. When the glue dries, it leaves a raised edge. (e) Scented markers can help the child differentiate between colors. Markers can be Braille-marked. (f) Use different-textured papers (see Figs. 3.22–3.24).

Paint and Brushes

CHILDREN WITH MENTAL RETARDATION. Use task analysis to determine the specific steps needed to teach painting skills and proper brush techniques.

Task analysis is discussed later in this chapter. Assist children who have trouble grasping brushes by thickening brush handles by taping or rubber-banding foam rubber to them. Having one brush per color prevents the need to continually clean the brushes before moving to another color (and prevents accidental color mixing when the child forgets to clean a brush before putting it into another color). It might help to have the children paint on paper that is taped to the table or that is taped inside a cookie sheet with raised edges (Figs. 3.11 & 3.22). This prevents paint from getting all over the table and helps provide some limits for the child.

CHILDREN WITH LEARNING DISABILITIES. Same as above. Set specific guidelines for use. Have the child tell you what these are in his own words (to check on how well he understands what he is to do).

CHILDREN WITH BEHAVIORAL DISORDERS/EMOTIONAL DISTURBANCE. Same as above. Be very clear about procedures and rules. Give clear directions and state your expectations in terms of art skills and behaviors. Be clear about the consequences of inappropriate behaviors *BEFORE* the child begins the art session. Check with the rest of the treatment team to insure that the methods they use (i.e., token economies, behavior modification, logical consequences, etc.) are the same as the ones you use. This will insure there is consistent treatment of inappropriate behaviors throughout the school.

CHILDREN WITH PHYSICAL DISABILITIES. Use a helmet- or mouth-holder for the brush. A simple holder for the mouth can be made using a length of plastic or rubber tubing that fits over the handle of the brush (Figs. 3.13 & 3.14). Once adapted, the brush mouth-holder should be sterilized and kept in an airtight container or plastic bag. The brush should be used ONLY by the same child (to prevent germs/viruses from spreading). Brush handles can be thickened with foam rubber or shortened as needed. A glove holder can be made using velcro (Fig. 3.18). A plastic gallon jug can be adapted to hold a brush (Fig. 3.19). A child with the full use of his toes can use them to hold a brush. A brush can be taped to a rubber spatula handle and then the spatula can be taped to a shoe. Paint and water containers can be anchored with strong tape, velcro, or by adding gravel (Figures 3.25 & 3.26). Paper should be taped to the table or easel or lap board. An autofocus camera can be used (Fig. 3.20), if the child cannot use an adapted brush. Also, computers with graphic art programs can be used. In this way the child still makes design and aesthetic decisions, but the "fine motor skills" are performed by the camera or the computer.

CHILDREN WHO ARE DEAF/HARD-OF-HEARING. Demonstrate skills using both "hands-on" and written directions. Analyze the art experience for key vocabulary words and capitalize on the art session to instruct/teach new vocabulary or to provide additional drill for familiar words.

CHILDREN WITH VISUAL IMPAIRMENTS. Use Braille-marked paint containers that are spill-proof. Scents can be added (a different one per color) to help the child distinguish between colors. Use one Braille-marked brush per paint container. Tape paper down and use an orientation or reference point to help guide the child. The paper can also be taped into a cookie sheet that has raised edges to provide parameters and orientation points (Figs. 3.22–3.24).

Three-Dimensional Media

Wood and Cardboard Sculpture

CHILDREN WITH MENTAL RETARDATION. Use precut, **pre-sanded** wood scraps or precut cardboard or recycled cardboard boxes. Limit the numbers of wood scraps or other three-dimensional media. Turn the activity into an academic skills reinforcement experience by giving the child a simple addition problem. The answer is the number of pieces of wood, cardboard boxes or shapes that the child will get with which to build a sculpture. (See Chapter 7 for more examples of art and mathematics activities.) Use task analysis to help the child learn appropriate gluing skills. Have the child hold two pieces of wood or cardboard that have glue on them and are to be glued together, and count to 30. By the end of the count, the glue will be dry and the pieces will have adhered. Consider different types of glues (glue sticks, white glue, etc.) and adapt the type of glue to the needs of the child. If painting a sculpture, limit the numbers of colors of paint so the child does not get frustrated when he is unable to cover one part of the sculpture without getting paint all over. It may be best to limit the color choices to only one.

CHILDREN WITH LEARNING DISABILITIES. Same as above. The art experience could also be academically oriented by having wood scraps or cardboard shapes cut into basic geometric shapes. This then could be a part of the way the child gets his shapes. For example, "You can select two squares, three triangles and two circles for your sculpture."

CHILDREN WITH BEHAVIORAL DISORDERS/EMOTIONAL DISTURBANCE. In addition to the above, the teacher or the art therapist could have the group work in teams (selected judiciously by teacher or therapist) and play a game. How high (or wide) can one group make their sculpture? (All teams will have the same number of pieces.) Be sure all wood scraps have at least one level (flat) surface that can be easily glued to other pieces. If using recycled cardboard, precut the shapes for the child.

CHILDREN WITH PHYSICAL DISABILITIES. Precut and presand all wood/cardboard. Work in teams that have one member with some fine motor skills. Glue could be sponged or brushed on. (Sometimes a glue gun will be easier to use.) Use large enough pieces so that they can be easily manipulated with a minimal amount of fine motor skills. Let the child do as much of the work as possible including the selection of wood or cardboard pieces that will go into the sculpture.

CHILDREN WHO ARE DEAF/HARD–OF–HEARING. None. Be sure to maximize the potential to teach/reinforce vocabulary. Show only partially completed examples (or remove completed examples before the child begins his own work). This prevents copying.

CHILDREN WITH VISUAL IMPAIRMENTS. Have completed examples that the child can explore. The examples should be small enough that the child can tactually "see" using both hands. Larger examples will be difficult to understand because the hands cannot grasp the entire sculpture. Provide a means for the child to go and get his own wood or cardboard pieces from a container in the room. Be sure all splinters are removed and all surfaces of each wood piece has been sanded. A glue stick may be easier to use than a glue bottle.

Clay

CHILDREN WITH MENTAL RETARDATION. Exploratory experiences will be important at first. It will help to demonstrate how to attach two pieces of clay and how to "pull out" appendages (legs, arms). Demonstrate clay skills BEFORE distributing the clay to the children. Clay is so motivating that many children will cease to listen/observe the demonstration. Tactile-defensive children might be helped via having them use clay tools at first. Positive reinforcement will also help. Determine what is reinforcing to the individual child and use this to help reward appropriate behaviors and art skills. The intrinsically motivating feature of clay will make this art experience especially powerful.

CHILDREN WITH LEARNING DISABILITIES. Same as above. Clay experiences can be used to reinforce other academic concepts (proportion, addition, subtraction, vocabulary, and sequencing), so analyze the experience to maximize the curricular interrelatedness. Have the child repeat your directions in different words to be sure he understands what is to be done.

CHILDREN WITH BEHAVIORAL DISORDERS/EMOTIONAL DISTURBANCE. Set clear rules and directions along with clear explanations of what will happen if the rules/directions are not followed. Coordinate consequences with the rest of the school educational team so there is a unified front. Teach specific skills to help the child successfully express himself in clay. Also provide choices in terms of where to sit, and what to make, so the child is empowered and is encouraged to be independent. Help intercept potential material failures and situations in which the child might get easily frustrated.

CHILDREN WITH PHYSICAL DISABILITIES. Have children "mix" clay by putting dry clay powder and water into a very strong garbage bag. Then the group can knead the bag. Preprepare mixed clay by rolling it into fist-sized balls. Then the children can flatten and texture the clay as they desire. Team up those children without fine motor abilities with children who have some fine motor abilities.

CHILDREN WHO ARE DEAF/HARD–OF–HEARING. No specific adaptations will be necessary except the need to utilize the clay experience as both an art activity and one in which the child learns new vocabulary. If necessary, show examples but remove them before the children begin so they cannot copy the example. Use the "secret" method (described above) to encourage children to make their own unique creations.

CHILDREN WITH VISUAL IMPAIRMENTS. Provide examples that the child can easily understand via tactile exploration with his hands. Do not hesitate to teach basic clay skills. See note about tactile defensiveness under "Children with Mental Retardation" above. The same principles apply here.

Adaptations in the Instructional Sequence

Art-Centered Learning

The third category of adaptations is in the instructional sequence. Among the ways that this is accomplished is by means of curricular integration/correlation. This means incorporating concepts from other content areas into art experiences so that they become art-centered learning. In Chapters 5–9 of this book there are many examples in which curricular integration is demonstrated in terms of art and reading, art and language arts, art and science, art and math, and art and social studies. This approach provides for repetition of academic concepts and reinforcement of learning through the visual arts. Art-centered learning is extremely powerful because art is an intrinsic reinforcer and motivator for all children. Moreover, this integrative approach puts art at the center of the school curriculum and, by example, may hopefully demonstrate that art belongs in the center of one's life (Anderson, 1992, 1979; Anderson & Morreau, 1986).

Additional Challenges

A second grouping under adaptations in the instructional sequence consists of providing additional challenges in an art experience. This approach provides for children who are "early finishers," or who are gifted and desire these challenges to their intellect and skill. For example, in printmaking, an additional challenge would be for a child to make a print that has a second or third color. This more involved task could be assigned when the child has demonstrated his competency in mastering printmaking with one color. It is understood that not all children will master the initial one-color print phase and want to go further by attempting the additional challenge of executing a two- or three-color print.

Other examples of additional challenges would be having children write and illustrate their own books (see Chap. 5), create a cover design and make several copies of their books. In puppetmaking, children could be challenged to construct a puppet that has arms that move—or facial features that can change expressions.

In doing a life-size portrait, the child could be challenged to construct a figure that stands on its own, i.e., by attaching it to a large piece of cardboard on which he would work directly. In this challenge the child must also figure out a way to make the cardboard stand on its own without leaning against the wall. Another challenge for older children would be to have them create a life-size portrait of a celebrity or famous storybook character (see Fig. 3.27). A further challenge might be to turn the cardboard figure into a chair or piece of furniture in the spirit of what some of the avant-garde artists have done.

Task Analysis

Another approach that falls into the category of adaptations in the instructional sequence is task analysis. In task analysis all the steps necessary to complete a task are isolated and described and put in their most logical sequence. Task analysis is especially helpful in teaching basic art skills to children with fine motor problems.

It is essential that steps in a task analysis are observable. To check for observable steps consider the following: Can one see the behavior? Can the behavior be measured/evaluated? If two or three persons observed the activity, would they agree on what step(s) had occurred?

In analyzing a task, it is essential that the teacher or art therapist execute the task himself. It is also helpful to observe someone else as they physically demonstrate the task. It is helpful to field test the completed task analysis to be certain that no step is out of order or has been omitted.

Finally, it is essential that the learner has all the prerequisite skills he needs to execute each step in the task analysis. For example, if the child does not know how to hold scissors so that they are perpendicular to the paper he is cutting, then he will not be able to make a successful cut. Or if the child does not know about Valentine's Day, then he will need to be given information about the event before he is asked to construct a Valentine's Day card.

The task of creating a Valentine's Day card will illustrate how task analysis is accomplished. First the art experience is stated as a behavioral objective:

> Given construction paper, markers, paste and scissors, the child will construct a Valentine's Day card that includes two to six cutout heart

shapes (non-overlapping) and a three- to five-word (self-developed) written greeting.

The basic skills and concepts that the child needs to have mastered to complete the activity include: an understanding of Valentine's Day, an understanding of the purpose of a greeting card, the ability to cut, paste and write. Specifically, these prerequisite skills would be:

1. fold the construction paper in half
2. cut heart shapes out of the paper
3. select two to six heart shapes
4. place shapes on the card so none overlap
    a. pick up one shape
    b. spread a thin coat of glue on one side of the heart
    c. turn over the glued side of the heart and place it on the folded paper card
    d. wipe off any excess glue
5. repeat step 4 as needed
6. select words from a list provided for a greeting for the card
7. write a greeting on the card
8. clean up, throw away paper scraps, close glue bottle, recap markers
9. send card (Morreau & Anderson, 1986)

Let us assume that in our example the child has all the skills for the construction of the card except cutting skills. One of the most frequently cited problems that children with disabilities have is in cutting skills (Anderson, 1980; Anderson, McAnally, & Colchado, 1978). Here is an example of the steps involved in a task analysis of using scissors to cut paper.

The task should be stated as a behavioral objective so that the task is clearly defined in observable terms. (For information on ways to write behavioral objectives, see Chapter 4.) So for our purposes we will begin with the following behavioral objective:

> Given a paper with a line, and a pair of scissors, the child will use the scissors to cut along the line so that the paper is not torn and the cut does not deviate from the marked line.

The following are subcomponents the child needs to master to be able to cut as described above in the behavioral objective:

1. Pick up scissors and place the thumb of the dominant hand through one hole and the second finger of the dominant hand through the other hole. (The first finger rests on the outside of the hole.)
2. Rotate the wrist of the dominant hand so the scissors are pointing straight out from the hand parallel to the floor or table.
3. Lift thumb until scissors blades are completely open.
4. Pick up the page with the guideline marked on it (with the subdominant hand) so that

the hand is turned up with the page held flat (the thumb is set on top of the page and the rest of the fingers hold the bottom of the page).

5. Position the line on the page so it is directly in front of the hand holding the scissors.
6. Place the lined paper (with the subdominant hand) between the fully opened scissors (held in the dominant hand).
7. Hold the page firmly against the opened scissors (with the subdominant hand) and hold in position (do not move away from the apex of the open scissors).
8. Push the dominant thumb down (while holding the scissors blades perpendicular to the line being cut).
9. Close the scissors blades completely.
10. Pull up on the scissors blades with the thumb to open the scissors.
11. Pull the page and the cut area with the other hand.
12. Repeat steps 7–11 until the entire drawn line is cut. (Morreau & Anderson, 1986, p. 53)

Task analysis is an important method to teach basic skills (art or any other). The approach helps the child to master art skills. Once the child has mastered art skills, he then has the ability to express himself with a variety of art media and can fully participate in art.

> Task analysis is not the end of an art activity, rather, it is the beginning of art instruction. The major goal of art instruction is to provide the learner with the means to go beyond a simple demonstration of art skills, such as the ability to cut, paste, or draw marks on a page, to the creation of a fully developed artistic statement demonstrating skill mastery and individuality in the art work produced. (Morreau & Anderson, 1986, p. 54)

Discipline-Based Art Education

Discipline-Based Art Education (DBAE) is a reality in many art programs around the country. Art teachers will need to consider adaptions in their instructional approach to accommodate children with disabilities that have been included in the regular art classes. DBAE and ways of adapting this curricular approach are discussed in Chapter 5.

Technological Adaptations

The fourth major category is technological art adaptations, most of which have evolved from the use of personal computers. The advantages of the use of a computer include:

1. The computer is neutral. It does not criticize and is therefore much less threatening as a instructional aid than another person might be. Students can be free to make mistakes and practice in a personal, private manner (Kirk & Galligher, 1989).
2. The computer can be intrinsically motivating. Students who may be highly distractible have been able to become extremely focused and engaged in using a computer.

3. The computer can provide immediate feedback and reinforcement and has an almost limitless amount of patience.

4. The computer software often presents information in a game format which also can be extremely motivating to students.

5. The computer allows students to work at their own pace, permitting individualized learning.

6. The computer can foster a sense of independence in children who may have few opportunities to be in control of their surroundings. This mastery and sense of control are especially important for children with disabilities, particularly those with physical disabilities (Johnson, 1987; Kirk & Galligher, 1989).

7. The computer can be equipped with art software and can become the "hands" for children with limited hand use. They still have the experience of making aesthetic decisions without the frustration of trying to do art tasks requiring very fine motor skills (*Art Education,* 1983; White, 1985; Ettinger & Roland, 1986).

8. The "primary visual mode of learning the computer represents is especially helpful to students with hearing impairments." (Anderson, 1992, p. 296)

9. With good software, the computer can foster discovery and problem-solving skills learning.

10. The computer can remediate short attention problems that children may have.

11. The computer can also assist with the development of "eye-hand coordination, visual motor skills, logical reasoning processes, creative decision making and interpersonal relationships" in children with behavioral and emotional problems (Canter, 1989, p. 314).

12. The computer can also provide a careful and minute record of a child's movements in image-making as well as the development of those images (Anderson, 1992; Weinberg, 1985).

ADAPTATIONS, THE AMERICANS WITH DISABILITIES ACT, AND THE INDIVIDUALS WITH DISABILITIES EDUCATION ACT

The Americans with Disabilities Act (ADA) became law on July 26, 1990. As yet the implications of this landmark legislation are not fully known. Among the provisions of this law is one for the "acquisition or modification of equipment and devices" (PL 101-336, 1990). Therefore, adaptative equipment is one of the mandates of this legislation (and most likely can be funded via this law).

On September 29, 1992, the regulations for Individuals with Disabilities Act (IDEA) (the reauthorization of PL 94-142) became law. One of the provisions of the IDEA is in the area of assistive technology devices and services. "Assistive technology devices and services should be made available to a child with a disability if it is a required part of the child's special education, or a related service or a supplemental service or aid" (*Federal Register 57*(189), p. 44813). Therefore, technological assistance in the form of computers or specially designed adaptative equipment could be funded under the mandates of the IDEA.

REFERENCES

Anderson, F. E. (1979). *Art Adaptations: A slide tape instructional program* [slide tape]. Normal, IL: Illinois State University.

Anderson, F. E. (1992). *Art for all the children: Approaches to art therapy for children with disabilities.* Springfield, IL: Charles C Thomas.

Anderson, F. E. (1980). *Art in secondary schools in Illinois.* Unpublished manuscript, Illinois State University, Normal, IL.

Anderson, F. E., Colchado, J., & McAnally, P. (1979). *Art for the handicapped.* Normal, IL: Illinois State University.

Callan, E. (1987). Art adaptations. Paper presentation at the National Art Education Association Conference, Boston, MA.

Canter, D. S. (1989). Art therapy and computers. In H. Wadeson (Ed.), *Advances in art therapy* (pp. 296–315). New York: John Wiley and Sons.

Canter, D. S. (1987). The therapeutic effects of combining Apple Macintosh computers and creativity software in art therapy sessions. *Art Therapy, 4*(1), 17–26.

Ettinger, L., & Roland, C. (1986). Using microcomputers in the art curriculum. *Art Education, 39*(1), 48–51.

Federal Register (September 29, 1992). 57(189) part 11 Department of Education. 34LFR parts 300 and 301. Assistance to States for the Education of children with disabilities Program and preschool Grants for children with disabilities; Final Rule.

Johnson, B. G. (1987). Using computer art in counseling children. *Elementary School Guidance and Counseling, 21*(4), 262–265.

Kirk, S., & Galligher, J. (1989). *Educating exceptional children.* Boston: Houghton Mifflin.

Mini-Issue: A microcomputer in every art room? (1985). *Art Education, 38* (2), 4–27.

Morreau, L., & Anderson, F. E. (1986). Task analysis in art: Building skills and success for handicapped learners. *Art Education, 39*(1), 52–54.

Public Law 101-336. Americans with Disabilities Act. July 26, 1990.

Public Law 101-476. Individuals with Disabilities Education Act. October 30, 1990.

Susi, F. G. (1989). The physical environment of art classrooms: A basis for effective discipline. *Art Education, 42*(4), 37–43.

Weinberg, D. J. (1985). The potential of rehabilitative computer art therapy for the quadriplegic, cerebral vascular accident and brain trauma. *Art Therapy, 2*(2), 66–72.

Chapter 4

INCLUDING ART IN
THE INDIVIDUALIZED EDUCATION PROGRAM

In 1975 Public Law (PL) 94-142, the Education for All Children Act, became law. There were several provisions in this law that profoundly influenced special education. One mandated children with disabilities be educated in the least restrictive environment (LRE). One of the best definitions of the LRE was provided by the Council for Exceptional Children. They defined a LRE for a child with disabilities as an educational placement

> in which his educational and related needs can be satisfactorily provided. This concept recognizes that exceptional children have a wide range of special educational needs, varying greatly in intensity and duration; that there is a recognized continuum of educational settings which may, at a given time, be appropriate for an individual child's needs; that to the maximum extent appropriate, exceptional children should be educated with nonexceptional children; and that special classes, separate schooling, or the removal of an exceptional child from education with nonexceptional children should occur when the intensity of the child's special education and related needs is such that they cannot be satisfied in an environment including nonexceptional children, even with the provision of supplementary aids and services. (*Council for Exceptional Children*, 1976, p. 43)

Since the mid 1970s there has been increasing demand that children with disabilities be normalized, and whenever possible be placed in regular education classes (Blandy, 1989; Lilly, 1988). In the 1990s this demand has been replaced by a strong belief that *all* children with disabilities be totally included in regular education classes. The inclusion concept virtually eliminates special education classrooms and resource rooms. Inclusion means that all support services and special education occur in the regular education classroom (the placement being the grade level and neighborhood school that the child with disabilities would typically have if she were not disabled) (Peters, n.d.; Minnesota Inclusive Education Technical Assistance Program, n.d.).

While the debate over the efficacy of inclusion continues, the reauthorization bill for PL 94-142, PL 101-476, was passed in 1990. This law, the Individuals with Disabilities Education Act, continues the mandate that children with disabilities be placed in the LRE. The new law continues to require the development of an Individualized Education Program (IEP) for every child with disabilities that receives special education. The IEP must be developed on an annual basis. This IEP is based on an assessment of the student's abilities and skills in six major areas: academic/cognitive, communication status, motor and perceptual skills, self-help skills, social/emotional status, and prevocational/vocational.

The present level of educational performance is established for each of these six areas. Then a staffing is held at which parents or guardians, all teachers who have the child, a representation from the school district or unit who supervises the delivery of special education and, when possible, the child are present. It is during this staffing that the child's IEP is developed.

Art is not one of the subjects specifically included in the six major areas in which annual goals are written. Art may be included in the IEP in several ways. First, the child may be recommended for placement in a regular art class (if she is not already included in all regular education programs).

Art may be listed as a related service that can be used to assist the child in achieving a specific level of performance in any subject area. And art might be used to remediate a particular problem that the child may be having in one of the six major areas in which annual goals are written. There is a growing body of research that documents the positive use of the arts as vehicles for learning and for remediating academic and social problems in school. Chapter 5 includes a brief discussion of some of this research and is followed by examples of how art can be integrated into the reading, language arts, science, math and social studies curricula—i.e., how the entire school curriculum can be an art-centered approach and how art can be used to remediate other academic problems.

THE SEVEN PARTS OF AN IEP

All IEPs must include the following seven parts (Morreau & Anderson, 1984; Anderson, 1992):

1. the current level of performance of the learner
2. annual goals
3. short-term instructional objectives
4. the educational services and experiences that will be provided, as well as the dates that these begin and the period of time that these experiences and services will be provided
5. the nature of the child's participation in regular education programs
6. schedules, procedures, and objective criteria for annual evaluation
7. a transition plan (only required for students 14 years and older)

One can begin the IEP planning process by responding to the following questions (Morreau & Anderson, 1984):

1. The learner is working toward what ends? (What are the annual goals and short-term objectives?)
2. What is the learner's present level of artistic abilities and skills?
3. In what way(s) will the learner achieve these objectives and in what contexts? (What are the services and experiences offered, and what is the extent to which the individual will participate in regular education art programs?)
4. How effective is the IEP in accomplishing the goals set for the learner? (What are the evaluative criteria, the methods, and the schedule for assessing the effectiveness of the art experiences being provided to the learner?)

While special educators must determine a learner's needs and may conceptualize annual goals well in advance of the staffing at which an IEP is developed, and while there are many commercially available or district-wide available lists of such goals, these goals simply do not exist in the visual arts (Morreau & Anderson, 1984). Even if they did exist, most likely IEP planning would begin with a general idea of what an individual student needed to acquire in terms of basic art concepts and skills. Teachers who do not have background or training in art would have some difficulty with this task. Most special education teachers lack specific training in the visual arts or an understanding of what a typical child could expect to do in art or expect to know in art at a specific age. However, there is general agreement about what basic art skills a child typically should have at normal ages, and there is general agreement that children do move through a general developmental sequence in art (Chapman, 1978, 1985; Gardner, 1990; Kellogg, 1970; Lowenfeld & Brittain, 1987; Piaget & Inhelder, 1956; Salome & Moore, 1979).

Art Assessment

Some sort of art assessment will be called for prior to the IEP staffing. There are few standardized art measures available. Most likely the teacher will accomplish this assessment in terms of some sort of observational checklist. Such a checklist may include the child's response to standard two- and three-dimensional media, as well as the child's ability to recognize basic colors and basic art tools and to use them appropriately. It also might be helpful to make use of a starter sheet (see Figs. 4.1–4.3) to determine the child's ability to draw a figure and what her figure concept is.

It is important to realize all children have good and poor days and that children may behave differently at different times. This shift in behavior may show up in any drawing or art task that might be used for an assessment. Indeed one art educator (Kellogg, 1970) pointed out that a child drew in five

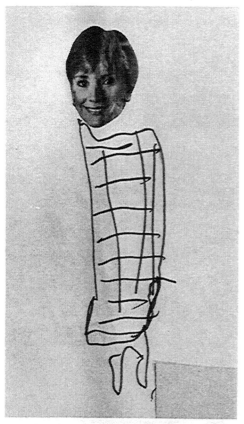

Figures 4.1 and 4.2. A starter sheet can be used as an art-based assessment task. The child is given a page with a head cut out from a magazine or pattern book. The head should be the same age, sex and ethnicity as the child who is to complete the picture. The child should be observed as she completes the picture using markers or other drawing tools. Observations would include how the child approaches the task (with enthusiasm, reluctantly, slowly, etc.) and what the child says during her drawing. Upon completion, the child can be asked to tell something about the person she has drawn. Figures 4.1 and 4.2 are starter sheets by an 11-year-old girl with moderate mental retardation. The activity can be presented in a game format by asking the child to draw what is missing. A second starter sheet (Fig. 4.2) that has a body, but no head, should also be given to the child to complete. As in the first starter sheet, the body should be the same age, sex and ethnicity as the child who is to complete the picture. The person drawings in the completed starter sheets can be compared with figure drawings that children typically would draw (see Chap. 2) in order to determine at what artistic developmental level the child may be functioning. This can provide an art age for the child that can be compared with her chronological age and her mental age, if this information is available. Larry S. Barnfield is acknowledged as the source for the starter sheet concept. Figure 4.2 is from Frances Anderson's, *ART FOR ALL THE CHILDREN: Approaches to Art Therapy for Children with Disabilities* (Springfield, IL: Charles C Thomas, Publisher), 1992.

Figure 4.3. This starter sheet has been completed by a boy who is 14 and has moderate mental retardation and deafness. Note how he has included details to his picture which depicts himself bowling. These details and the figure indicate that he is operating at a Schematic level of artistic development (typically *c.* seven to nine years of age). This and other starter sheets provided the first evidence that he was brighter than special educators first thought. (He had no expressive or receptive language and could not be evaluated using standard intellectual assessments.) From Frances Anderson's, *ART FOR ALL THE CHILDREN: Approaches to Art Therapy for Children with Disabilities* (Springfield, IL: Charles C Thomas, Publisher), 1992.

different ways during a single week. The point is that one should be aware of the possibility of variation in art tasks and should collect and base an evaluation on more than one piece of artwork. It also will be helpful to collect artwork done at several times during the school year. Such data will help in documentation of ability level and growth during the year.

What follows in Table 4.1 is an example of a simple checklist that can become the basis for an art observation/assessment. The art skill sheet developed by Troeger (Table 4.2) offers another example of an art assessment that has been successfully utilized in the IEP planning process for special needs students.

TABLE 4.1
GETTING STARTED IN ART
(A BEGINNING CHECKLIST)

Child		Yes	Sometimes	Not Yet
Knows	1. How to hold paint brush and use paint			
	2. How to hold scissors and cut paper with them			
Can	3. Spread glue evenly, using appropriate amount			
	4. Pick out the right colors when given their names			
	5. Name 3 colors			
	6. Identify 3 or more colors by name			
	7. Complete a starter sheet			
	8. Hold a crayon correctly			
Knows	9. How to clean up			
Can	10 Name 3 art activities completed last year and describe the processes			
Comments:				

Note. From <u>Art for All the Children: Approaches to Art Therapy for Children with Disabilities</u> (pg. 191) by F. E. Anderson, 1992, Springfield, IL: Charles C Thomas. Copyright 1992 by Charles C Thomas. Adapted by permission.

In doing an assessment of a child for an IEP one must note both the child's strengths and weaknesses. In 1992, Troeger refined a field-tested model for implementing IEPs in art (Anderson, 1992; Troeger-Clifford, 1981). In the model, Troeger stressed that a child must be evaluated within her own maturation and learning context. Observation and a review of the child's files will be an important part of the process of assessment. Troeger recommended the following tasks if the child seems to be developmentally behind normal children: a drawing, a painting using tempera, an art experience using cut-and-paste construction paper and a clay activity. If the child seems to be functioning in the schematic developmental level, then she recommends the following tasks: a person drawing, a drawing of a geometric form, a painting about which the artist writes or dictates a story, a cut-paper picture and a sculpture out of clay. While the child works, notes should be taken about how she approaches the tasks and what is verbalized during the activities.

Troeger developed an art skill sheet to record the child's artistic developmental levels and skills (Troeger-Clifford, 1980; Anderson, 1992). The Art Skill Sheet is presented in Table 4.2.

Annual Goals In Art

The next step that occurs in developing an IEP is that annual goals and short-term objectives are established. The short-term objectives will indicate when the child has mastered the annual goal. Annual goals will include skills, attitudes, and knowledge in a general way, and they do not have to be framed in terms of observable behaviors. Some annual goals in art might be:

1. The learner will demonstrate appreciation for her own and other student's artwork.
2. The learner will use art skills to express herself creatively.
3. The learner will demonstrate cooperation in doing group artwork.
4. The learner will learn the use of scissors, crayons and paint.
5. The learner will know the primary and secondary colors.

For each annual goal, there probably will be several short-term (behavioral) objectives.

Behavioral Objectives As A Part of Art Learning and Assessment

There are some limits to behavioral objectives. They are not a panacea, and they should not be used as *the* only means of evaluating a child's progress, the teachers' effectiveness, or the art program's success. The very nature of art and its focus on divergence and individualistic search for unique solutions does not easily lend itself to a series of specific behavioral or performance objectives.

Moreover, some art behaviors such as aesthetic responses cannot directly or overtly be easily measured (McAshan, 1970). Thus, covert and unobtrusive means must be sought to provide some index of aesthetic response (Webb, Campbell, Schwarts, & Sechrest, 1966). At best, these are gross indicators and do not really touch, explain, or assess the tremendous complexity of aesthetic response. Such behaviors as facial expressions, long undistractible attention, verbal or written expressions such as *wow, fantastic, astounding,* and *awesome,* or even dead silence in a class can give some clues about artistic response. Until more sophisticated measures are developed, these indirect means will have to be used.

Behavioral objectives often do not allow for the long-term assessment of

TABLE 4.2
ART SKILL SHEET

NAME: DATE: AGE: SEX:

DRAWING

_____ establish hand/eye contact with marker
_____ manipulate large marker on flat surface
_____ draw a circle
_____ draw a triangle
_____ draw a square
_____ draw a face
_____ draw a person
_____ draw a person with head, arms, legs
_____ draw a person with head, body, arms, legs
_____ draw a person beyond schematic level
_____ draw objects in front of or behind others
_____ utilize variation of shapes and details
_____ utilize different kinds of lines
        (continuous, short, thin, wide)
        to convey contours or texture

PAINTING

_____ control handling of brush
_____ paint freely on paper with large brush
_____ paint areas of color
_____ paint horizontal lines
_____ paint vertical lines
_____ recognize and choose colors:
        _____ red   _____ green   _____ black
        _____ yellow   _____ purple   _____ brown
        _____ blue   _____ orange   _____ white
_____ mix colors to create new colors
_____ paint representational symbols
        _____ house   _____ person   _____ car
        _____ tree   _____ animal   _____ others
_____ paint shapes, lines, and colors as
        designs
_____ utilize language to describe painting

CUT PAPER

_____ hold scissors
_____ open and close scissors
_____ cut on straight line
_____ cut out a circle
_____ cut out numerous shapes
_____ place paste on back of shape
_____ attach shape to design surface
_____ experiment with a few shapes, cutting
        and pasting at random
_____ combine shapes in simple patterns
_____ use papers varied in texture, color, and
        shape to make complex designs
_____ construct three-dimensional forms by
        folding, fitting, and fastening

CLAY

_____ grasp clay
_____ break clay into pieces
_____ change shape of clay
        (patting, poking, kneading)
_____ roll clay into a ball
_____ roll clay into a coil
_____ pinch or pull shape from lump of clay
_____ roll clay into slab with rolling pin
_____ join two or more shapes by smoothing,
        scoring, and use of slip
_____ add appropriate amount of water to
        keep clay in good working condition
_____ construct familiar objects (animals,
        people, cars, pots) with uniform
        thickness
_____ use simple tools to create texture

Other Helpful Data

Note. From Art for All the Children: Approaches to Art Therapy for Children with Disabilities (p. 191) by F. E. Anderson, 1992, Springfield, IL: Charles C Thomas. copyright by Charles C. Thomas. Printed by permission the effects of instruction. The assumption is that learning is a continuous cumulative process, and to determine that learning has occurred, some overt response must be made. However, incidental instruction occurs at all times through the observation of others. It may be years before a particular student behaviorally demonstrates what she has learned (Effland, 1974).

Writing Behavioral Objectives in Art

There are three main requirements for an objective to be behaviorally stated (Mager, 1962; Timitz-Wolf, 1985). First, the final *outcome* of the behavior is specified by name. For example, a child paints a card, builds a pot, or mixes a secondary color. Second, the behavioral objective must describe the *conditions* that are important and necessary for the performance or behavior to occur. Thus the child will build a pot, using clay; the child will print a card, using waterbase printer's ink and rice paper; the child will mix green when given a brush, and yellow and blue tempera paint; or the child will offer positive statements about one artwork on display that was created by a classmate. While the conditions of a behavioral objective will often include the art materials or instructions to perform, other conditions might be: a discussion of prints made by Japanese artists, a paint-spotted workspace, or an assigned group of students who are making murals. Or the conditions can include the natural circumstances in which the behavior is expected to occur (Morreau & Bruininks, 1991), for example, given leisure time in her home, the learner will be able to paint.

The third part of a behavioral objective is the *criterion*. Criterion statements may be cast in terms of quality, frequency, duration, or a combination of these factors. The criterion-measure provides a means of assessing when the child has demonstrated the desired behavior or mastered the particular developmental goal.

Generally, behavioral objectives begin with a statement of the conditions under which the performance will occur for the child using a "Given" statement. Thus, our examples of behavioral objectives could be stated as follows (criterion statements are in italics):

> Given clay, the learner will make a pot *having smooth concave sides, one quarter to one-half inch thick, and having no holes.*
> Given waterbase printer's ink and rice paper, the learner will print one print on the paper that is *centered and has an even covering of ink.*
> Given blue and yellow tempera paint and manila paper the learner will mix *equal parts of both primary colors of paint resulting in green.*

One art experience may have several intermeshed learning experiences. The criterion would depend on the child's need and developmental characteristics (Morreau & Bruininks, 1991). For example, in a painting activity the criterion for one child might be related to controlling the dispersal of paint on the paper; for another child, the criterion might be demonstration of skills for cleaning up; while for a third child, the criterion might be engaging in an activity continuously for a period of time (i.e., expanding her attention span). These three behavioral objectives with differing criteria would be stated behaviorally as follows:

> Given paint and paper and a half-hour art period, the child will paint a picture *without running colors of paint together on the paper.*
> Given a paint-spotted worktable, the child will wipe the table *without prompting so that all paint spots are gone.*
> Given paint, paper, and a half-hour art period, the child will paint for *20 minutes without engaging in a non-related activity.*

Thus, in writing a behavioral objective that would be applicable for several children, the conditions and the outcome may be the same, but the criterion statement might vary depending on the particular child's abilities and the specific goals for that child. Additionally, while in many school activities behavioral objectives may be written with criteria statements that include measures such as a percentage of accuracy, they may be difficult or impossible to evaluate. For example, let us rephrase the same three examples to include criterion statements with percentages:

> Given paint and paper and a half-hour art period, the child will paint a picture *without running colors of paint together on the paper 100 percent of the time.*
> Given a paint-spotted worktable, the child will wipe the table *without prompting, removing all paint spots 100 percent of the time.*
> Given paint, paper, and a half-hour art period, the child will paint for *20 minutes without engaging in a non-related activity 100 percent of the time.*

These three examples now restated appear to be much more precise. However, the question arises as to who will be determining the percentages of compliance and against what measure the learner's performance will be appraised . . . against the child's prior performance? Against all children in the class? Against all children who have ever engaged in that activity?. Generally, in art activities a child may be assessed against her personal level of performance, efforts or standards toward which she is working.

Also when criterion statements are posed that relate to complete mastery of the task, then the inclusion of 100 percent accuracy statements may be redundant, but they would be unlikely to pose problems determining completion or mastery. However, criterion statements that indicate a percentage of less than 100 percent may cause other types of problems. Let us again restate the three examples of behavior objectives including percentages of less than 100.

Given paint, paper, and a half-hour art period, the child will paint a picture *without running colors of paint together on the paper 80 percent of the time.*

Given a paint-spotted worktable, the child will wipe the table *without prompting 90 percent of the time, removing all paint spots.*

Given paint, paper, and a half-hour art period, the child will paint for *20 minutes without engaging in a non-related activity 75 percent of the time.*

Now the issue of determining when a child has met the objectives becomes more difficult. The implication in all of these criterion statements is that the teacher or art therapist will make the determination based on her observations. However, there is no way of knowing the context in which these observations will be made. Will they be based on the teacher's years of experience in working with children having a particular disability? If so, then how would the teacher with little prior experience appraise the objective? Will they be based on the teacher or art therapist's prior observations of the particular child? If so, then how would a teacher or art therapist that had little or no other experience in working with the particular child appraise her?

Therefore, it is more sensible to omit criterion statements that include percentages of completion based on adult observation. Clearer criterion statements can be written that avoid the percentage of accuracy issue altogether. Let us rewrite our examples, eliminating percentages and replacing them with more activity-specific criterion statements.

Given paint, paper, and an art period, the child will paint a picture *without running colors of paint together except one or two places on the paper.*

Given a paint-spotted worktable, the child will wipe the table *with less than three prompts from the teacher.*

Given a paint-spotted worktable, the child will *wipe the paint spots from the table removing all visible* spots.

Given paint, paper, and a half-hour art period, the child will paint for *20 minutes without engaging in a non-related activity for more than 15 minutes of the time.*

Finally, in the example of the child cleaning the worktable, note that the initial behavioral objective has been restated in the form of two behavioral objectives. This is done because the task involves two criterion statements for which a teacher or art therapist might select; one relating to attending to the task and the other relating to how clean the table will be wiped. Thus the percentage of accuracy issue has been replaced with criteria that can readily be assessed, and there is likely to be less confusion in deciding when the child has completed the task and accomplished the behavioral objective.

There is a great need to write precise behavioral objectives for specific children. It is also necessary to define art vocabulary and art activities more precisely. Verbs such as *to make, to appreciate, to do, to create, to explore, to enjoy,* and *to become aware* are not precise enough, do not often incorporate knowledge of artistic process, and often do not imply or result in overt activity. Therefore, such statements as "the child makes a picture," or "the child will do a sculpture," or "the child will make a pot" are inappropriate. It is more precise and appropriate to state: "The child *paints* a picture, *sculpts* a figure, or *pinches* a pot."

A list of verbs that are more appropriate for use in writing behavioral objectives in art may be found in Table 4.3 (Salter, n.d.):

TABLE 4.3
LIST OF PRECISE AND VAGUE VERBS (Salter, nd)

Precise Action Verbs		Vague Verbs that Fail to Specify Activity or Fail to Result in Overt Action
to pull	to roll	to create
to construct	to slot	to enjoy
to throw a pot	to stain	to appreciate
to sew a puppet	to glaze	to make
to cut	to melt	to express
to paste	to nail	to explore
to glue	to mold	to examine
to stitch	to pour	to recognize
to paint	to rub	
to build	to sand	
to select	to saw	
to choose	to smooth	
to arrange	to stamp	
to collect	to trace	
to list	to trim	
to illustrate	to wipe	
to draw	to wrap	
to sketch	to carve	
to compare	to dab	
to measure	to fold	
to contrast	to drill	
to crush	to describe	
to locate	to frame	
to weave	to print	

The abstract, less precise verbs (to explore, enjoy, appreciate, express, create, make, examine, and recognize) need operational definitions, such as:

To explore	Find by accident a different (new) way of doing an art activity; use an art media in two or more different ways.
To enjoy or *to appreciate*	Say words of pleasure, for example, *Wow, this is fun! This is awesome. I want to do this all afternoon.* Observe behavior such

	as totally undistractible attention being given for a longer than average period for this particular child.
To express	Fill the page with one or more drawn figures, tell a story about one's artwork, or paint shapes and figures with colors that have never been used before by that child.
To create	Paint or draw a picture, build a sculpture or a pot, or construct a puppet by sewing or cutting and pasting, that is not copied or that includes something about the creator (a favorite color, a favorite topic, or an event that made the child happy). Select materials, subjects, or page placement that differ from others in the class.
To make	To draw, to paint, to construct by cutting or pasting, to glue, to print, to pinch, to sculpt, to weave, to color, or to fingerpaint.
To examine	To look at from at least three different vantage points, to taste, to touch, or to manipulate.
To recognize	To identify by calling an object its specific name or to select one word from a given list.

To summarize, the three major components of a behavioral objective are the conditions, the outcome, and the criteria. Behavioral objectives in art for an IEP must be specific to the learner and must utilize action verbs that result in overt behaviors or in behaviors that can be measured unobtrusively. Ultimately, the overall goal is to determine ways a child's development can be assessed. If the procedures being used with that child are not working, then they can be altered and/or changed to better assist that child in successful performance of these tasks (Bruininks, Morreau, Gilman, & Anderson, 1991).

Finally, not all behavioral objectives encountered on IEPs are written in the way described above. The examples and the approach used to frame the outcome, conditions and criterion statements reflect the author's philosophical bias toward a behavioral approach in writing, implementing, and assessing behavioral objectives. There are those who will not agree with this approach. Whatever approach one uses will be determined by one's own philosophical orientation and the directives of the agency, school or administrative structure within which one works.

Educational Services and Experiences

Every IEP must include not only short-term behavioral objectives, but also a description of the specific educational services and experiences that are to be provided, as well as the time frame for their provision. This section of the IEP may include related services such as special adaptive art or art therapy. Parents and teachers (especially art teachers) should be aware that these related services can be requested and will be provided (and funded) if requested in many states.

Placement of Learner

Once annual goals and short-term objectives based on an assessment of the learner's performance are established, decisions will be made relative to the placement of the learner in either regular education or self-contained classrooms. The mandates of PL 101-476 (the reauthorization bill for PL 94-142) stress that learners with disabilities must be placed in their least restrictive environment (LRE). The LRE is now being interpreted to mean that *all* children with disabilities should be included in the regular education classroom (the classroom and school in which they would have been placed were they not disabled) (Peters, n.d.; Minnesota Inclusive Education Technical Assistance Program, n.d.; O'Brien & Forest, 1989).

This inclusion philosophy is a worthy ideal, however, there may be some realities that need to be considered in including children with disabilities in regular education classrooms. For example, the regular art education classrooms may be already overcrowded and the art teacher may already be dealing with classes of 40 or more regular education children. In view of the "hands-on" nature of many art experiences, the art teacher may be already in an almost impossible situation. Also, the art teacher may lack the special training needed to successfully instruct children with a variety of disabling conditions. While inclusion means all support services occur within the context of the regular education program, funding for consultants and specialized services may not be forthcoming. On the other hand, inclusion may mean increased opportunities for art therapists to assist regular education teachers in providing the support services necessary for a child with a disability to fully participate in the regular education program. Finally, art teachers are rarely present at staffings at which individualized education programs are developed for students with disabilities (Anderson, 1980; Anderson, Colchado, & McAnally, 1979). It would benefit both the special learner as well as the art teacher to be a part of the IEP staffings where these decisions are made. This part of the IEP also specifies the anticipated dates for the initiation and the expected length of the services that will be provided to the learner.

Schedule for Annual Evaluation

The final part of the IEP includes the objective criteria, evaluation methods, and the time frames for determining whether the short-term

TABLE 4.4
AN EXAMPLE OF AN IEP THAT INCLUDES ART

Name:	James Smith		S.E. Program: MMR	Grade: Inter	Parents: Mr. & Mrs. James Smith
ID#:	342		Teacher(s): Jones Murphy McKown		Guardian:
Address:	55 Main Street	Zip: 61761			Phone: 442-2687 School: Main
Date of Birth:	11/2/82	Age: 11			

PRESENT LEVEL OF PERFORMANCE

SKILL AREA	INFORMATIONAL ASSESSMENT			REGULAR PROGRAMS		SUPPORT SERVICES			
	DATE	TYPE	RESULTS		TYPE	PERSONNEL	INITIATED	DATE COMPLETED	
Art	10/5/93	Situational pretest Observation Direct Question	Motor deficit (cutting) Negative toward others Lacks color concepts	100% 5th grade class	Adapted Art	Anders	10/16/93	6/7/94	

AREA OR SUBJECT	ANNUAL GOALS	SHORT-TERM OBJECTIVES	EVALUATION	
			INITIATED	COMPLETED
Art	The student will master basic cutting skills	Given a pair of blunt-nosed scissors, the student will place his fingers in the holes and place the blades in the correct position for cutting on four occasions.	Situational checklist 10/25/93	
		Given scissors and paper, the student will cut a marked piece of paper in half without deviating from the line more than 1/16" and leaving no jagged edges.		
		Given a pair of scissors and 10 printed geometric shapes, the learner will cut all the shapes so they are smooth and not more than 1/16" off the printed lines.		
	The student will positively critique the works of others	Given a painting produced by a peer, the student will state one or more positive characteristics consistent with the criteria presented by the teacher.	Situational pretest 10/25/93	
	The student will know the results of mixing basic colors	Given ten sets of two randomly selected colors, the student will state the color which will result when they are mixed without error.	Oral pretest 10/25/93	

From "Individualized Education Programs in Art: Benefit or Burden?" by Lanny Morreau and Frances E. Anderson, 1984, *Art Education 32* (p. 11). © 1984 by the National Art Education Association. Adapted with permission.

objectives are being accomplished. This is to be established for at least an annual evaluation.

With the parts of an IEP in mind and some discussion of how to translate annual goals into behavioral objectives, let us look at an example (Table 4.4) of a completed IEP that includes a placement in art.

From these examples the reader may now be more aware of how to incorporate art into a child's IEP. While these examples demonstrate ways to include methods of assessing a child's art skills and how to include an art component in an IEP to facilitate that child's learning of basic art skills, there are other ways that art can be an important component in an IEP. The next five chapters demonstrate many ways that art can be used to remediate and to instruct children in the following curricular content areas: reading, language arts, science, math and social studies (Anderson, 1981, 1983, 1988, 1991; Anderson, Ash, & Gambach, 1982). The information that follows demonstrates how central art experiences can be to the educational core for children. All of the examples that follow have the potential to be written into a child's IEP, with art being the vehicle to that child's learning in ALL school subjects.

REFERENCES

Anderson, F. E. (1992). A review of the published research literature on arts for children with disabilities. Unpublished manuscript, Illinois State University, Normal, IL.

Anderson, F. E. (1992). *Art for all the children: Approaches to art therapy for children with disabilities.* Springfield, IL: Charles C Thomas.

Anderson, F. E. (1983). A critical analysis of *A Review of the Published Research Literature on Arts with the Handicapped: 1971-1981,* with special attention to the visual arts. *Art Therapy, 1*(1), 26–35.

Anderson, F. E. (1980). The effects of mainstreaming on secondary art education in Illinois. Unpublished paper, Illinois State University, Normal, IL.

Anderson, F. E. (1988). A review of the published research literature on arts with the handicapped. Unpublished manuscript, Illinois State University, Normal, IL.

Anderson, F. E., Ash, L., & Gambach, J. (1981). *A review of the published research literature on arts and the handicapped: 1971-1981.* Washington, DC: National Committee Arts with the Handicapped.

Anderson, F. E., Colchado, J., & McAnally, P. (1978). *Art for the handicapped.* Normal, IL: Illinois State University.

Blandy, D. (1989). Ecological and normalizing approaches to disabled students and art education. *Art Education, 42*(3), 7–11.

Bruininks, R. H., Morreau, L., Gilman, C., & Anderson, J. (1991). *Adaptive living skills curriculum.* Allen, TX: Developmental Learning Materials.

Chapman, L. (1978). *Approaches to art in education.* Englewood Cliffs, NJ: Prentice-Hall.

Chapman, L. (1985). *Discover art* (Vols. 1–6). Worcester, MA: Davis.

Council for Exceptional Children. (1976). Least restrictive environment. Reston, VA: Council for Exceptional Children.

Effland, A. (1974). Evaluating goals for art education. *Art Education, 27*(2), 8–10.

Eisner, E. (1976). *The arts, human development and education.* Berkeley, CA: McCutchan.

Gardner, H. (1990). *Art education and human development.* (Occasional Paper number 3). Los Angeles CA: The Getty Center for Education in the Arts.

Kellogg, R. (1970). *Analyzing children's art.* Palo Alto, CA: National Press.

Lilly, M. S. (1988). The regular education initiative: A force for change in general and special education. *Education and Training in Mental Retardation, 26*(12), 253–260.

Lowenfeld, V., & Brittain, L. (1987). *Creative and mental growth* (8th ed.). New York: Macmillan.

Mager, R. F. (1962). *Preparing instructional objectives.* Palo Alto, CA: Fearon.

McAshen, H. H. (1970). *Writing behavioral objectives.* New York: Harper and Row.

McFee, J. (1970). *Preparation for art.* Belmont, CA: Wadsworth.

Minnesota Inclusive Education Technical Assistance Program. (n.d.). *Inclusive school communities.* Minneapolis, MN: University of Minnesota.

Morreau, L., & Anderson, F. E. (1984). Art and the individualized education program: Benefit or burden? *Art Education, 32*(6), 10–14.

O'Brien, J., & Forest, M. (1989). *Action for inclusion.* Toronto Ontario: Inclusion Press.

Peters, B. (n.d.). Definitions of mainstreaming, integration and inclusion. Unpublished manuscript.

Piaget, J., & Inhelder, B. C. (1956). *The child's concept of space.* New York: Humanities Press.

Public Law 94-142, The education for all children act, 1975.

Public Law 101-476, The individuals with disabilities education act, 1990.

Salome, R. A., & Moore, B. (1979). *Development of figure concepts in the graphic art work of children from different countries.* Chicago, IL: International Film Bureau.

Salome, R. A., & Moore, B. (1979). *Development of spatial concepts in the graphic art work of children from different countries.* Chicago, IL: International Film Bureau.

Salter, M. (n.d.). A categorized "shopping list" of verbs useful in making objectives more precise. Champaign, Il: East Central Region for the Hearing Impaired.

Thorne, J. H. (1990). Mainstreaming procedures: Support services and training. *NAEA Advisory.* Reston, VA: National Art Education Association.

Timitz-Wolfe, V. (1985). Writing behavioral objectives: Some pitfalls. *Exceptional Children,* pp. 20–35.

Troeger-Clifford, B. (1981). The development of a model to include art in the individualized education program for physically handicapped and health impaired students. Unpublished Doctoral Dissertation, North Texas State University, Denton, TX.

Webb, E. J., Campbell, D. T., Schwarts, R. D., & Sechrest, L. (1966). *Unobtrusive measures.* Chicago: Rand McNally.

Chapter 5

LEARNING AND GROWING THROUGH ART

The value of the visual arts as facilitators of creative, aesthetic, emotional and intellectual growth has been clearly documented (Anderson, 1978, 1985; Hobbs, 1990; Hodsell, 1984; Lowenfeld & Brittain, 1987). In spite of budget cuts at the elementary level which have eliminated many arts specialists, classroom teachers continue to teach art to their students. Some research has documented how powerful the visual arts can be in teaching other academic concepts to typical public school children. In a five-year study of the impact that an integrated art and reading curriculum might have on the reading skills of normal fifth grade students, Catchings (1984) found that this approach resulted in participants making statistically significant gains on reading tests. Van Buren (1986) reported that art was found to enhance both the reading, communication vocabulary and self-expressive skills of children. Caldwell and Moore (1991) found that drawing activities were more effective practice for narrative writing with second and third grade children than the traditional verbal discussion.

VISUAL ARTS RESEARCH ON CHILDREN WITH DISABILITIES

Increased attention has been given to the potential of the visual arts as facilitators of the development of children with disabilities. In 1969 the American Art Therapy Association was founded. In the mid 1970s the National Committee Arts for the Handicapped (NCAH) was formed. Renamed Very Special Arts a decade later, this enterprise has been and continues to be a strong advocate of arts experiences as a means to enrich the quality of life of individuals with disabilities. Research on arts and learners with disabilities buttresses this fact.

Systematic research on the visual arts with individuals who are disabled is somewhat sparse. A ten-year comprehensive literature review sponsored by Very Special Arts considered over 300,000 studies and identified only 53 experimental studies of which 19 were in the visual arts (Anderson, Ash, & Gambach, 1982). From this review, it was clear that the arts could be used to identify perceptual and emotional problems; to reinforce academic concepts, motor skills, and more appropriate social behaviors; and to assist in remediating learning problems (Anderson, 1983).

Two updated reviews of the literature published since the 1982 Very Special Arts study yielded 60 additional experimental studies in the visual arts which reinforce the earlier research findings (Perez, 1989; Anderson, Kolano, & de la Cruz, 1993). These studies also document that mastery of an art skill can enhance the self- and body-concept of children with disabilities. In addition these studies suggest that persons who are disabled can participate in regular classroom situations while holding their own artistically.

Art as a Vehicle for Learning Academic Concepts

Greene and Hasselbring (1981) found significant gains on concept attainment when children who were prelinguistically deaf were taught through art activities by the regular classroom and special education teachers. Pontius (1983) studied the drawing abilities of normal children and children with dyslexia and mental retardation. She concluded that drawing instruction especially focusing on spatial relationships can help children in learning literacy skills.

Art as a Reinforcer of Social Skills

The visual arts have also been used to reinforce more appropriate social behaviors. Schennum (1987) studied the effects of a six-week art and dance/movement therapy program on the behaviors of 42 children who were 6 to 12 years old. Children were randomly assigned to each of three groups: no expressive therapy, one hour of expressive therapy and two hours of expressive therapy. Staff, who were unaware of the special expressive therapies program, rated all 42 children on the Devereux Child Behaviour Rating Scale (Spivack & Spotts, 1966) to assess problem behaviors. Children that received the expressive therapy program had significantly diminished acting-out behaviors and were significantly more emotionally responsive.

Hardison and Llorens (1988) found that participation in a six-week crafts program resulted in delinquent girls making improvement on measures of sensory integration, motor, cognitive, psychological and social skills. Tibbets and Stone (1990) found that short-term art therapy with adolescents who were seriously emotionally disturbed resulted in an increase in positive self-concept and ability to realistically view their environment. Art therapy also helped depressed students reduce severe anxiety and feelings of rejection.

Art as a Means of Enhancing Positive Self- and Body Concepts

De Chira (1982, 1990) found that involvement in a visual arts program, which focused on the human figure, enhanced the body images of elementary children with learning disabilities. She used a variety of art activities in which children produced both two- and three-dimensional artworks. These art activities focused on an awareness of body images. Post-treatment scores of the experimental group on the Human Figure Drawing Test, the Imitation of Postures Test and the Self-Identification of Body Parts in response to verbal instructions were all significantly different from the control group. Hiltunen (1989) found that a combined art and drama therapy approach resulted in the improvement of knowledge of body parts and body concepts held by the participants who were mentally retarded.

Art as a Means of Inclusion/Integration of Children with Disabilities

Schleien, Ray, Soderman-Olson, and McMahan (1990) found that students with moderate to severe mental retardation were able to participate in a special museum program when paired with regular second graders. The program included "hands-on" art experiences as well as gallery tours and interactive art exhibits. Staff observed and tallied social interactions between the groups of children, documenting a significant increase in these social interactions. Appropriate social behaviors in the museum program context improved significantly for the children with mental retardation. Additionally, there was an increase in the positive attitudes of the nondisabled children toward the children with mental retardation.

ART–CENTERED LEARNING

Children with disabilities learn best in a multisensory hands-on approach. They also learn best when there are many opportunities to practice skills and apply newly learned concepts. Art provides the framework for both a multisensory "hands-on" approach and many opportunities to practice newly learned concepts in a framework where boredom and repetition is eliminated.

When art is *infused* into the content of as many subjects as possible, it offers a highly motivating context for learning. Every subject covered in school has the potential for an interrelated/correlated visual art experience (Anderson, 1975; Anderson & Barnfield, 1974).

This approach works best when an alliance is created between the child's classroom teacher and the art therapist or art teacher. Additionally, it will help the art specialist to peruse books and curricular materials that the children are using in their other classes.

In art-centered learning, there must be a good balance between the art concepts, media and content, and the concepts and information from the other academic areas. Just utilizing art media in a regular classroom activity such as using crayons to color in sets in a mathematics lesson, or using clay to make a mountain range in a geography lesson, or cutting out a predrawn pattern for a jack-o-lantern does not make these activities valid art experiences. What would make them art-centered lessons would be to incorporate more open-ended outcomes. For example, the child could draw *his own* sets in the mathematics lesson, he could *design his own flag* for a country in the geography lesson and he could design his *own unique* jack-o-lantern. Then these experiences would be examples of valid art activities.

By taking concepts that a child is learning in the other academic areas and using these as a basis for an art experience, the art teacher or art therapist will be reinforcing academic concepts of which the child is already knowledgeable. Opportunities to practice these concepts and reinforce them in the art activities will be provided. For example, if a group of children who are deaf are studying the science concept of what happens when heat is applied to a solid — i.e., the idea of melting — this concept can be carried into the art activity by having the children make crayon/waxpaper laminations of leaves or tissue paper shapes. (Crayon/waxpaper laminations are discussed in Chapter 8.) Crayon shavings are made and become the "glue" in the lamination. When the lamination is ironed (between two pieces of newspaper), the crayon melts and holds the lamination together.

In this example, artistic concepts of design organization can also be covered through a discussion of where to place the nature objects or tissue paper shapes before the laminating is completed. Compositional concepts of center of interest and repetition of shapes can also be discussed. Thus we have an example of an art-centered lesson that includes concepts about artistic design principles, as well as a discussion of a scientific concept. Other concepts including transparency and opacity can be discussed.

A group of children might be involved in learning basic painting skills. They can be given step-by-step instruction in the use of a brush. The lesson can also become a discovery lesson (discovery is an important learning approach used in science and is discussed in Chapter 8) about color if the children are only given red, blue and yellow paint. They will soon discover the secondary colors of orange, green and purple.

Sometimes topics or themes for artwork can come from the experiences the children have had on a field trip, or in reading a story, or in relationship to some curricular activity occurring in their regular classroom. This art-centered approach provides an economy of means because the art teacher does not have to spend as much time discussing possible topics for the child's artwork. These topics instead can be directly related to what is happening in the rest of the school day.

This art-centered approach can also flow back to the regular classroom if the art teacher or art therapist continues to be aware of what is happening in the rest of the child's school day. This reciprocity and flow between the art room and the regular classroom is the core idea behind art-centered learning. This approach is also compatible with the whole language approach to learning currently espoused in many elementary classrooms *and* compatible with Discipline-Based Art Education.

THE WHOLE LANGUAGE APPROACH TO INSTRUCTION

The whole language approach is based on the premise that children learn best when instruction is *not* broken down into subject areas.

> Whole language in its more comprehensive definition is an attitude, a belief, about how all the processes of human communication (listening, talking, reading and writing) develop, about how they are acquired, and about the most effective instructional practices that promote their acquisition. As such, whole language is *not a method* of teaching. It is a consideration that guides instructional decision making. It cannot be canned, packaged, or programmed.
>
> A whole-language philosophy underlies much of the natural literacy learning that occurs in the home environment, and the same premises should also apply in the school setting: (1) the child is central; (2) children are innately motivated to learn; (3) literacy is best acquired through doing literate things (talking, reading, and writing) with real purposes and not through activities *about* them; (4) reading and writing are progressive — development occurs through strongly parallel stages toward closer approximations of standard forms. (Jewell & Zimtz, 1990, p. 303)

The list of human communication modes provided by Jewell and Zimtz (1990) omits communication via the arts — sound, visual art and movement. Visual expression is also an important form of human communication. Indeed, children draw before they write! In fact, children who have difficulty with written communication may more easily express themselves visually. As earlier mentioned, a recent study (Caldwell & Moore, 1991) documented that second and third grade students wrote significantly better narratives when they first drew as a rehearsal prior to writing (as opposed to just verbally discussing the content for a narrative writing task). Visual communication in the form of drawing, painting and creating with three-dimensional materials may have more power to motivate children with disabilities than communicating via talking, writing, and reading.

The concept of a whole language approach to the curriculum needs to be expanded to include art. In so many instances, it is *art* which *links* learning in reading, writing and talking. In the pages that follow, there are ample illustrations of the potentially central role that art activities can play in a child's learning to read, to write, to do math, to understand science and to comprehend social studies.

In conveying information to the reader about language arts, reading, social studies, science, and mathematics, each of these content areas have been separated. However, in any one example of an art learning experience presented, the child does not solely learn about art or one of the other major curricular areas. Art can help *integrate* concepts and become the powerful *motivational glue* that helps children learn about language arts, reading, science, math and social studies. Thus, a whole language approach is not whole without the addition of art to the list of subject areas included.

THE CONTENT OF ART

Including art in a whole language approach does not mean that the content of art is compromised. Art does have its own structure and content which is based on design elements and principles. Professionals in art do not recommend an undue instructional emphasis on these elements and principles, for they can become a block to artistic expression (Lansing, 1969; Art Therapy Training, n.d.). However, everyone should be aware that these elements and principles exist and that the art lessons described in this book are built on line, color, shape, and texture. These design elements are integral parts of each learning situation presented. For example, in Chapter 7 the section on geometry focuses on two- and three-dimensional shapes and colors, while in the shape game segment, texture is emphasized.

Design principles of harmony, unity, balance, proportion, and contrast have also been carefully considered in the way that each art experience is structured and in the materials selected for these activities. For example, a limited palette is a necessary component to insure harmony and unity in an art activity. Therefore, using synthetic packing pieces, uncooked pasta, rice, and paper scraps in a mosaic or texture picture offers too many different materials in one activity. The result: a picture with too much variety. A better choice would be to limit the materials to a variety of the same class of items. An example of this would be a mosaic or picture made with only two to four different sizes and shapes of the same kind of synthetic packing material.

A limited palette may mean using only different types of paper in a composition or a mural, or offering only one or two colors of paint to cover a sculpture or a clay piece. It may imply limiting a wood sculpture to components of two or three basic geometric shapes and insuring contrast by providing a variety of different sizes of these shapes. Further limits might be set by specifying a *minimal* number of pieces that the child might use (for example, at least ten shapes, three of which must be triangles and three of which must be squares). There is not any fixed formula. However, some limits and some freedom are needed in an activity to enable individual solutions in a diverse range of possibilities. A certain honesty and truth in materials selection and use is the guiding principle. In every instance, this kind of implicit design consideration has been given in specifying the materials and in planning the art learning situations presented in this book.

If the aim of the art activities is primarily cathartic and self-expressive, then it may not be appropriate to focus unduly on the art content. However, by adhering to some of the limitations suggested, the outcome of the activity will be more aesthetically pleasing and thus more acceptable and more self-affirming to the child engaged in the activity.

DISCIPLINE-BASED ART EDUCATION

Since the mid 1980s there has been a curricular revolution occurring in art education. With the strong advocacy (both moral and financial) of the J.P. Getty Center for Education in the Arts, Discipline-Based Art Education (DBAE) has been adopted in many schools. In DBAE, in addition to a focus on the creative production of artwork in public schools, art specialists are also emphasizing the historical, critical and aesthetic aspects of the visual arts (Broudy, 1987; Duke, 1983, 1988).

A study of art history enables the learner to put artists and their work in the appropriate chronological and social context. Art criticism is the systematic discussion of a work of art through four parts: describing, analyzing, interpreting and evaluating. "Art criticism directs attention to what is in the work, how it is organized, what it means and how successful it is" (Hobbs & Salome, 1991, p. 9).

Aesthetics is the

> study of sensory responses to art works [and] is closely related to criticism. . . . When students are encouraged to analyze the visual, formal and expressive qualities of artworks and then to examine their personal responses to works of art, they are involved with aesthetic qualities (Hobbs & Salome, 1991, p. 9).

Art viewed in these four dimensions is an academic discipline which can be a means of developing critical thinking, of understanding cultural differences, of studying history, and a means of introducing a discussion of philosophical values. This means that in addition to developing appropriate media and materials adaptations for the child with disabilities who is included in the regular art class, the art teacher must also adapt curricular materials in art history, art criticism and aesthetics. In some cases with some children with disabilities this task is feasible, with other children an undo focus on art history, criticism, and aesthetics is not appropriate (Art Therapy, n.d.), for it may interfere with the expressive aspects of the art experience.

A detailed discussion of DBAE is beyond the scope of this book. Fortunately, there are several graded art textbook series that have been developed with DBAE in mind. The reader is urged to consult these and other similar sources for detailed information. These include: *Discover Art: Grades 1-6* by Laura Chapman (1985), Davis Publications, Worcester, MA); *The Visual Experience* by Jack Hobbs and Richard Salome (1991, Davis Publications, Worcester, MA); *Discovering Art History* by Gerald Brommer (1989, Davis Publications, Worcester, MA) and *Understanding and Creating Art* (books one and two) by Ernest Goldstein, Robert Saunders, Jo Kowalchuk, and Theodore Katz (1986, Garrard Publishing Company, Dallas, TX).

With the availability of these materials, art specialists can also consider an art-centered approach in which art is redirected *back into the regular school classroom* by working with classroom teachers to develop social studies activities centered around art that was produced during various historical periods in the development of the United States, or by providing information about artworks and artists from other countries, cultures and subcultures — i.e., multicultural approaches. Additionally, critical thinking skills can be reinforced in the regular classroom through extended discussions of art masterpieces and how these are valued, as well as how to describe, analyze, interpret and evaluate them (Broudy, 1987; Eisner, 1983; Ennis, 1987; Feldman, 1987, 1985, 1970; Hobbs & Salome, 1991).

Adaptations Enabling Children With Disabilities to Participate in Discipline-Based Art Education

Art teachers who are using the DBAE approach may find difficulty in adapting DBAE for children with disabilities who are included in the regular art classroom. The following suggestions and examples of ways to adapt DBAE are provided to demonstrate ways children with disabilities can participate in DBAE (whether their least restrictive educational alternative is a regular art class or a self-contained classroom).

CHILDREN WITH MENTAL RETARDATION. Consider mental age in presenting information about art history, art criticism and aesthetics. Provide hands-on/multisensory approaches in class discussions. Break down lessons into short segments that are sequenced and concepts that are repeated throughout, moving from simple to more complex concepts. Select artists and/or masterpieces that can be related to the lives of the children.

For example, children can relate to artists who choose to include simple everyday items in their still life painting. Actual items can be brought into class that are examples of those included in the masterpiece under discussion. Always try to integrate a "hands-on" art experience that directly relates to discussion of an artist. For example, show a reproduction of Van Gogh's painting *Twelve Sunflowers in a Vase* (Arles, 1988, 456; Hulsker, 1977). Bring in a vase of sunflowers. Have the child touch and smell the flowers. How would he describe the color, texture and smell of the sunflowers? What does the color yellow mean to the child? What other items do we associate with the color yellow? Does the child have a favorite flower? Why is it his favorite? What does it smell like? Have the child paint a picture of the flowers.

Go on a field trip to an art gallery. Have a section of the room set up as a small gallery; discuss how to display artwork. Set up a display of reproductions. Which reproduction would the child like to have hanging in his room at home? Develop a list of words to describe one of the reproductions. Some words might be *colorful, happy, weird colors, ugly.*

CHILDREN WITH LEARNING DISABILITIES. Use a multisensory approach as in the example above. There is a commercially available laser disc on the life and art of Vincent Van Gogh (*Vincent Van Gogh: A Portrait in Two Parts,* 1982). If it is possible to show this disc it would provide an exciting and motivational means of understanding the life and times of Vincent Van Gogh.

Play some art games such as art concentration using pairs of artworks by well-known artists. With the help of the class, develop an art trivia pursuit or art wheel of fortune or art jeopardy game. Have a gallery set up in the room. Have learners form a gallery committee and decide which of 8 to 10 reproductions of art by several well-known artists should be included in a special art exhibit. Develop a list of selection criteria (reasons why a painting might be liked or disliked) for including artwork in the show. Have children write a review of the art show.

CHILDREN WITH BEHAVIORAL DISORDERS/EMOTIONAL DISTURBANCE. A multisensory approach is also recommended (see examples above under "children with mental retardation" and "children with learning disabilities"). Select artists who were especially expressive such as the Abstract Expressionists or Van Gogh. (Van Gogh also used vibrant colors and very thick paint.) Some information about Van Gogh's life will illustrate his expressive factor. Discuss his relationship with his brother, Theo. Use the discussion as a springboard for talking about the child's sibling relationships (Hulsker, 1977; McCarter & Gilbert, 1985; Phillips, 1983; Pickvance, 1984).

Learners might make a painting of sunflowers (or some other subject about which they feel especially passionate). The teacher can build in some controls by discussing possible topics and making a list of them on the chalkboard. Include reasons why topics are chosen. Discuss color and how it can express moods and feelings (Silberstein-Storfer & Jones, 1982). Create mood pictures using colors.

CHILDREN WITH PHYSICAL DISABILITIES. Adapt brushes so they can be easily grasped, or use a helmet or mouth-holder for brushes. Pair up children so that strengths are complimented. Choose artists such as Toulouse-Lautrec (Piper, 1984) who had disabilities, and research their lives and how they overcame their disabilities. Consider using artists whose work is more expressive and less representational. Jackson Pollack, Franz Kline, Willem de Kooning are examples of Abstract Expressionistic artists whose work can be easily modeled. In many cases these artists just poured paint onto a canvas lying flat on the floor (Janson & Cauman, 1971; McCarter & Gilbert, 1985). Learners can easily create similar poured paintings—some can even use their wheelchairs to "run" across the paint surface. Discuss how the learners felt doing the paintings and whether these feelings are conveyed through the artwork they have created. Utilize the art gallery ideas described above. Have a group of learners mount a show of the classes' Abstract Expressionistic paintings. Discuss placement of artworks in the gallery. Have other learners write a review (positive critique) of the show. (Be sure that all children have at least one of their paintings in the show.)

CHILDREN WHO ARE DEAF OR HARD–OF–HEARING. Watch the Van Gogh disc and discuss his life and times afterwards (Phillips, 1982). Make a list of new vocabulary from the disc. Have learners try drawing some of the vocabulary definitions. Then try and match the symbol with the vocabulary word (McCarter & Gilbert, 1985).

Play some art games using reproduction postcards or some of the commercially available games including: American Art Quiz (Safari Unlimited, 1989); Art Lotto (Safari Unlimited, 1990); Let's Make a Painting (National Gallery Publications, 1991); and In the Picture (Intempo Toys, 1990).

Divide the group into pairs. Have each child select 20 paintings he likes from a pile of art reproduction postcards and 20 that he does not like. Arrange these in a montage and share reasons for the selections with his partner and other classmates (Ratcliff, 1977).

CHILDREN WITH VISUAL IMPAIRMENTS. A focus on some of the famous twentieth century sculptors will perhaps be most meaningful. Brancusi, Calder, Moore and Smith and are some examples (Janson & Cauman, 1971). Have examples/models of artworks done in the style of each of these artists. Examples should be small enough so that a child can hold it in one or both hands. Use different-textured materials that reflect each material the artist used (wood, smooth metal or glazed or burnished clay surfaces). Smith used metal in his sculpture. A mock-up could be made using metal screws, nuts and bolts.

Team the child who is blind with one who can see and have this child verbally describe one of the sculptures. This will increase the awareness of visual qualities in both learners. Develop descriptors for the different qualities felt in each example. Then have the learners apply these descriptors to their artwork. Which piece was the most surprising, most pleasant to touch, most angular or had many straight edges, etc.? Be sure that each completed sculpture can be placed in a category.

Have the learners try to construct a piece of sculpture using the same style and materials as the examples. The cardboard geometric shape mobile and the slotted shape sculptures discussed in Chapter 7 can be related to the work of Alexander Calder.

Discuss the concept of the tactile aesthetic (Rubin, n.d.). This concept is the pleasing (or unpleasant) feel of a piece of sculpture and the fact that some pieces that feel wonderful do not look wonderful.

ART ACROSS THE CURRICULUM

We now turn to *specific examples* of the ways that the visual arts can be utilized as an equal partner in helping the student with disabilities to learn basic skills and concepts in reading, language arts, mathematics, science, and social studies. Because he is a specialist, the art teacher may not be as aware of curriculum content in other areas, and the classroom teacher may not be fully aware of the role art can play in the rest of the curriculum. Also, the art therapist may find this information helpful as he works with children who have been recommended for art therapy as a means of remediating social-emotional and learning problems. An attempt is made to present a strong case for utilizing art in *other* learning and vice versa. Ways that this has been accomplished with disabled children are discussed and demonstrated. As elsewhere, very few if any assumptions are made about the prior knowledge which the reader might bring to this chapter.

ART AND READING

The reader should be aware that there is a direct link between a child's artistic developmental level and his ability to recognize words and to read simple sentences. Lowenfeld (Lowenfeld & Brittain, 1987) noted that the first link between art and reading occurred in the Scribbling stage when the child began to label or name his symbols. This represents the initial link between words and symbols. They also noted that it was during the Preschematic stage of development (typically between the ages of four and six years) that word recognition began. When the child included a baseline in his drawings and paintings and placed objects along this baseline, this was an indicator that he could begin a full reading program. Baselines typically occur in a child's drawing when he is in the Schematic stage of development at around six or seven years of age.

Art can be a rich source of opportunities for students to practice their reading skills (Tanner, 1984). Every art lesson can become a lesson in reading comprehension and vocabulary. When students are able to read sentences and simple paragraphs, then art experiences can be written in a self-instructional format. Art appreciation can also become a topic through

which reading skills can be taught (Rowell, 1983). Art teachers or art therapists may need to know the basic skills necessary for students to be able to
read, so that they can develop integrated art and reading experiences.
Classroom teachers may already be familiar with these basic reading skills.

There are several available resources that outline the reading skills needed
in a sequential way from pre-first grade level through the middle school
level (Barbe, 1979; Bowen, 1985).

For the purposes of our discussion these basic skills will be taken from the
Clinical Reading Instruction Handbook (Bowen, 1985). At the prereading level
there are five major skill areas: Cognitive Prerequisites, Pre-Word Attack/
Structural Analysis, Vocabulary, Comprehension, and Oral/Silent Reading.
What follows is a breakdown of skills in each of these areas and *some
suggested* art experiences that can facilitate learning these skills. The reader
should keep in mind that some of the suggested art activities necessitate the
child's functioning artistically at the PreSchematic or Schematic level since
he will be asked to draw a recognizable picture of items.

Pre-Reading Level

I. Cognitive Prerequisites

Recognizes likenesses and differences in pictures, sounds and shapes
Discriminates between colors and color combinations
Knows basic concepts of right-left, up-down, over-under, top-bottom, etc.
Shows attention span of five seconds and longer for auditory and visual stimuli
Classifies objects and pictures by category (Bowen, 1985, p. 73)

Discussion

Similarities and differences can be infused into the dialogue both prior to
beginning an art activity and after the activity has been completed.

Obviously many art experiences can focus on color. Just learning to
identify the three primary colors and how to mix the secondary colors are
basic not only to prereading skill development but are also basic to art
learning. One suggestion is a lesson in which the children first name a color
and do a color search around the room, trying to find all the red objects in
the room and all the blue objects, etc. This kind of discussion can develop
into a color search game. The activity and discussion also could incorporate
the concept of grouping or classifying objects by category (i.e., find all the
blue objects in the room or on the table or in the picture being shown to the
children). Additionally, the lesson could incorporate position words by
having each child tell where a color is located in an illustration or in the
room (i.e., the blue part is above the red square, the blue square is to the left
of the bulletin board). The teacher or art therapist could read directions for

children to find various colors in a game format. This activity would also provide some practice and opportunity for the child to develop his attention span.

After the initial color identification and color search game, the children might participate in a painting experience in which only the primary colors were provided. By simply painting with these colors the students would discover the secondary colors. This discovery could be an opportunity for the teacher to discuss how one mixes secondary colors (equal parts of two of each of the primary colors).

II. Pre-word Attack/Structural Analysis Skills

"Identifies some words through picture clues" (Bowen, 1985, p. 73)

Discussion

This skill can be developed and reinforced through a perceptual training game approach which might include visuals of words that are clues to identifying a specific word. An example might be showing picture clues leading to the word *apple* — first the children are told it is something to eat, it is a (show pictures of fruits), it is red (show picture of red), and it grows on trees (show picture of tree). If the children in the group are able to draw recognizable items, they can try drawing the answer to the riddle . . . or select the correct answer from visual options.

II. Pre-word Attack/Structural Analysis Skills

"Identifies rhyming elements in letters and words"
"Recognizes some high frequency words by sight" (Bowen, 1985, p. 73)

Discussion

Young children like rhymes. They enjoy making up rhymes and singing or repeating them. This language learning process can be taken further by encouraging the child (if he is developmentally able to draw recognizable objects) to draw or illustrate the rhyme (Bowen, n.d.). For example:

"One, two, buckle my shoe"
"A tisket, a tasket, a green and yellow basket"

Most young children are eager to read and are highly motivated to call words from story and picture books, from signs found in the community, and from common labels. Initially, the teacher may place or tape labels on common objects in the room such as a desk, chair, door, window, mirror, etc. After such words have been associated with their concrete representations, the teacher may ask students to select a word card from a stack of such cards and ask for the word to be drawn rather than pronounced. A game could be made in which children's illustrations are mounted on one set of cards and are matched with separate word cards. (This activity should be done only if the child is functioning at an artistic level of a typical five- or six-year-old and can draw recognizable objects.)

III. Vocabulary

Understands spoken meanings of place, quantitative, function and descriptive words
Demonstrates adequate receptive language skills (listening vocabulary)
Expresses self orally through spoken language (expressive language)
Describes objects and activities orally
Labels common items (Bowen, 1985, p. 73)

Discussion

Every art experience is an opportunity to develop these aforementioned vocabulary skills. In fact, each and every art activity should be scrutinized for the opportunities to extend the child's understanding of spoken vocabulary for quantitative words, function and position words, and descriptive words.

For example, large and small as well as position words could be emphasized in a clay activity. This kind of art activity—as most art activities—also provides practice in receptive language skills because the children must follow oral directions. Since art (and particularly clay) is highly intrinsically motivating for children at this level, the practice in listening skills will be especially potent. Before the teacher gives any clay out, he should show the children the two sizes of clay that they each will receive. Next the teacher could show the class how to flatten the large ball of clay and, using the fingers, "draw" a face in the clay and add the small ball of clay as a nose. While emphasizing the importance of each child making his own unique face, the teacher could then distribute the larger ball of clay to each child. The teacher could next have the children each put the clay (on a paper towel) *in front of* them. It will be important to have the children follow step by step the directions that the teacher gives about what to do next (i.e. "Using the flat or palm of your hand, gently flatten the clay ball into a pancake; raise your hands when you are finished. Next make eyes, ears, mouth and hair with one finger by using it like a pencil and drawing with it.") Finally, the teacher would distribute the smaller ball of clay and have the children add it for the nose by sticking it into the center of the face.

After each child is finished, the teacher can discuss what they did and have each child stand up and show his clay project. The teacher can ask for someone to verbally explain how he made the clay face and how the clay feels in his hands. (Again, this activity assumes that the child is artistically developmentally able to make a face—i.e., that the child is functioning on a typical five- or six-year-old level.)

This example should give the reader some idea of how vocabulary skills at the prereading level can be developed and reinforced through a clay experience.

IV. Comprehension

"Follows simple oral directions" (Bowen, 1985, p. 73)

Discussion

The same clay activity described above is also an example of how one could provide opportunities for the child to practice following simple oral directions.

IV. Comprehension

"Orders events in a short sequence"
"Recalls descriptions from stories read aloud"
"Identifies time-order sequences in a picture story" (Bowen, 1985, p. 73)

Discussion

Much of the learning process reflected in the above named skills entails recall and sequence. The development of these skills can be aided greatly through art experiences. The teacher can facilitate correlated reading and art experiences in some of the following ways:

1. Type (or cut and paste) the text of short stories so that major story events or actions are segmented on different sheets of paper or cards. Ask the children to draw actions to match each story event or element. The printed segments and illustrations are randomly mixed. Children then are asked to place each segment in correct order.

2. The recall of character descriptions and other types of descriptions (objects in particular) is of paramount importance in building comprehension skills. Children's stories abound with descriptions of colorful, exotic and fanciful characters. The teacher may collect descriptions of such objects and creatures, from children's literature, read them to the child and then ask him to draw, paint, or illustrate one or more details that were heard in the description. Some objects that children enjoy illustrating are dinosaurs, all kinds of monsters, frogs, cartoon characters, animals and storybook characters.

3. The use of artwork, i.e., illustrations, has been overlooked as a diagnostic procedure for determining how well a child comprehends what was heard or seen. Identifying sequences and details, and translating them into drawings or illustrations, is as valid a process for checking comprehension as is requesting a verbal or written answer. (If a teacher uses illustrations by

children as a diagnostic to determine comprehension, then the children should be developmentally and physically able to draw recognizable objects.)

V. Oral/Silent Reading

"Follows left to right sequence of printed letters, words" (Bowen, 1985, p. 73)

Discussion

There are many art activities that provide practice in sequencing from left to right. Printing with sponges or vegetables or stamp printing with yarn tied around blocks of wood can be structured so that the child must move in a pattern from left to right across the page in several rows. Drawing or painting experiences can be structured so that the child is asked to begin with the left side of the page and move to the right as he works.

If the child can draw recognizable persons and objects, then he can illustrate simple two- or three-word sentences such as: "See Mark jump." "The dog barked." "Bill hit the ball." "See Spot run."

First Grade Level

At the first grade level the first area of the All-Purpose Reading Skills List (Bowen, 1985) in which art can be integrated is III. Comprehension. (Table 5.1 presents a breakdown of all the reading skills at the first grade level.)

III. Comprehension

(First area of art integration at first grade level.)

Interprets simple graphic material such as maps
Recalls material which has been read aloud
Places events in correct sequence
Organizes ideas in logical order (Bowen, 1985, p. 74)

Discussion

An example of an art experience that can provide practice in all the skills listed above under comprehension would be a lesson in which a story was read aloud. Students are asked questions about the events in the story and then they are asked to draw a cartoon strip of the story (if the students were able to draw recognizable objects and persons, i.e., stick figures that resemble people). This could be done as a group using large pieces of paper taped to the chalkboard with volunteer students drawing in various events of the story. Next they discuss in what order their drawings should be to tell the story, and the teacher orders the drawings in the correct sequence. After some practice with this group activity, the students do a similar cartoon-type

TABLE 5.1
THE ALL-PURPOSE READING SKILLS LIST
First Grade Level

I. Word Attack/Structural Analysis
____ Identifies upper case letters
____ Identifies lower case letters
____ Identifies beginning consonant sounds
____ Identifies ending consonant sounds
____ Identifies simple consonant diagraphs
____ Knows sounds of short vowels
____ Knows sounds of long vowels
____ Identifies vowels in 3-letter combinations
____ Identifies consonant sounds in relation to position
____ Recognizes common word families, i.e., -all, -at, -eel
____ Recognizes basic sight words and high frequency words from the Dolch, Johnson and other such word lists
____ Identifies base words and some endings

II. Vocabulary
____ Chooses correct word meanings for context usage
____ Identifies references to words such as his, her, it, them
____ Identifies contractions and the words that form them
____ Identifies compound words and their meanings
____ Identifies inflections and implied meanings
____ Understands meaning of simple punctuation marks, i.e., period, comma, and question mark

III. Comprehension
____ Follows simple oral directions
____ Recalls details in short stories
____ Draws conclusions from short stories
____ Answers specific questions about characters
____ Interprets simple graphic material such as maps
____ Recalls material which has been read aloud
____ Identifies main idea from short story
____ Places events in correct sequence
____ Interprets negative sentences
____ Organizes ideas in logical order
____ Chooses the best title for a passage

IV. Oral/Silent Reading
____ Follows left-to-right sequence of letters and words
____ Reads short passages orally
____ Reads text with punctuation such as comma in a series, colon, quotation marks, appositives, etc.
____ Reads end punctuation such as exclamation point, dash, parentheses

Note. From Clinical reading instruction handbook. by M. Bowen, 1985, Normal, IL: Illinois State University, Copyright, 1985 by M. Bowen. Reprinted by permission.

drawing individually or in small groups. Students then share their artwork, and the class discusses the story drawn and how correct it was in terms of sequence of events. After doing this several times, the students try telling a simple story using cartoon drawings and see if others understand the visual story. (Note: this idea requires more abstract thinking and might be more appropriate at the second or third grade level. Hoff [1982] and Fuller and Pribble [1982] have documented the value of cartooning in art and in integrated art and social studies activities with middle school age children.)

Second Grade Level

At the second grade level, vocabulary is the first area in which art can be correlated.

II. Vocabulary

"Introduction to use of dictionary to obtain word meanings" (Bowen, 1985, p. 75)

Discussion

At this level, the teacher can incorporate art activities into reading lessons in several ways because children typically are operating at a Schematic level of artistic development—i.e., can typically draw recognizable persons and things. The children can, as individuals or groups, make a pictionary—that is a picture dictionary of key words that are easily drawn. The teacher might want to list such words on the chalkboard. Specific words to be drawn can be assigned to individual children. Next, the definition of the word can be given orally. Such items might be: occupations, foods, types of transportation, pets, zoo animals, etc.

III. Comprehension

Recalls details from short story

Places events into correct sequence

Understands sequence of action in short stories

Follows simple written directions

Organizes ideas into logical order (Bowen, 1985, p. 74)

Discussion

In addition to carrying over the idea of doing cartoon drawings of short stories described under grade level one, students at the second grade level of comprehension can do more elaborate picture stories and can also begin to create their own stories. These can be dictated into a tape recorder, transcribed later and illustrated. These created stories can then be made into books which can be traded and read by classmates.

This is exactly what one elementary school in Florida did and the results became the Chattahoochee Publishing Company. Two groups of special needs classes of students, who had learning disabilities and developmental delays, engaged in a special bookmaking project.

Based on material and approaches recommended by J. Turnbull in *No Better Way to Teach Writing* (1982), the two classes of students with learning disabilities spent nine weeks working on a bookmaking project.* After looking at books in the school library, the teacher and students had brainstorming sessions. At times it was hard to get across that *any idea* or approach was acceptable. This meant the students could begin with their own drawings that related to a story or start with a story and then illustrate it (Fig. 5.1). Initially, students had difficulty in getting past the concept that it was more important to get the idea down than to have words spelled correctly.

Figure 5.1. Two students with specific learning disabilities draw some of their ideas for their stories. Photo credit: Tom Anderson.

Stories were read to the students; some saw film strips; others listened to audiotaped stories. The picture in Figure 5.2 is from a book titled *Reptiles* by a nine-year-old boy who had average intelligence and a specific learning

---

*While these students were for the most part older than regular second grade students, their artistic developmental levels and some of their academic levels were more typical of second grade children. Therefore, the work of these students is discussed in connection with reading abilities typical of the second grade level.

Snakes eat eggs and then in the stomach
it cracks and then the snake spits out the
egg shell.

Figure 5.2. A page from a book titled, *Reptiles,* that was written and illustrated by a nine-year-old boy of average intelligence who had difficulty with auditory processing. Note that in terms of artistic development, this child's graphic work as reflected in this drawing is in the early Schematic stage of development. This book and the books in Figures 5.3–5.6 were created and published at the Chattahoochee Publishing Company, Chattahoochee Elementary School, Chattahoochee, FL. Photo credit: Tom Anderson.

disability related to auditory processing. He had difficulty remembering details from a brief (no more than two-sentence sequence) story.

In writing this story the boy listened to a *National Geographic* tape/book about reptiles. He was very interested in reptiles. He told his story to the teacher and she wrote it down. Later, the text was corrected and typed out, and the boy illustrated his story. The story was bound using cardboard, and a library card pocket and card were added. The bookbinding, library card and pocket were done for all the stories the class wrote. Later, the students read each other's books. These became the publications of the Chattahoochee Publishing Company.

Other examples (Fig. 5.3–5.6) that are included in this section are: *The Bird and the Boy* by a female student who was ten years old with a specific learning disability involving speech problems (Fig. 5.3). *The Boy that Kept on Changing Cars* (Fig. 5.4) was by a nine-year-old second grade boy with specific learning disabilities and behavior problems (in part resulting from verbal and physical abuse). *The Girl Who Changed Colors* (Fig. 5.5) was created by a 10-year-old boy with specific learning disabilities in receptive language and in arithmetic. He functions at the fifth grade level in reading and is very slow in completing all his tasks. *Me Being Kool* (Fig. 5.6) was created by a nine-year-old boy with specific learning disabilities.

Third Grade Level

At the third grade level, the initial reading skills area in which art can be related is III. Comprehension.

III. *Comprehension*

Begins to interpret meaning of simple figurative words and expressions, i.e., similes, metaphors, idioms
Uses context to obtain meaning of unfamiliar words
Predicts outcomes from a given passage (Bowen, 1985, p. 76)

Discussion

If children are able to master the ability to interpret, find meaning from the context of unfamiliar words, and predict outcomes from passages, then they can also visualize. Being able to visualize requires complex mental processes and the ability to abstract visually (Cardinale & Anderson, 1979). If students can read a story and are able to visualize what the story is about, then they can draw appropriate pictures to accompany that story. Additionally, they can take a verbal concept and visualize it. For example, students who were deaf were asked to visualize a picture from partial visual information that was provided. They were given a sheet that had only two large triangles and two small triangles drawn on it. From this visual information, one student drew two children flying kites (Fig. 5.7); another student took a triangle on a sheet of paper and made it into a package by adding the words "This Side Up" (Fig. 5.8).

In another integrated art and reading activity, nine-year-old learners

Figure 5.3. This is a page from the story, *The Bird and the Boy,* written and illustrated by a ten-year-old girl. Her specific learning disability involved speech problems. Note that in terms of artistic development this child's graphic work as reflected in this drawing is in the Schematic level of development. The text reads, "One day a little boy went swimming close to the birds." Photo credit: Tom Anderson.

Figure 5.4. This is a page from the book, *The Boy that Kept on Changing Cars.* The book was written and illustrated by a nine-year-old second grade boy with specific learning disabilities who has some behavior problems due to physical and verbal abuse. Note that in terms of artistic development this child's graphic work as reflected in this drawing is in the Schematic stage of development. The text is, "I like to drive a car. One day there was a race. A boy named Reggie was racing with the racing car." Photo credit: Tom Anderson.

Figure 5.5. This page is from the book, *The Girl Who Changed Colors*, written and illustrated by a fifth grade boy with specific learning disabilities in receptive language and arithmetic. Note that in terms of artistic development this child's graphic work as reflected in this drawing is in the Schematic stage of development. The text is, "There once was a girl who changed colors every time she saw a fish." Photo credit: Tom Anderson.

Figure 5.6. This page is from the book, *Me Being Kool*, by a nine-year-old boy with specific learning disabilities. Note that in terms of artistic development this child's graphic work as reflected in this drawing is in the early Schematic stage of development. The text is, "One day I was in my tree house. I looked oh so cool. My tree did say I was cool." Photo credit: Tom Anderson.

Figure 5.7. Completion drawings can help children develop their visualization skills which are necessary in the development of reading skills. In this example, the nine-year-old boy with deafness was asked to complete the drawing which had four triangles (two large ones and two little ones). As we see, the boy transformed the four triangles into two children flying kites.

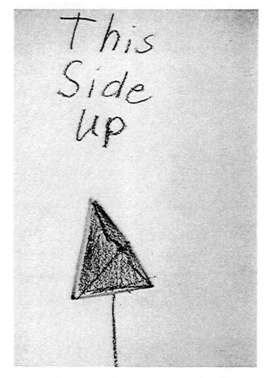

Figure 5.8. In this completion drawing, one triangle was already drawn on the paper. Another nine-year-old boy who is deaf transformed the triangle into a package and added the words "This Side UP." (Quite a creative solution to the drawing task!)

with learning disabilities were asked to combine animal words to form new unique creatures (Fig. 5.9 & 5.10). Examples of two of these are the *dinowolf* and the *tuck*. Next, the students drew these strange creatures and wrote sentences about them. Since this activity also is a language arts activity, the students later read orally what they had written. This would also reinforce the skill area of Oral/Silent Reading and the subskills: "Reads material orally with appropriate expression as related to text" and "Pronounces words accurately" (Bowen, 1985, p. 76).

Figure 5.9. Having fun with words and combining two nouns can motivate children both to be creative and to see reading and language arts as a fun learning experience. This is the mighty Dinowolf which was created by a nine-year-old boy with learning disabilities. He wrote this about the Dinowolf: "He eats grass. He is part wolf, part dinosaur. Its body is green & he's [sic] head is brown. It is 30 feet high and 100 feet long. He is shigh [sic] and is hard to find."

Finally, art and reading can be integrated by having students create verbal and visual narratives through the genre of cartoons (Craven, 1981; Fuller & Pribble, 1982; Hoff, 1982). Cartooning begins to occur naturally in children at around nine years of age (Wilson & Wilson, 1982). A cartoon activity will be most effective if students are functioning at the Schematic level of artistic development (which occurs typically between seven and nine years of age) and have the skills to organize visual symbols on a page. The students could be read a story. Then they could draw a cartoon strip that illustrated the key points in the story. Another approach might be to have

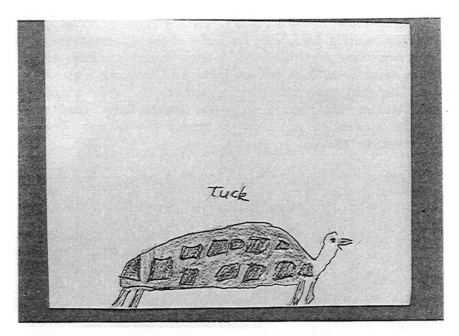

Figure 5.10. This is a picture of the Tuck, created by a nine-year-old boy with learning disabilities. He wrote this about the Tuck: "He live [sic] in the water. They eat insects, smails, [sic] frog, fish, grains and grass. They lay eggs in nest and hollow trees. His head is like a duck. His body is like a turtle."

the students develop their own cartoon characters and stories, produce these and then have classmates read the cartoon stories.

If students are able to follow simple written directions, then special free-time art experiences can be made available in an art book (or teacher-authored series of art activities) in which the child must read and follow printed directions in order to complete an art project. There are in fact several commercial graded texts available in art that have just this kind of art lesson. Two examples are *Art: Meaning, Method and Media* by G. Hubbard and M. Rouse (1972) and *Discover Art* by L. Chapman (1985). An example of one such graded art lesson for the third grade level appears in Figures 5.11 and 5.12. In this example and for all succeeding levels in the graded text, students are expected to read the text themselves and then to undertake the art activity explained in the text.

Fourth Grade Level

At this level two areas in which art can be related are vocabulary and comprehension.

Preparation

- pencils
- tracing or other semi-transparent paper (like lightweight typing bond), at least 2 sheets per student, about 4½" × 6" (11.2 cm × 15.2 cm).
- (desirable) many photographs of insects or a film on insects.
- display area and thumb tacks or tape to put up the drawings.

Note: Paper is small because the drawings that students create will serve as ideas for prints in Lesson 46.

Objectives

Vocabulary: symmetry, view
Students will:
a) understand that art is often inspired by nature.
b) appreciate the variety of lines, shapes and patterns found in nature.
c) understand that various subjects can be seen and drawn from different views.
d) create a drawing of a familiar or an imaginary insect.

45

Drawing
Insects

Artists like to study nature. They look for lines and shapes in nature. They study textures and patterns, too.

Study these insects as an artist might. Look for different kinds of lines. What patterns do you see? Is the body of each insect the same shape?

Look at the insects shown in this lesson. Seven are shown from the top view. The top view shows their symmetry. **Symmetry** means that one half is like the other half.

One insect is shown from a side view.
Can you find it?

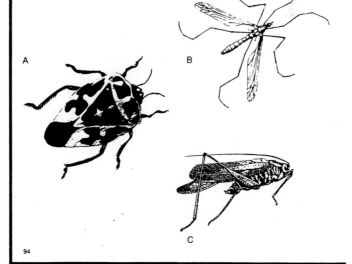

A

B

C

94

Exploration

about 5 minutes

1. Open the lesson with a discussion of nature's beauty. Call on students to describe some of the most beautiful natural things they have seen. Answers might include sunsets, rainbows, flowers, etc. Point out that artists often study the lines, colors, shapes and textures found in nature.
2. Explain that students will make drawings of insects. Ask the students to name varieties of insects. The list might include crickets, grasshoppers, ants, caterpillars, butterflies and beetles.
3. Work through the text on the left-hand page. Allow time for children to answer the questions in the text.
4. Review the concept of symmetry. Stress that a symmetrical design has the same shapes located in the same position on both sides of a midline. The average human body and the bodies of most animals are symmetrical. You may wish to remind the class of symmetrical shapes or designs they have cut from folded paper.
5. Have students focus on the illustrations. Help them notice such details as wing shapes and positions, body markings, curves of antennae. Discuss the concept that insects and other subjects can be seen and drawn from different viewpoints — top, side, front and back. Note that the grasshopper is shown in a side view.
6. Read through the remaining text. Preview the next lesson. In the next lesson students will make art prints based on drawings they make in this lesson.

Figures 5.11 and 5.12. (Next page) These are two pages from the *Teacher's Edition* of *Discover Art: Level 3* by L. Chapman (Worcester, MA: Davis), 1985. Copyright 1985 by Davis. Reprinted by permission. This activity not only reinforces reading skills but also is an example of an integrated art and science lesson.

D

E

F

G

Draw a real insect or an imaginary insect. Draw the top view or the side view.

Make your drawing very dark. You will use your drawing in the next lesson. You will use it to make an art print.

This is a drawing of a make-believe insect.

95

Extensions

Perceptual Awareness: You may wish to have students try to draw very large symmetrical lines and shapes on the chalkboard. Have them place chalk in both hands, stand very close to the board with arms outstretched, and draw with both hands simultaneously. Have them begin with wide arcs, then try swinging their lines in, up and around to make more complex symmetrical designs. (This chalkboard activity was popular early in this century. It was believed to improve handwriting.)

Science: Contrast the way an artist and a scientist might study insects. Point out that scientists and artists are both very keen observers of nature. The artist is more likely to study insects to discover the beauty or the strange lines, shapes, colors, etc. The scientist may look for the same features, but is more likely to want to explain their purpose — e.g. protection, reproduction, food gathering, etc.

Cleanup

about 2 minutes

1. Make sure that names are on the artwork. Collect the drawings and consider displaying them. Artwork will be needed for the next lesson.
2. Collect and save the unused drawing paper.

Evaluation

about 4 minutes

1. Refer to objectives a–d to review the lesson and to evaluate the results.
2. You might use the classroom to display the drawings. Have the children note and describe some of the differences they see (top, or side view, varieties of body shapes, and so on).

Activity

about 25 minutes

1. Distribute the paper for drawings. Explain that everyone is to draw one imaginary insect or one insect from memory. If you have photographs of insects, students may use them for reference, but should not copy.
2. Suggest that students fold their paper if they wish to draw the top view of an insect. Demonstrate or call on students to explain how to draw half of the insect on one side of the fold with very dark lines. Refold the paper so the drawing is inside.

The lines should be visible enough to trace the other half of the insect. (If not, students might try to darken the lines or use the light from the window to trace the other half of the insect).
3. Encourage students to think about the lines, shapes and patterns in their insects. Stress that the drawings should have dark lines.

Figure 5.12.

II. *Vocabulary*

"Interprets meanings of descriptive words such as similes, metaphors, idiom" (Bowen, 1985, p. 78)

III. *Comprehension*

Identifies main idea of passage
Interprets meaning of descriptive and figurative words, i.e., similes, metaphors, hyperbole, idiom
Identifies the setting of a story or content reading passage
Identifies cause-effect relationships
Predicts outcomes from a story
Identifies character traits (Bowen, 1985, p. 78)

Discussion

Again, at this level a student could have these comprehensive and vocabulary/interpretation skills reinforced by illustrating key points of stories or the story settings. Another approach might be for the student to draw a portrait of a key character in a story. Or the learners might play a visual/character descriptor game (Cardinale & Anderson, 1979). In this kind of a game, body parts and visual descriptors as well as personality descriptors are placed in three hats or boxes. Students draw one word from each box and then individually or in teams draw or sculpt the three-word descriptive combinations they have. For example, three words selected might be: courageous prickly ear, or scary bumpy nose, or happy rough eyebrows, or grumpy bumpy mouth. These then are drawn and eventually put together to form a most unusual portrait of someone. Students must agree (with the teacher's help) whether each team has accurately or appropriately solved the problem of illustrating each three-word combination.

Thus, we can see from these numerous examples some of the ways that the visual arts can be utilized *in the best sense* to facilitate instruction and the development of reading skills on many levels.

REFERENCES

Anderson, F. E. (1975). Mainstreaming art as well as children. *Art Education, 28*(8), 26–27.

Anderson, F. E. (1983). A critical analysis of *A Review of the published research literature on arts for the handicapped: 1971-1981. Art Therapy, 1*(1), 26–39.

Anderson, F. E., Ash, L., & Gambach, J. (1982). *A Review of the published research literature on arts for the handicapped: 1971-1981.* Washington, D.C.: National Committee Arts for the Handicapped.

Anderson, F. E., & Barnfield, L. S. (1974). Art especially for the exceptional. *Art Education, 27*(4/5), 8–10.

Anderson, F. E., Colchado, J., & McAnally, P. (1979). *Art for the handicapped.* Normal, IL: Illinois State University.

Anderson, F. E., Kolano, M., & de la Cruz, R. (1993). *A review of the published research literature on arts for persons with disabilities: 1981-1992.* San Francisco, CA: Abbey Gate Press.

Art therapy training, information brochure. (n.d.). Houston: American Art Therapy Association.

Bowen, M. (n.d.). Patterns of interest development. Unpublished manuscript, Illinois State University, class handout, Normal, IL.

Bowen, M. (1985). *Clinical reading instructional handbook.* Normal, IL: Illinois State University.

Brommer, G. (1989). *Discovering art history.* Worcester, MA: Davis.

Broudy, H. S. (1987). The role of imagery in learning. *Occasional Paper 1.* Los Angeles, CA: The Getty Center for Education in the Arts.

Caldwell, H., & Moore, B. H. (1991). The art of writing: Drawing as preparation for narrative writing in the primary grades. *Studies in Art Education, 32*(4), 207–219.

Cardinale, R., & Anderson, F. E. (1977). Art games and learning problems: Or, what does a courageous prickly ear look like? *Art Education, 32*(1), 17–19.

Catchings, Y. P. (1984). Art joins the reading circle. *Instructor, 44*(10), 150–152.

Chapman, L. (1978). *Approaches to art in education.* New York: Harcourt, Brace, Jovanovich.

Chapman, L. (1985). *Discover art 1-6: Teacher's editions.* Worchester, MA: Davis.

DeChira, E. (1982). A visual arts program for enhancement of the body image. *Journal of Learning Disabilities, 15*(7), 399–405.

DeChira, E. (1990). Art for special needs: A learning disabled child in a special art program. *Art Therapy, 7*(1), 22–28.

Duke, L. (1983). The Getty Center for education in the arts. *Art Education, 36*(5), 4–13.

Duke, L. (1988). The Getty Center for Education in the Arts and discipline-based art education. *Art Education, 41*(2), 7–12.

Ennis, R. H. (1987). Critical thinking and the curriculum. *National Forum, 65*(2), 60–65.

Eisner, E. (1983). The kinds of schools we need. *Educational Leadership, 41*(2), 54–58.

Feldman, E. B. (1970). *Becoming human through art.* Englewood Cliffs, NJ: Prentice-Hall.

Feldman, E. B. (1985). *Thinking about art.* Englewood Cliffs, NJ: Prentice-Hall.

Feldman, E. B. (1987). *Varieties of visual experience.* Englewood Cliffs, NJ: Prentice-Hall.

Fuller, M. J., & Pribble, D. A. (1982). "Cartooning," drawing the line in art and social studies. *Art Education, 35*(1), 9–11.

Goldstein, E., Saunders, R., Kowalchuk, J., & Katz, T. (1986). *Understanding and creating art.* Book one and two. Dallas, TX: Garrard.

Greene, J., & Hasselbring, T. S. (1981). The acquisition of language concepts by hearing impaired children through selected aspects of an experimental core art curriculum. *Studies in Art Education, 22*(2), 32–37.

Hardison, J., & Llorens, L. A. (1988). Structured craft group activities for adolescent delinquent girls. Special issue: Group process and structure in psychosocial occupational therapy. *Occupational Therapy in Mental Health, 8*(3), 101–117.

Hiltunen, S. S. (1989). The effects of art/drama therapy experiences on rigidity, body concept and mental maturity in graphic thinking of adolescents with mental retardation. *Art Therapy, 6*(3), 18–25.

Hobbs, J. (1990). *Art in Context* (4th ed.). New York: Harcourt, Brace, Jovanovich.

Hobbs, J., & Salome, R. A. (1990). *The visual experience.* Worcester, MA: Davis.

Hobbs, J., Salome, R. A., & Willis-Fisher, L. (1991). *The visual experience. Teacher's edition.* Worcester, MA: Davis.

Hodsoll, F. (1984, March 29). Art Education: One of the basics. *The Christian Science Monitor,* p. 4.

Hoff, G. R. (1982). The visual narrative: Kids, comic books and creativity. *Art Education, 35*(2), 20–23.

Hubbard, G., & Rouse, M. (1972). *Art: Meaning method and material: 1-6 Teacher's edition.* Westchester, IL: Benefic.

Hulsker, J. (1984). *The complete Van Gogh: Paintings, drawings, sketches.* New York: Harrison House/Harry N. Abrams.

Intempo Toys. (1990). *In the picture: The kids' art game.* Palo Alto, CA: Intempo Toys.

Janson, H. J., & Cauman, S. (1971). *A basic history of art.* Englewood Cliffs, NJ: Prentice-Hall.

Jewel, M. G., & Zimtz, M. (1990). *Learning to read naturally.* New York: Macmillan.

Lowenfeld, V., & Brittain, L. (1987). *Creative and mental growth* (8th ed.). New York: Macmillan.

The National Gallery. (1991). *Make a painting: A game for up to eight players.* Washington, DC: The National Gallery.

Perez, J. (1989). Abstracts of research on arts used with children who are handicapped. Unpublished manuscript, Illinois State University, Normal, IL.

Piper, D. (1984). *Looking at art.* New York: Random House.

Pontius, A. A. (1983). Links between literacy skills and accurate spatial relations in representations of the face: Comparison of preschoolers, school children, dyslexia, and mentally retarded. *Perceptual and Motor Skills, 57,* 659–666.

Ratcliffe, E. R. (1977). The old masters art collage: An art therapy technique for heuristic self-discovery. *Art Psychotherapy, 4*(2), 29–32.

Rowell, E. (1983). Developing reading skills through the study of great arts. In J. Cowen (Ed.): *Teaching reading through the arts* (pp. 55–68). Neward, DE: International Reading Association.

Rubin, J. A. (n.d.). Film guide to *We'll show you what we're gonna do.* (Art for multiply handicapped blind children.) Unpublished manuscript, Pittsburgh Child Guidance Services, Pittsburg, PA.

Schennum, W. A. (1987). Expressive activity therapy in residential treatment: Effects on children's behavior in the treatment milieu. *Child and Youth Care Quarterly, 16*(2), 81–90.

Schleien, S. J., Tipton, R. M., Soderman-Olson, M. L., & McMahon, K. T. (1990). Integrating children with moderate to severe cognitive deficits into a community museum program. *Education and Training in Mental Retardation, 22*(3), 112–120.

Silberstein-Storfer, M., & Jones, M. (1982). *Doing art together: Discovering the joys of appreciating and creating art as taught at the Metropolitan Museum of Art's famous parent-child workshop.* New York: Simon & Schuster.

Spivack, G. H., & Spotts, J. (1966). *The Devereaux Child Behavior (DCB) Rating Scale.* Devon, PA: The Dereuc Foundation.

Sturgess, P. (1986). Exploration of the character, expressive qualities and attitudes towards arts activities of exceptional adolescent students. Toronto: Canada Ontario Institute for Studies in Education. (ERIC Document Reproduction Service No. ED 277209)

Tibbets, T. J., & Stone, B. (1990). Short-term art therapy with seriously emotionally disturbed adolescents. Special Issue: The creative arts therapies with adolescents. *Arts in Psychotherapy, 17*(2), 139–146.

Tanner, M. (1984). Artistic reading: Comprehension with a flair. *Art Education, 37*(1), 17–23.

Van Bruen, B. (1986). Improving reading skills through elementary art experiences. *Art Education, 39*(1), 56, 59, 61.

Vincent Van Gogh: A Portrait in two parts. (1982). (Laserdisc). New York: North American Philips.

Chapter 6

ART AND LANGUAGE ARTS

Lynne Raiser

COMPARISON OF THE READING AND WRITING PROCESS

Before presenting specific activities integrating art and language arts, let's examine the difference between the reading and writing processes. Reading is a process that decodes symbols to discover meaning. Conversely, written composition is an encoding process that pulls from visual and auditory memory the groups of squiggles that express meaning.

Decoding the words, "The boy hid under the house all night," is a different process from spelling those words and arranging them in the order demanded of English syntax. For example, the word *night* sounds like *nit* with a long *i*. If the reader does not have the *ight* pattern in her visual memory, she cannot spell the word correctly. When she reads the sentences she has visual clues to help her decode the message. Even if she can only read some of the words, she may be able to figure the others out by using context clues. Suppose she can read, "The boy *?* under the house all night." She knows the boy did something under the house all night. Did he play? Did he sleep? Did he hide? Maybe there is a clue in the next sentence, "He was afraid of the big dog." But the reader does not recognize the word *afraid*.

At this point, the reader has decoded this: "The boy *?* under the house all night. He was *?* of the big dog." Now she knows that the boy did something under the house all night because of a big dog. Big dogs are scary. A boy wouldn't play under the house with one. Or sleep with one. Maybe he was scared and hid from him. Even if the reader does not decode the words exactly and reads, "He *hide* under the house all night. He was *scared* of the big dog," she can understand the sentences.

Trying to pull those words out of memory and write them in correct order with correct spelling is more difficult. The child must remember how to make each letter. She must remember to put the letters in the correct order so her spelling is accurate. She must use correct verb tenses, capital letters and periods. She must remember the peculiar spelling pattern in night. If

Note: Some of the material in this chapter is from *Earthshine* by L.S. Raiser (Jacksonville, FL: Very Special Arts Florida, 1991). Copyright 1991 by L.S. Raiser. Adapted by permission.

she has never seen the word *afraid,* she has to ask someone how to spell it or she could look it up in the dictionary (which is hard to do if you cannot spell the word). Or she could try to sound it out. With some knowledge of long *a* spelling patterns, she might spell it *frade* or *ufraid.* Only about half of English words can be sounded out, assuming the child knows how to spell the 43 sounds in all their variations and sequence them correctly. The other half must be learned by visual memorization.

It is not difficult to understand why written language is the last language skill mastered. Juggling the requirements of letter formation, letter order, word order, spacing between words, spelling, grammar, capital letters, punctuation, and organization of the content is an overwhelming task for many beginning writers. Children who know they are inefficient learners typically avoid as much written work as possible and delay mastery of basic language arts skills, usually indefinitely.

LANGUAGE ARTS AND VISUAL ART

Language arts and visual art are natural partners in the education of special children. Young children discover early that they can express themselves by making their mark, beginning when they learn to feed themselves and discover the joy of smearing strained carrots all over the highchair and themselves. Many parents experience the horror of their toddler painting the wall with a lipstick or papering a door with Band-Aids. Even nonverbal children can say, "SEE WHAT I CAN DO," by discovering ways to validate their existence by making their mark. Special children may learn to express themselves differently, and they may do it later, but they still do it.

Experimentation with carrots and lipstick gives way to markers, crayons, pencils, and paints as parents and teachers provide art materials to children. As they become aware of the symbols of their language, children discover that one of the most important words in the world to them, their name, can be written. When developmentally ready, the special child will try to write her name. In the beginning, it may be more of a drawing as the child tries to copy her name without careful step-by-step instruction in letter formation. Still, the scribbles are hers—her very own name. She can draw a picture of herself that looks like a spider and she can draw squiggles that look like her name. She is on the road to written composition as soon as she sees the connection between the spoken word and the written word. Developmentally, in art this is the process that occurs in the named scribble stage when the child begins to label her drawings even though the scribbles do not really look like the object that she names. This process naturally grows out of the early scribbles that evolved into the pictorial representation of herself and her world.

Many children with disabilities have disorganized, illogical approaches to learning. Visual clues are very important to inefficient readers who get so bogged down in decoding words that they lose the meaning of the message. A picture can convey a great deal of information quickly. Many highly verbal picture readers are able to fool their teachers into believing they are reading and comprehending when they are really understanding the story from the pictures. If they have good auditory memories, they can often memorize what they hear another child read and then acceptably "read" the same passage. By incorporating art into language arts activities, the power of the visual-motor stimulation of drawing and other art activities can help bridge the gap between the spoken word, life experiences, and their symbolic representation in written language.

Children who are easily frustrated and those who fear failure can be enticed to participate in learning activities that are nontraditional and don't look like "school." The child with language impairments who makes a paper plate stick puppet and then dictates her puppet's words into a cassette tape recorder for later transcription by her teacher will likely enjoy and complete this task. Conversely, she may resist standing in front of the class to share what she did over the weekend. As she puts the eyes, nose, mouth, and hair on her puppet she is developing its personality so that when she speaks into the recorder she loses her self-conscious identity as a shy, fearful little girl with poor language skills and becomes another, more competent communicator.

The author conducted a playwriting project with a group of elementary students with learning disabilities. A hyperactive child with rapid-fire, poorly articulated speech was chosen to play the turtle who had to move and talk very, very slowly. Another extremely shy boy with a severe speech problem was chosen to be the brave, proud, majestic eagle because he looked the part. Both boys interpreted their characters with great success. When they lost their own identities and became their characters, their speech disabilities and natural speaking styles were nearly eliminated.

Similarly, schoolwork that does not look like schoolwork is less threatening. Playwriting for puppets is less threatening than writing a report about a book that was difficult to read and full of words difficult to spell. Writing a poem about a whale in the shape of a whale is not a language arts lesson, it is art. And everybody knows that in art, reading and spelling do not matter. Writing cartoons is far more motivating than using spelling words in sentences which for some children with disabilities is the sum total of their written language experience in the elementary school grades.

Visual art can be the catalyst, the link between attempting academic tasks and academic success. The extra time the teacher spends in developing creative, arts-based language arts activities pays off in less reluctant children who are less fearful of failure because the spotlight is not on the correctness of the task but on the creative expression and the artistic risk-taking. For some children, successful risk-taking in an art-based lesson may carry over later into more risk-taking in the traditional learning experiences so frequently avoided or feared.

LEARNING CHARACTERISTICS OF CHILDREN WITH DISABILITIES AND LANGUAGE ARTS

Before presenting specific activities, let us look at some of the learning characteristics of special children as they relate to language arts.

CHILDREN WITH MENTAL RETARDATION (MR). Learners with mental retardation process information very slowly and need lots and lots of repetition and practice. A student with educable mental retardation (EMR) can be expected to learn to read between the second and sixth grade level by the time she graduates from high school, so intermediate elementary students will have some degree of literacy. These students tend to have poor memories and do not generalize well. Concept development is difficult, and they learn best through concrete, real-world experiences. Drawing and writing cartoons about real people doing real activities will have more carry-over than using fantastic talking animals to illustrate a message. It takes a student with EMR so long to learn concepts that, for example, excessive time spent in developing an illustrated story about the family life of polar bears is difficult to justify. Real-life situations can be explored through art and written language, offering the EMR student the opportunity to develop daily living skills, problem-solving abilities, literacy, and her imagination. Activities do not have to be fanciful and removed from experience to be creative and imaginative.

Learners with trainable mental retardation (TMR) will rarely be able to write thoughts independently, but they can develop group stories with the teacher who can recast their ideas into coherent sentences. Some students with TMR can verbally express a complete experience as the teacher writes it.

CHILDREN WITH LEARNING DISABILITIES (LD). Learners with learning disabilities often share with EMR children the characteristics of poor memory, inadequate problem-solving skills, difficulty generalizing learning from one situation to another and need for extensive practice. Many learners with EMR and LD have severe visual perception difficulties which interfere with handwriting and drawing ability. They may have figure-ground disturbances that interfere with interpretation of pictures.

In art activities the teacher can be quite frustrated by a child with LD who seems intelligent, but cannot "see" design elements. The student with this type of LD may have difficulty learning by watching the teacher model an art activity in front of the class. She may learn best one-on-one with clear, verbal, step-by-step instructions by the teacher as the activity is demonstrated. Sometimes it is necessary to talk such a child through the activity several times before letting her attempt it, to avoid unnecessary frustration. There are some children with visual perception difficulties who find art a very frustrating experience. If they have good verbal skills, the emphasis in the art/language arts activity should be on language expression rather than expecting a quality art product.

Severe reading and written language disabilities are common among children with LD. Since most of them have normal intelligence, they are often extremely frustrated that they are so "dumb." They often suffer from lack of motivation and frequently become behavior problems. Finding new and novel ways to teach and reteach the same skills and concepts is a constant challenge to the teacher.

CHILDREN WITH BEHAVIORAL DISORDERS (BD). Although many learners with BD have normal intelligence and no discernible learning deficits, motivation is a common problem. Most learners with BD have been referred because of acting-out, noncompliant behavior. Even withdrawn, nonaggressive children can test a teacher's patience with quiet, stubborn refusal to participate in any class activities. Many teachers of students with BD hold that they cannot teach these children academics until they get their behavior under control. The activities in a class of children with BD frequently include art and music activities, games, and other low stress activities so that these children can learn appropriate classroom behaviors before moving into more challenging academic tasks. The use of art-based language arts activities is well-adapted to BD classrooms organized according to the "control first—academics second" philosophy. The art/language arts link allows learners with BD to take risks and experience success in a nontraditional, creative atmosphere that can still be structured to encourage self-control and appropriate social interactions.

CHILDREN WITH PHYSICAL DISABILITIES (PD). Learners with PD can use three-dimensional materials such as clay and larger, more controllable drawing pencils, markers, or paintbrushes. Written work can be typed or done on a computer with appropriate adapters. Students with severe PD can select magazine pictures or photographs to illustrate written work if they cannot hold drawing or painting tools.

CHILDREN WHO ARE DEAF OR HARD-OF-HEARING (D/HH). Learners who lose their hearing acuity before they develop language usually have great difficulty learning written language. If they have been taught sign language, they are speaking another language with a different structure which makes the teaching of standard written English difficult. Visual art can be a bridge to standard English for these students. Students who lose their hearing after developing language may learn skills in written expression more easily. In either case, communication between the teacher and student will be difficult unless the teacher is trained to communicate with students who are D/HH. Clear, step-by-step, visually enhanced directions will be necessary for these students. A carefully illustrated lesson plan can be given to students who are D/HH to help them follow along with teacher instructions. Many art-based language arts activities may appear more complicated than they really are to learners who are D/HH because of the nontraditional approach which requires the student to shift mental gears and understand how to do an academic task in an unexpected way. The comfort of sameness is gone and communication becomes more challenging for the learner who is D/HH and the teacher.

CHILDREN WITH VISUAL IMPAIRMENTS (VI). Learners with VI can participate in visual art/language arts activities with some modifications. In a cartoon activity, for example, a child with severe VI can model clay figures instead of drawing them. The words the student with VI writes or dictates can be attached to the mouths of the clay figures with toothpicks. Another adaptation would be to allow the student with VI to draw larger figures with a black marker instead of smaller, more detailed, colored cartoon characters. Black on white is easier for a learner with VI to see. Her favorite color might be added as an accent after her figures are drawn. Too many colors may confuse the student's perception of the picture so that adding the speaker tags later may be difficult.

With this background information in mind, let us now discuss appropriate language art and art activities for children with disabilities. Only those activities that are truly valid art and language arts (that is those experiences that call on about an equal amount of art concepts and skills and language arts concepts and skills) endeavors will be covered in this segment.

VISUAL VOCABULARY ACTIVITIES

Visual vocabulary exercises encourage special children to see the richness of their language. Many inefficient learners have poor memories and weak visualization skills. Although these activities focus on visualization, some also consider the auditory and tactile properties of words. Experiencing the look, sound, and feel of words helps children remember word structure and word meaning. Additionally, a final part to most of these activities is to have the children draw pictures of *their* visualizations of these visual vocabulary activities.

Shape Words

Shape words challenge children to write words the way they look, feel, or sound (Fig. 6.1). Adjectives, adverbs, and verbs make the best shape words because they have clear, precise concepts that can be expressed visually. Some suggestions are: scary, rough, splash, swirl, bumpy, buzz, bubble and sharp.

Words with opposite meanings (antonyms) add the interesting dimension of contrast (Fig. 6.1). Words can be written in different colors with different thicknesses of marker, pencil, or paintbrush to further illustrate the opposite meanings. Some antonyms to get learners started are: hard, soft, under, over, big, little, tall, short, near, and far.

With many of these shape words and antonyms, the child can create drawings or three-dimensional sculptures with wood or clay to illustrate these words or word pairs.

Also, you could make a game or problem out of the art experience by assigning drawings that have examples of some of the shape words and opposite words. The problems posed might be, "Today, you are asked to draw something High and Low and Heavy."

Word Pictures

Word pictures are "drawn" using the word to illustrate its meaning. Nouns work best because they are naming words that represent persons, places, or things and can be more easily depicted (Fig. 6.2). Have the children lightly sketch a pencil outline of the subject of the word picture. Using a marker or pencil, they write the word over and over until the outline of the sketch is completely covered. They can fill in the picture of the word in a different color. Children with undeveloped fine motor coordination may need to draw larger word pictures with fat pencils or crayons. Some nouns for word pictures are: table, giraffe, banana, volcano, feather, rainbow, waves and seagull.

By combining two or more words, children can create more complex word pictures (Fig. 6.3). After the word pictures are completed, the light pencil sketches can be erased with an art gum eraser.

Pictionary

Beginning readers benefit from creating their own picture dictionary or "pictionary." Assemble a construction paper booklet with 32 pages, one for each letter of the alphabet plus *ch, sh,* and *th* which sound differently than *c, s,* and *t.* For children who are easily frustrated, hand out only the pages they

Figure 6.1. These are examples of shape words. Learners are asked to write words the way they look, feel or sound. These visual vocabulary activities help children with disabilities to gain an awareness of the richness of their language. These examples include simple shape words (afraid, book, falling) as well as opposing shape words with opposite meanings (large/small, high/low, thick/thin and in/out).

need each day. Print both the uppercase and lowercase letter at the top of each page, one set of letters to the page. Collect a supply of magazines and ask the children to search for pictures that begin with the sound they are learning. Be sure to check their pictures before they glue them into their pictionary. Have the children add new pictures to pages previously started as they find them in their search for new sound pictures. If the children have the drawing skills (are functioning at the Preschematic artistic level at four or five years of age typically or above), they can draw their own pictures of the words included in their pictionary. Later they can add the words above or under the pictures to develop spelling awareness. As children begin to

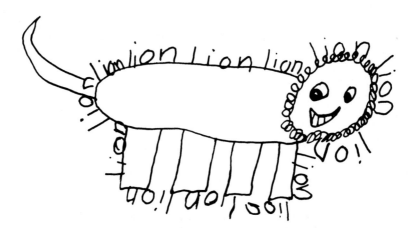

Figure 6.2. This example of a word picture was drawn by a second grade boy with learning disabilities.

write the words to go with the pictures, many of them will be quite intrigued with their newfound skill in "spelling" and ask how to spell the words (Figs. 6.4 & 6.5).

WRITING FLUENCY ACTIVITIES

Before children can express complete thoughts in writing they must be able to write most of the letters of the alphabet and spell a few words. It is not necessary to wait until children can write all the letters or spell extensive lists of words. They can dictate stories and poems. The children can write independently, spelling words the way they think they look and sound. Too often inefficient learners receive so many red marks on their papers because of lack of capital letters and periods and poor spelling that the job of creating with words is quickly dashed. Correctness of form, punctuation, and spelling come later. First, children must become comfortable exploring the ideas in their heads through written expression. Beginning writers need to experience the easy flow of written language when no strings are attached. Some of the written fluency ideas in this section have been adapted from Tiedt, Bruemmer, Lane, Stelwagon, Watanabe, and Williams (1983).

Free Association

Words about pictures can be used to develop fluency of ideas through free association. Have the children draw a picture of a person, animal, or object at the top of a piece of construction paper. Then ask them to list all the words they can think of that describe the picture. Remind them that spelling

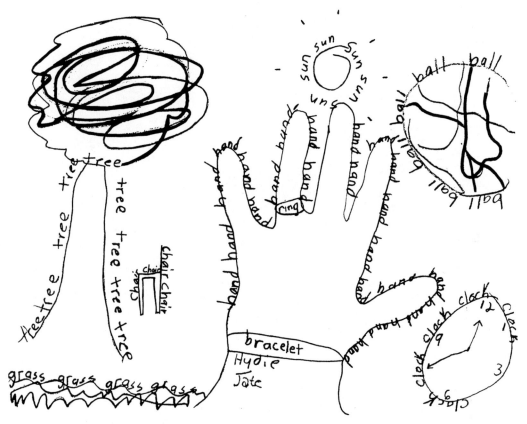

Figure 6.3. This is an example of a combined word picture. Here a third grade girl with specific learning disabilities has combined several words and made a complex word picture.

does not matter. The purpose of the activity is to think and write ideas, not write and spell perfectly. Ask them to write the words quickly, listing all thoughts that come into their minds about the picture. If they cannot think of how to spell a word, tell them to draw a picture or write the beginning sound, or any other sounds they hear in the word, and go on to the next word. Later, if they remember the word by the picture clues they drew or the sound clues they wrote, you can help them spell it. Children are often amazed to see how many words they can think of, especially when spelling does not count.

Magazine pictures can be used in place of original drawings, especially for activities using free association to explore specific content lessons, such as nutrition, jobs, or transportation. As children get comfortable with using free association to make lists of words about a picture, they will often begin

Figure 6.4. Children who are deaf and six years old make books by stamp printing construction paper for the cover design. These covers are then "filled" with blank pages of drawing paper. Then the empty book can become a pictionary.

to write sentences in their lists instead of strings of unconnected words (Fig. 6.6). The sentence lists become first attempts at expressing complete written thoughts.

Picture Brainstorming

Picture brainstorming asks children to think of as many solutions to a problem as they can. Then instead of writing their solutions, they draw them. Give the children a problem such as, "There is an elephant on the roof of the school. No one knows how he got up there, but we must think of ways to get him off. Draw as many ways to get the elephant off the roof as you can think of."

In Figure 6.7 a nine-year-old boy with LD has drawn his solutions to "How many different ways could you get a porcupine out of a box?" Brainstorming encourages children to think creatively as they develop problem-solving skills. Brainstorming through drawing offers a motivating alternative to writing for reluctant or inefficient writers.

Figure 6.5. Here a child who is deaf shows her drawing of a nurse for her pictionary. Not only is the book a pictionary—it also is a pictionary specifically of community helpers.

Rhebus Writing

Rhebus writing combines words and pictures to tell a story (Fig. 6.8a & 6.8b). The pictures are usually the nouns and verbs. The children write the rest of the words in between their pictures. Several group rhebus stories should be written before children attempt to do them in groups of two or individually. Children who are not comfortable drawing may use magazine pictures. Another alternative is to have the children draw the main characters in their story for the teacher to photocopy several times. Then as they develop their stories they can use the copies when they want their cat or dog to look EXACTLY the same each time. Some perfectionistic children are easily frustrated when they discover it is almost impossible to draw each figure exactly the same each time it is needed in the story. Children can also trace the original figure several times.

Rhebus stories make stimulating bulletin boards and class books. Children enjoy trying to read each other's stories which are like deciphering codes.

For children who are just beginning to write stories, introduce rhebus writing with a parallel story format such as:

If I found a ____ (draw a picture of animal or object),
I would ____ (draw a picture of the action).

TRUCK
BIG
YELLOW
FAST
WHEELS

TRUCKS
ARE
BIG
AND
GO
FAST
ON
THE
STREET

Figure 6.6. This illustration shows how free association looks. The first list of words under the car are words related to the car using free association. The next list (on the right side) shows how these words can be connected into complete written thoughts.

Parallel story formats give the children the words they need so they can concentrate on drawing their pictures to express their ideas. Later they can create their own stories. Other parallel story formats are:

***

Once upon a time there was a   (picture),
who liked to   (picture).

***

If I ever saw a   (picture),
I would   (picture).

How to Get a Porcupine Out of a Box

Figure 6.7. This is a drawn solution to the problem "How many different ways could you get a porcupine out of a box?" The illustration is by a nine-year-old boy with learning disabilities.

Puppet Plays

Puppet making is a popular project with children. Children can create puppets out of paper bags, paper plates, old socks or spoons (Anderson, 1978, 1993) and act out shows together (Figs. 6.9 & 6.10). Puppets can be an early introduction to creative writing.

Beginning writers often write stories that are really conversations without quotation marks. The following example was written by a sixth grade girl with LD:

> T.T. I said you are nuts. Don't say that said T.T. While I was in New York I ate 3 Nutty Buttys and I got sick. "Oh" I said and you are fed up with Nutty Buttys right right said T.T.

1's there was a

_ _ _ _   _ _ _ :

This lived on ST.

_ _ _   _ _ _ _ _ _ _

So, -the had a problem.

_ _ _ _

The

_ _ _ _   _ _ _ _ _

 the poor .

_ _ _ _ _   _ _ _ _ :

The 🐿️ was very mad.

___

He tried 2 the INK of

a plan, so that the 🐊

🪵   〰️   🐊   🐿️

___   ___   ___

him.
Then he had a real good idea.
He moved 2 🐭 ST.

___   ___

Figures 6.8a & b. This is an illustration of rhebus writing. The pictures that are included are usually the nouns and verbs. The connecting words are written out. If the child lacks the confidence or ability to draw the words, magazine pictures can be used. Or, multiple copies of the same noun can be made with a photocopier.

How much clearer her tale would have been if she had written it in playwright form as follows:

NANCY: T.T., you are nuts.
T.T.:   Don't say that. While I was in New York I ate three Nutty Buddies and I got sick.
NANCY: Oh, and you are fed up with Nutty Buddies, right?
T.T.:   Right.

Plays require no quotation marks. Just write the characters' names in capital letters followed by a colon. A colon! That is quite sophisticated and impressive for children who have not mastered periods yet. It is motivating to be considered ready to use colons and write in an unfamiliar form like a play or a poem. When teaching inefficient or reluctant learners basic literacy skills, teachers need all the tricks they can find to make learning novel and exciting.

Even if children are not developmentally ready or able to write, be sure to take the time to write some of their impromptu puppet shows so they can see that the words they have put in their puppets' mouths can be written and read. For some children this will be a revelation. Written words may seem alien to them, and certainly nothing they could ever have anything to do with creating. To capture the children's puppet play dialogue, turn on a tape recorder during the free play time. Later you can print or type some of the speeches for them to see.

Many teachers of children who are young or developmentally slow write experience stories about class happenings to help the children see the relationship between words that are said and words that are read. In play form a child's EXACT words are recorded. When read back to the child, those words increase in stature, and she can see and hear that her imagination can be written down and saved to enjoy later. Written in play form, words are more concrete because they are words that people and puppets say to each other in the present tense. When we write down in narrative form WHAT we DID, the past tense removes us from the immediacy of the communication. Writing plays instead of experience stories is a more sophisticated group writing activity for older children who are inefficient, reluctant writers. Playwriting is really easier, but the children who have never done it will likely think it is a mature writing form. The following bit from a play written by children with emotional disorders shows how witty youngsters can be:

RABBIT: Help! Mom! Dad! I'm scared. I don't know my way home. Come get me! I'm dirty and hungry.
LAMP POST: (Leans down and shines) Who are you? Where did you come from?

RABBIT: I'm Bucky Bunny. I live in the forest. I'm lost.

LAMP POST: I don't move much. I just stand and shine. I might know someone who can help you.

(LAMP POST shines on PARKING METER. PARKING METER ticks time away.)

RABBIT: I'm lost. Can you help me?

PARKING METER: I'm running out of time. Do you have any money? I can't help you if I run out of time.

RABBIT: Oh, no! What will I do? (RABBIT trips over GARBAGE CAN.)

GARBAGE CAN: Ouch! That hurt! Be more careful.

RABBIT: I'm sorry. I need help to get home. Can you please help me?

GARBAGE CAN: I just collect garbage. And I'm too full to move.

The Rabbit does get home. He was there all along having a bad dream.

(Play written by Judi Howell's class of children with emotional disturbances, Normandy Elementary School, Jacksonville, FL.)

Making Puppets

Begin playwriting by making paper plate puppets decorated with yarn, bits of paper, fabric and found objects. Be sure to use inexpensive real paper plates, not plastic or styrofoam, so the markers will write and the glue will stick. You can glue or staple a tongue depressor for a handle as an option. Children will hold them up, sometimes to their faces like masks, and talk. You can turn them into masks by cutting holes for their eyes as another option (Fig. 6.10). They will pretend they can see, and some children prefer to hide behind their paper plate puppets/masks so they can be freer to communicate what they imagine their puppets would say.

After the children make their puppets, let them play freely with them, developing their puppets' personalities and talking to other puppets. You will find that some of your most reluctant communicators talk more easily when holding a puppet near their faces. A child with a puppet in her hand assumes a new identity. The puppet can risk saying those things that the child may not feel comfortable saying.

With paper plate puppet in hand, children can talk to each other and you can write their puppet conversation as a play to be performed again and again. Encourage them to go beyond the usual "Hi, how are you?" "Fine, how are you?" If they cannot think of anything else to say, have them tell jokes which most children enjoy doing. Puppet plays are a good introduction to more elaborate pupil-written and produced plays that will be possible when children become more adept at dictating or writing dialogue.

Figure 6.9. These are spoon puppets created by two girls with moderate mental retardation. Note that the pipe cleaners are used both for the hands of the puppets and to hold the dresses on to the spoon. By twisting pipe cleaners to hold on the material for the dresses, there is no need to do any sewing in constructing the puppets.

Cartoons

Cartoons are similar to plays in that cartoon characters talk exactly as puppets and actors do. Puppet plays and cartoons are parallel activities that offer two options for developing beginning writing skills.

Ask the children to draw a picture of a person, animal, or object. Glue their drawing in the upper middle of their paper. Then ask them to write or dictate to you what the person, animal, or object is saying. You might structure the activity by asking that they draw a particular figure; allowing them to choose will lead to more varied cartoons. You may also let them choose a picture from the newspaper or a magazine instead of drawing their own.

When you make your first magazine picture cartoon, it is fun to ask the children to select a picture of an animal or an object. After they glue it on their paper, ask them to write what the figure in the picture, such as the

Figure 6.10. A ten-year-old girl with auditory impairments has created this paper plate mask/puppet.

lemon or the goat, is saying. Children will likely respond enthusiastically to this ridiculous request. Silly assignments often help children remember processes. When introducing two-character cartoons, you might say, "Remember when we wrote the cartoons about the lemons and the goats? Well, today we are going to create a new kind of cartoon. The lemon and the goat are going to talk to each other!" Now this is sillier than ever and should encourage some completely foolish dialogues as they draw or select totally unrelated pictures. Silly assignments allow inefficient learners to have fun taking risks because all the cartoons will be foolish, even the one the teacher makes to show them how to do it.

After drawing or selecting two pictures, have the children write what the characters are saying to each other. Be sure that the children write the words that the characters say before they draw the balloons around the words. Drawing the balloons first will cause great frustration for children who cannot judge how much room they will need. Also, the first character in the picture to speak is the one on the left. This assures that the cartoons can be read from left to right as books are read.

POETRY

Poetry is painting with words. Poetry creates images of what is seen, felt, and heard. Poetry is also music, using words to create rhythmic, flowing sounds. Because of the economy of words, poetry appeals to children with special needs. Students who are not good readers or writers may find poems enjoyable to create because they do not have to dictate or write many words to express their thoughts or feelings. Success in activity completion comes quickly.

The challenge in writing poetry is choosing precisely the words that express the images in the writer's mind. The previous exercises that develop visual vocabulary and writing fluency lead naturally into writing poetry. Being familiar with visual and auditory words helps children see and hear poetic images.

Many children are not aware that the words of their favorite songs are poems. Chants and raps are also poems. Singing and chanting are natural introductions to the study of poetry. Sing the songs. Then say the songs, listening for the best and flow of the words without the music.

Follow singing and saying the words of songs with nursery rhymes and other poems that appeal to children. There are many lovely books that combine poetry and art to inspire children to create illustrated poems. *Talking to the Sun* (Koch & Farrell, 1985) combines classic poems and artwork from the Metropolitan Museum of Art and would make an excellent model for a class book of poetry.

Poetry is meant to be shared aloud. Children need to hear their own poetry read by their teacher with the same eloquence as we would read work by master poets. Poems should also be typed or carefully rewritten by the children or the teacher and displayed attractively in personal or class books or on the bulletin board. A poem is both a visual and auditory experience and needs to be appreciated through both modalities. The huge success of the greeting card industry is evidence of the perfect match of poetry and visual art. The poetry forms that follow lend themselves well to greeting cards as well as books and bulletin board displays. Publication in some form, including bulletin boards, gives students an incentive to rewrite, an often dreaded chore for any writer.

As in all the creative writing activities, be sure to do at least one group poem, possibly several. Sometimes teachers are unsuccessful with creative writing activities because they expect their students to produce a poem or play independently after one teacher demonstration. Children with disabilities profit from the support of the teacher doing a group poem with them, followed by one-to-one help as they develop their own. Some low functioning children may never be able to write a poem alone, but can make a contribution to a group effort to co-author a poem with their teacher serving as scribe. All creative writing activities present the potential for the children to illustrate many of the verbal descriptions that have been written. There is also the potential of making a booklet or magazine that includes the children's creative writing and illustrations.

Before presenting various forms of poetry, a comment is needed about the use of formulas in creative activities for special needs children. If you find the restrictions imposed by haiku, diamante, lanterns, cinquains, and parallel poems bothersome, please remember that structure exists in all art forms in some way. Structure can free children to explore within the confines of the poetic form while offering guidelines to provide a measure of security to the explorers. Certainly children should explore free verse, but beginning writers may find an open-ended poetry assignment too threatening for enthusiastic risk-taking. Experiment with these poetry forms and experience the excitement of children emerging as painters with words.

Some of the poetry activities have been adapted from *Teaching Writing in K-8 Classrooms* by Tiedt, Bruemmer, Lane, Stelwagon, Watanabe, and Williams (1983) and teacher consultants from the South Bay Writing Project. This book will be useful to readers in developing a writing program for special needs children.

Haiku and other poetry forms help children creatively learn the difficult concept of syllables. Before writing haiku, the children need extensive practice in counting syllables in words. Begin with their names, having them clap out the syllables with their hands, tap them with pencils, and slap them on their desks and thighs. Let them beat out the syllables in as many ways as they can imagine. Counting syllables through clapping, tapping, and slapping is like chanting. It is like keeping time in music. Noise is necessary for learning syllable counting. Many children have difficulty understanding the concept of syllables because they are not encouraged to learn them through sound and movement. Children with disabilities will find it difficult to master syllables with worksheets and quiet counting under their breath.

After the children can clap, slap, and tap the syllables of all the names of the children, adults, and pets in the class, take on the objects in the room, what they see out the window, and their favorite TV shows. Then beat out syllables in sentences, words to songs, nursery rhymes, and poems in books. As they beat out syllables, they can also chant them in a singsong, two-note "song:"

We	clap	syl
are	ping	lables

Haiku

Haiku is a Japanese poetry form that celebrates nature and the seasons. The challenge of haiku is to capture the essence of ideas or to describe scenes or events in three nonrhyming lines with a total of 17 syllables. The first and third line have five syllables and the middle line has seven. Haiku poems can be the stimulus for drawings or paintings of nature and the seasons.

The example that follows is by an eight-year-old girl with special needs.

Frost

The frost makes me cold.	(five syllables)
It's foggy on the windows.	(seven syllables)
Frost makes me shiver.	(five syllables)

Lanterns

Lanterns are poems in the shape of a Japanese lantern in a five-line pattern. The following lantern poem was written by a third grade boy with special needs.

Line 1	I	(one syllable)
Line 2	threw the	(two syllables)
Line 3	string in the	(three syllables)
Line 4	water and caught	(four syllables)
Line 5	fish.	(one syllable)

Diamante

Diamante poems are diamond-shaped and require specific types of words. A pure diamante begins and ends with opposite concepts, but the form can be used to describe one concept. Diamantes can be used to explain concepts in science or social studies (Pino, 1983). Begin by choosing two nouns with opposite meanings. Here is the pattern:

Line 1 Write a noun that is the opposite of the line seven noun
Line 2 Describe noun with two adjectives
Line 3 Describe noun with three -ing or -ed words
Line 4 Two nouns related to line one
   Two nouns related to line seven
Line 5 Describe noun in line seven with three -ing or -ed words
Line 6 Describe noun in line seven with two adjectives
Line 7 Write a noun that is the opposite of line one noun

CHILDREN
wide-eyed, eager
willing, loving, trusting
youngsters, funsters, oldsters, grumps
complaining, regretting, suspecting

jaded, tired
ADULTS

The following poem is an example of writing a diamante as part of an ecology unit:

CONSERVATION
precious, earthwise
protected, treasured, honored
jewels, resources, trash, junk
spoiled, wasted, tossed
ugly, murky
POLLUTION

Cinquains

Cinquains are five-line poems that describe or tell a story:

Line 1 A noun for the title
Line 2 Describe the noun with two adjectives
Line 3 Write three verbs telling what the noun does
Line 4 Write a short phrase about the noun
Line 5 Write a word that means the same as the noun (a synonym)

The following cinquain would also easily lend itself to being illustrated by student's drawings of lions.

LION
growling, hungry
chases, pounces, attacks
brings down his prey
FATCAT

Limericks

Limericks introduce rhyme in a five-line poem. The three "a" lines rhyme and have the same meter. The two rhyming "b" lines are shorter and have the same meter. Here's the pattern:

Line a There once was a _____
            There once was a girl named Shirley
Line a Who _____
            Whose hair was awfully curly.
Line b He/She _____
            She poured on some glop,

Line b _____
        Turned her hair into a mop,
Line a _____
        And everyone thought Shirley was squirrelly.

Definition Poems

Definition poems define a word in poetry form. The word can be defined once or several times in the poem as follows:

> Success is trying to do
>   something you really want to do
>   and making it.

> Success is being afraid of failure
>   but trying anyway and reaching
>   your goal.

> Success is never saying "I quit"
>   even with failure staring you
>   in the eye and telling you
>   "You can't."

Color Poems

Color poems are versions of definition poems in which colors are defined. These poems can be written on colored paper to stimulate colorful images. Encourage the children to use all their senses to describe a color. Color poems also lend themselves to visual illustrations. Once written, encourage the children to draw pictures to illustrate parts of their poems.

> Yellow is butter dripping
>   over the edge of my
>   stack of pancakes.

> Yellow is the chirp of
>   a sparrow outside
>   my window.

> Yellow is the feel of
>   my kitten as she
>   rubs against my leg.

Shape Poems

Shape poems are poems written within the outline of a shape related to the ideas in the poem. The surfing shape poem in Figure 6.11 by a sixth grade boy with severe learning disabilities makes you feel the surfer's experience as he glides down the wave.

Figure 6.11. This is a surfing shape poem written by a sixth grade boy with severe learning disabilities. He has captured the gliding feeling that a surfer has when he rides down the wave.

The arts-based creative writing activities presented in this chapter will be just the beginning—a jumping off place—for the creative teacher. Teaching children with special needs is a constant challenge. These children need more practice in learning skills and concepts than other children. There is no reason to make practice a dull, boring drill when there are so many alternative ways to learn. For some reason we educators seem to believe the brightest, most competent learners should have the most creative teaching. On the contrary, if every child with special needs was taught with the same energy and creativity as a gifted child we might see far more enthusiastic, energetic progress. There is no excuse for boring any learner of any age with dull, uninspired teaching. Our special children need it far more than any others because they have so much farther to go. Arts-based academic learning can make the journey a joyful experience.

REFERENCES

Anderson, F. E. (1978). *Art for all the children: A sourcebook for the impaired child.* Springfield, IL: Charles C Thomas.

Anderson, F. E. (1993). *Becoming, being and expressing through art.* San Francisco, CA: Abbey Gate Press.

Florida Times-Union. (1990, May 18). The heart and soul of the muppets is gone, p. 1.

Florida Times-Union. (1990, May 17). The muppet man, p. 2.

Fuller, M. J., & Pribble, D. A. (1982). "Cartooning," drawing the line in art and social studies. *Art Education, 35*(1), 9–11.

Koch, K., & Farrell, K. (1985). *Talking to the sun.* New York: Henry Holt.

Pino, Cynthia L. (1983). *RX for formula poetry in the content area. A curriculum guide from the School Board of Volusia County,* P. O. Box 1910, Daytona Beach, FL 32015.

Tiedt, I. M., Bruemmer, S. S., Lane, S., Stelwagon, P., Watanabe, K. O., & Williams, M. Y. (1983). *Teaching writing in K-8 classrooms.* Englewood Cliffs, N.J.: Prentice-Hall.

Chapter 7

ART AND MATHEMATICS

Art can be an important link between mathematics skills, active learning, and the real world. Active learning is recommended in developing mathematics skills and concepts (NCTM, 1989). Moreover, in learning mathematics the child needs to see the relationship between the real world and mathematics (Hill, 1990). Art provides active, hands-on involvement with materials that are a part of the child's world.

PROCESSING SKILLS

Mathematics educators stress the importance of four processing skills in the mathematics curriculum: problem solving, reasoning, making connections and communicating (Crosswhite, 1990; NCTM, 1989). These skills are essential to developing mathematics literacy.

Problem Solving

In learning about mathematics, problem-solving abilities are imperative. In problem solving from a mathematics perspective, the emphasis is on relating to the child's world, holding his interest, and actively manipulating materials. Moreover, the problems that are posed should be significant mathematically and should have several levels of possible solutions. Finally, the child should be aware when he has solved the problem (Worth, 1990). All of these qualities of problem solving are not unique to mathematics learning. They are essentials of art learning situations as well. The necessary addition of artistic significance to a problem provides the final ingredient to a valid problem-solving activity in art and mathematics.

Reasoning

Included in the processing skill of reasoning are the abilities to draw conclusions using inductive and deductive thinking, to recognize patterns and to extend pattern concepts, and to see the way in which mathematics is pervasive in the many things that one does on a daily basis.

Verbal Problem Solving and Reasoning

Verbal problem solving relies on reasoning, and there are numerous ways of calling on the application of these skills in an art activity. For example, in a cut paper lesson the following questions may be posed: "I have 30 pieces of blue paper, and there are 15 children in our class. How many pieces of paper does each child get?" Or, "I have 20 pieces of paper for our art lesson. How many pieces will be left if each child gets one piece of paper?" Or, "I have 10 pieces of green paper, and everyone wants to use green in his art picture. What can we do to solve this problem?" Thus the concepts of addition, subtraction, division, and fractions are utilized at a very concrete level (Carpenter, Carey, & Kouba, 1990). Most importantly, the problem situation becomes a part of the art lesson.

Having the child solve problems before he gets additional art materials is another way of using verbal problem solving in art. For example, the child adds two plus two, and the result is the number of wood pieces he gets for building his sculpture. Or the same may be done with a subtraction problem. Finally, this approach can be used each time the child solves a mathematics problem. He would get another piece of wood for each correct answer. These wood parts can then be used to make his construction. This same approach may be used with other art media, too. Such an approach should be used occasionally and only to reinforce skills rather than as a punitive activity.

Prenumber Activities

Classifying, sorting, comparing, and ordering are necessary prenumber activities (Trafton & Bloom, 1990) and are skills important to developing logical thought processes and reasoning (Payne, 1990). These prenumber activities are necessary in developing pattern concepts fundamental to higher math functioning (NCTM, 1989). Pattern concepts can easily be taught in art activities by using simple everyday items such as buttons, metal nuts, cotter pins, and washers. The child can string these in a variety of sequences to make body adornment (jewelry). The more mature child may develop this activity further by creating intricate beads and patterns using earth or salt clay. Printmaking, seed mosaics and tabby weaving are also examples of art experiences that require an understanding and use of pattern concepts.

In these pattern activities, it is important that the materials differ noticeably in color and/or size. It may be confusing for the child who is learning pattern concepts if he has too many choices of objects from which to make his body adornments. It is also more aesthetically valid to have jewelry from a limited palette, i.e., buttons with buttons, metal nuts with metal washers, or clay beads with clay beads. Weaving can also help in showing number patterns and odd-even concepts (Payne, 1990). Printmaking and seed mosaics are other examples of art experiences that require an understanding and use of pattern concepts.

Communicating

Students should be able to convey mathematics concepts in terms of the written word, spoken word and illustration by drawing. Communication also involves receptive language including reading abilities. In a mathematics lesson, a child can draw sets of things such as balls or trees or flowers. He can make rubbings of various coins. This would also help him identify money. These are *not* art activities per se, but they are examples of art readiness activities that reinforce art skills.

Communication skills can be stressed across the curriculum. Being able to communicate can be especially important not only in integrated art and mathematics activities but also in integrated art and science activities. Science educators also stress the importance of communication, and this processing skill is also discussed in Chapter 8.

Making Connections

The art-centered approach illustrates how art can be integrated with other academic subjects so that the children can make connections between mathematics, science, reading, language arts and social studies, and art. There are a number of ways that children can make connections between mathematics and art in counting, measurement, spatial relationships and geometry.

COUNTING

Counting can enter an art activity in a variety of ways (NCTM, 1989). Often by suggesting that the child have five or more things in his drawing, he may be encouraged to consider composition and filling the whole page. This can also provide appropriate limits for the child. Otherwise, the child may be frustrated by being asked, after the fact, to put more things in his picture. The child can count other items in his picture such as the colors, the geometric shapes, and the lines.

Finally, counting may be of great use in gluing and pasting activities. Children can be told to hold the wood or paper and count to 30 or whatever number is appropriate. This may be easier for them and for the instructor than telling them to wait for the glue to dry.

MEASUREMENT AND PROPORTION

Measurement is an important aspect of living (Liedtke, 1990) and measurement in art is no exception. There are many ways that measurement is used in art experiences (Neufeld, 1989). Children will find it necessary to learn how to measure in art activities, including making a frame for a puzzle or a matt for their two-dimensional artwork. In the process of making a bracelet, a hat or mask, it will be necessary to measure their wrists for a bracelet, or the circumference of their heads. Measuring will also be necessary in mixing salt/flour clay or wheat paste for papier-maché. Moreover, the children will be really motivated to do such measuring and mixing if afterwards they can sculpt an animal, some beads, or some other meaningful creation. The dress-up and draw art activity described in Chapter 9 requires measurement skills (Neufeld, 1989).

Learning to mix colors involves addition and proportion concepts. In introducing color mixing, the child can start by painting with only the three primary colors (red, yellow, and blue). Then he may discover other colors. Or the activity can be a problem situation such as "Today we have three colors for our painting. Can you make a fourth color by adding two of the colors together?" Finally, the children can be given the three primary colors and asked to make as many other colors as possible for their painting.

An older class can be encouraged to make the secondary colors by adding *equal parts* of two primary colors. If the class is fairly advanced, they can mix the tertiary colors by adding *two parts* of each primary color to *one part* of each secondary color (that is, two parts of red are added to yellow to make the tertiary color red-orange; two parts of blue are added to yellow to make the tertiary color blue-green).

PLEASE NOTE: Before reading further, examine carefully these visual examples of art and mathematics activities. These illustrations are preparation for the discussion which follows.

Figure 7.1. Comparing, classifying, sorting and ordering are necessary prenumber skills in completing a seed mosaic. Here an eight-year-old boy who is deaf is selecting seeds to complete his seed mosaic.

Figure 7.2. Different sizes of seeds and pasta were sorted and ordered in a specific pattern to make this picture. This is a very well-designed picture that was completed by a teenager with moderate mental retardation.

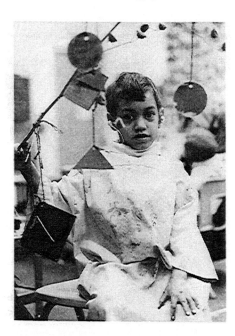

Figure 7.3. This four-year-old child who is deaf has included circles and triangles in his shape mobile. The art lesson focused on shape identification and on color words. The child verbalized and signed the correct color word before being given that color of tempera paint for painting each shape.

Figure 7.4. After discussing shapes and looking for shapes in the classroom environs and in photos or magazine pictures, this eight-year-old girl who is deaf is composing her own picture using geometric shapes cut from construction paper.

Figure 7.5. This cardboard slotted sculpture is a team endeavor. Four children who are deaf in a primary group are trying to find out how wide they can make their construction. An adult made the cardboard shapes by cutting discarded cardboard into a variety of geometric shapes and sizes. Slots have been cut in each edge of the cardboard shapes. (The width of the slots must be slightly wider than the thickness of the cardboard.)

Figure 7.6. These slotted cardboard shape sculptures were made by: lower left, a nine-year-old boy with visual impairments; middle, a 12-year-old boy with noncategorical disabilities; and right, a nine-year-old boy who is blind. Each student was given the same number of preslotted shapes and encouraged to produce individual sculptural statements. This art activity can be integrated into reading readiness lessons (shape recognition) and mathematical activities. Note: From F. E. Anderson, *Art, Children, and Disabilities* (San Francisco: Abbey Gate Press), 1993. Copyright 1993 by F. E. Anderson. Reprinted by permission.

Figure 7.7. A nine-year-old girl with physical disabilities glues her geometric shapes wood sculpture by brushing on white glue using a short-handled ½-inch flat brush.

Figure 7.8. Wood sculpture can become a very concrete creation. This particular sculpture has been titled "Robot." It is the creation of an eight-year-old boy who has perceptual learning problems and physical disabilities.

Figure 7.9. Children also can create abstract sculptural statements. Here is an untitled abstract construction by a nine-year-old boy with auditory disabilities.

Figure 7.10. A puzzle-making activity can integrate drawings and measurement skills. Some preplanning will be needed. After the topic of the puzzle is established, a black edge is drawn around the puzzle cardboard. (This black edge will make the puzzle easier to assemble.) *After* the black edge is complete, the rest of the drawing is made. Parents' occupations were the topic for this puzzle-making activity: thus, social studies was also a part of the art activity. After the puzzle picture is drawn and filled in, it is placed on top of a larger piece of cardboard. Then, one-inch wide cardboard strips are measured and glued onto the larger cardboard to make the puzzle holder. After the puzzle holder (frame) is made, the puzzle is divided into pieces and the pieces are numbered. These pieces are then cut out with a large pair of scissors.

Figure 7.11. This is a completed puzzle by a nine-year-old boy who is deaf, showing his father at work driving his tractor in the field.

GEOMETRY: THE WEDDING OF ART AND MATHEMATICS

Purpose/Rationale

The art learning sequence discussed at length in this section centers on geometry. Through these activities, the child's ability to recognize shapes and spatial relationships is developed. Children need to recognize the geometric shapes which are the building blocks of their environment (Shaw, 1990). This is necessary for their perceptual development as well. This series also requires the child to see the patterns of these shapes around him. The ability to perceive and identify shapes and spatial relationships is important in developing mathematics concepts and is also necessary to artistic development. In fact, Paul Cezanne, a famous French Impressionistic painter of the late nineteenth century, felt it was essential to view the world in terms of the basic geometric shapes, i.e., the cube and the cone and the cylinder. His idea was a revelation to the art world and was one of the major influences in the development in modern art (Janson & Cauman, 1971; Piper, 1984).

These art and geometric activities are presented in a series and lead to more complex art learning. The reader must decide at what point to enter this sequence with a child. It may be desirable to return to a simpler level for review or for reinforcement of the concepts.

SHAPE GAME

Materials

Brushes, ½ inch (*c.* 1 cm) wide
Cardboard cut in geometric shapes, 25 or more
Containers for paint and water
Hole puncher or scissors
Old newspapers
Paint shirts or smocks for each child
Paper towels
Sacks large enough to hold geometric shapes
String or yarn scraps
Tempera paint
Tree branches

Scrap cardboard can be used for the geometric shapes. It can be cut using a paper cutter, matt knife, or large scissors. Check before using the paper cutter because cutting cardboard can dull the blade. Pizza restaurants can supply cardboard circles.

Motivation

With the class or a small group in a circle, choose a child to be "it." First, he is given a shape and told its name. He is then asked to match this shape without looking and by searching in the bag. When the child has made a match, he keeps the shape. Tell the class that something will be made with their shapes later. Continue the game until all children have had a turn or until they know their shapes. Another game approach is to have each child and/or small group of children make the various shapes with their own bodies. Each child can be assigned a specific shape or can pick his own and have the rest of the class guess what it is.

Procedure

With the cardboard shapes that the children have earned in the Shape Game, they will make a mobile. (A mobile is a construction of a group of objects or shapes that hangs and moves or turns in the moving air.) Show the children an example. To avoid possible copying, the example should differ in some way from the mobiles that the children will make. A specific problem may be included in the activity such as, "In each mobile you must have three (or more) of your favorite shapes and three or more circles. You must also have two or more of the other shapes already discussed." These are then painted with tempera paint. After the shapes are dry, holes are punched into them, and these are hung on the branches that are suspended in the classroom. Balance can be discussed as the mobile is assembled. To help achieve balance, distance between parts can be measured. It will take about one-half hour to complete the mobile.

Adaptations

CHILDREN WITH MENTAL RETARDATION. Stress some specific words beginning with the shape names themselves. When the child can distinguish between two different shapes (or bigger and smaller sizes of the same shapes), he can proceed to the second part of the lesson. Have each child paint one or two shapes. All the children can then contribute to one group mobile.

CHILDREN WITH LEARNING DISABILITIES. Extend the movement aspect of the motivation. Large shapes may be marked on the floor with masking tape or made out of cloth. After doing the first part of the game described in the motivation section, have the children, either individually or in small groups, locate shapes as they are called out. The class and the teacher will probably think of other variations on these movement ideas. Weather permitting, the activity can be done on the playground and the shapes drawn with chalk.

CHILDREN WITH BEHAVIORAL DISORDERS/EMOTIONAL DISTURBANCE. In addition to the above, the children can work in small groups as they make their mobiles. Select those children who will work best together.

CHILDREN WITH PHYSICAL DISABILITIES. Secure the shapes with tape or a large stone so that they can be easily painted. Short-handled, stiff-bristled brushes are recommended. If the child cannot easily grasp the brush (even if it has been thickened with foam rubber), have him use a sponge instead. Paint that is thick (like the consistency of heavy cream) may be easier to use.

CHILDREN WHO ARE DEAF OR HARD-OF-HEARING. Special emphasis might be placed on specific words. Key words in this activity might be *large* and *small, both, hang,* and *color* names. There probably will be some other words the teacher will want to stress.

CHILDREN WITH VISUAL IMPAIRMENTS. Even though the totally blind child cannot distinguish colors, it is important that he paint his shapes. Color, even if experienced by name only, is still a part of this child's world. He has favorite colors also. Weight down the shapes with tape or a large stone before painting them. In stringing the mobile, incorporate small bells. Then the child can hear the mobile move.

Evaluation

POTENTIAL OUTCOMES. The child has played the Shape Game and identified the basic geometric shapes by touch and sight, making only one or two mistakes. The child has demonstrated his social skills and maturity by following rules and taking turns. The child has made a mobile using at least three of each kind of basic geometric shapes. He has painted these shapes with one or two of his favorite colors.

CLOSURE. Have the class review the names for the geometric shapes. Each child can show and share his work with the class. Then display the mobiles in the classroom.

SHAPE SEARCH

Materials

Cardboard examples of the geometric shapes: circles, squares, rectangles, triangles
Construction paper in assorted colors: 9 by 12 inches (*c.* 22 by 30 cm) and some scraps
Drawing paper about 9 by 12 inches (*c.* 22 by 30 cm) or larger
Examples of Paul Cezanne's paintings of landscapes and still lifes

Magazine pictures that have geometric shapes in them
Old newspapers
Paper towels, some slightly damp to wipe hands
Pencils or watercolor markers
Ruler or straight edge
Scissors
White glue in small bottles or potpie tins with ¼ inch or ½ inch (*c.* ½ or 1 cm) wide brushes

Motivation

Begin by playing a recognition game with the class. Hold up the shapes and have the children identify them. Next select one child and have him point out examples of geometric shapes in the classroom. Then tell the class the story of Super Shape. Super Shape has discovered many, many geometric shapes, and he has hidden them in the classroom somewhere. Have the children find places where Super Shape has hidden his shapes. The same approach can be done by using magazine pictures and art reproductions by Paul Cezanne, Piet Mondriane, Pablo Picasso, Constantin Brancusi, Henry Moore, etc. (Janson & Cauman, 1971; Piper, 1984). When they find geometric shapes in the pictures, the children can draw around them with pencil. This approach may be more motivating for older children. Finally, the class is asked to make their own picture of geometric shapes cut from construction paper.

Procedure

If the child does not readily comprehend how to make a shape picture, then partially demonstrate what is to be done by cutting out some shapes and pasting them down. After the demonstration, distribute the materials. Another approach would be to begin by building some objects from the shapes left over from the Shape Game. It is assumed that the children can cut out the various geometric shapes. If the child has difficulty cutting, he may need some practice. Or provide some shapes already cut out. Finally, some starter sheets with several shapes already pasted down might provide the beginning point for the activity. This activity should take about one-half hour.

Adaptations

CHILDREN WITH MENTAL RETARDATION. Extra practice in finding shapes and in seeing them in objects, such as houses, doors, windows, etc., may be needed. For those who do not have the cutting skills, it may be helpful to have shapes already cut for them. However, let the child choose the shapes he wants to use in his picture. This will help insure that the pictures are all different. Language can be emphasized; for example, after asking "How many circles do you want?" have the child respond using a full sentence, "I want five circles." Or one limitation may be placed on the activity, such as, "Use as many shapes in your picture as you want, but only use two triangles."

CHILDREN WITH LEARNING DISABILITIES. Using highly contrasting colors of papers may help this child distinguish between shapes. Squares can be cut from one color and rectangles from another. If there is one shape that is giving particular trouble to the child, cut that shape from a textured paper such as sandpaper.

CHILDREN WITH BEHAVIORAL DISORDERS/EMOTIONAL DISTURBANCE. Select several children to work together on a shape picture or mural. If the children are working individually, have them decide what shape(s) they want and begin with one or two of these. Having too many shapes from which to choose may be confusing.

CHILDREN WITH PHYSICAL DISABILITIES. It probably will be necessary to use precut shapes. Shapes that are cut from posterboard or cardboard will be more durable. It is suggested that students work on a cardboard background that can survive a lot of wear. The children can then brush on white glue with a short-handled stiff brush or use a glue stick. Finally, shapes are placed on the glued cardboard background surface.

CHILDREN WHO ARE DEAF OR HARD-OF-HEARING. It is important that the child really comprehends what he is to do. As the lesson is presented, have one or two of the children come forward and construct shapes on the felt board or draw them on the chalkboard. They may not understand a starter sheet with just a shape on it unless some pictures that have been completed are also shown. Throughout, emphasize that each child's work is to be different from the examples made in the class demonstration.

CHILDREN WITH VISUAL IMPAIRMENTS. Have some shapes precut. It may help to have different-textured papers for the square and the rectangle. After he has explored the shapes and can recognize them, let the child try his hand at cutting the shapes himself. To get the idea across, bring in examples of items that have these shapes incorporated in them: toy trucks, sailboats, or cups, for example. Be certain that the background paper (which could be a piece of cardboard) is secured to the work area. Glue should be in a container which is firmly attached to the table. A glue stick or roll-on glue bottle might be easier to use. The partially sighted will need shapes cut out of highly contrasting paper to stimulate what vision they may have.

Evaluation

POTENTIAL OUTCOMES. The child has identified the geometric shapes by sight making only one error. He has analyzed and identified these same shapes in objects in the classroom and/or in art reproductions and magazine pictures making only one or two mistakes. He has made one (or more) cut paper picture and has used only the basic geometric shapes. His picture has three or more of these shapes in varying sizes. He has been able to cut out these geometric shapes making only one or two mistakes. He has demonstrated that he can use the correct amount of glue in attaching the shapes to his picture.

CLOSURE. The construction paper pictures can be displayed after each child shares what he has made with the class. Other pictures with geometric shapes highlighted can be brought in by the class members. A list of objects in the classroom that contain the various geometric shapes may become part of a continuing bulletin board display.

SLOTTED SHAPE SCULPTURE

Materials

Cardboard in assorted sizes of various geometric shapes, 10 to 15 shapes per child
Matt knife or paper cutter or scissors or single-edge razor blade

Scrap cardboard may be cut by the teacher into the various geometric shapes with a matt knife, scissors, or paper cutter. Check before using the paper cutter because cardboard can dull the blade. A local pizza restaurant can supply cardboard circles in various sizes. The geometric cardboard shapes are slotted with a cutting tool or paper cutter. The slots should be slightly wider than the thickness of the cardboard. (It is important that *slots* and not *slits* are cut in the cardboard shapes.) When cutting slots, cut on top of other scrap cardboard. Test the slots to be sure they work. Depending on the size of the shapes, there should be two to six slots (evenly placed) per shape.

Motivation

Give a review of the geometric shapes and then demonstrate how the pieces of cardboard fit together. Build some examples. Either concrete ideas or more free-form abstract statements can be presented. The class will realize that problems of balance will have to be solved as they build their sculpture.

Remove the class examples or take them apart and return the pieces to the cardboard shape pile before the children begin their own work.

Procedure

The class demonstration will immediately communicate the procedure involved. Some of the intermediate children can help in cutting the cardboard shapes that have straight edges. Encourage the class to experiment. If they do not like their first attempts, the children may pull their sculpture apart and start over. The activity should take about one-half hour.

Adaptations

CHILDREN WITH MENTAL RETARDATION. Begin with fewer shapes per child. When it is certain that the child understands what he is to do and has had a chance to experiment, he may use more shapes. Suggest some concrete things to make. However, the class does not have to be limited to concrete subjects; they may use totally abstract ideas. This depends on the individual child's response to the activity. Encourage each child to have a different subject for his sculpture.

CHILDREN WITH LEARNING DISABILITIES. Some children may need help in visualizing sculpture ideas. If a child wants to make a specific item, he may need help in determining the shape components of that idea. For example, if the child plans to build an airplane, some pictures of airplanes will help. Have the child locate the various shapes that make up the plane, and even mark these on the picture. Once he has analyzed the shapes, he can easily proceed to constructing his sculpture.

CHILDREN WITH BEHAVIORAL DISORDERS/EMOTIONAL DISTURBANCE. In addition to the above, after some exploration of the materials or after each child has built one sculpture on his own, the class may work in teams of two or three. Carefully choose the teams to insure good working relationships. It may reassure the children to know that if they do not like what they have made, they may take it apart and start over.

CHILDREN WITH PHYSICAL DISABILITIES. In addition to lots of practice in joining, these children will probably need to work in teams. The teams should be comprised of children with complimentary strengths and abilities. Have the children work from a larger cardboard base. This base with slots in it can be folded and attached to the worktable using C-clamps or a vise. Enough of the edges should be exposed so that other parts can easily be attached.

CHILDREN WHO ARE DEAF OR HARD–OF–HEARING. In this kind of activity, having visuals of various everyday items around as well as pictures of sculpture by such artists as Alexander Calder and David Smith will help. Since the materials which the class is using are so varied and may be assembled in so many different ways, there will be little chance of copying. Have each child decide on a topic for his sculpture after some exploration of the materials. Encourage the children to do their own work. Stress that each person is different, so each person's work will be different also.

CHILDREN WITH VISUAL IMPAIRMENTS. Have several examples already taped together to show the children. They can explore these and then practice joining the slotted shapes. Each child can identify the shapes he is to use by sorting and selecting them from a large box in the classroom.

Evaluation

POTENTIAL OUTCOMES. The child has identified a variety of geometric shapes by name without making a mistake. He has learned to construct with these shapes by interlocking the slots. He has made one (or more) construction by using ten or more different types and sizes of geometric shapes. He has made an artistic decision about whether he will keep his construction or take it apart and build another. He has been able to work with at least one other student and do a group construction.

CLOSURE. After all the constructions are made, the children can show their work. Counting skills may be reinforced by having each child count the number of shapes in his sculpture. The rest of the class can check on his accuracy. The class may work in larger groups and see how wide or how tall their sculpture can become before it falls over. The constructions which the children particularly like can be glued together. Language arts may be tied in by writing words on each slotted shape. The child then tries to build various sentences. (The words and/or parts of speech can be shape-coded. For example, verbs can be on circles only, etc.)

WOOD SHAPES

Purpose/Rationale

The child lives in a three-dimensional world. To avoid visual chaos, it is important that the geometric shapes in the environment be identified (Buktenica, 1968). This activity enables the child to explore the basic geometric shapes in wood and then to build with these. During the activity some related mathematics concepts can be discussed. For example, the children can be given all the same number of blocks and shapes and then asked whose building covers the most area. (None will.) Or the children may experiment with making a building as tall as possible or as wide as possible.

Materials

Brushes, ½ inch (*c.* 1 cm) wide
Containers for water and paint, or water and water base wood finish
Old newspapers
Paint shirts or smocks
Paper towels
Sandpaper, fine flint paper in about 6 by 6 inch sheets (*c.* 15 by 15 cm), 1 sheet per pair of children
Tempera paint or waterbase (nontoxic) wood stain
White glue in small bottles or potpie tins with ½ inch (*c.* 1 cm) brushes
Wood, in assorted shapes, 5 to 15 shapes per child
Wood base (or cardboard) about 5 by 10 inches (*c.* 12 by 24 cm), one per child

A local lumberyard usually has a scrap box and gives away wood. The wood can be cut into shapes at the lumberyard or at the school wood shop. If a specific school does not have a wood shop, a nearby high school or the school district maintenance shop will have a power saw. Depending on how rough the wood is after cutting (the rough surfaces will need to be sanded with sandpaper or by using the belt sander), sandpaper may be optional.

Motivation

In this activity, the materials may be motivating in themselves. Have several boxes of sorted wood shapes. Hold up the various shapes and have the children identify them. Suggest that they will be building with these shapes. Ask what can be made with these shapes. A specific number of shapes may be given to each child for his construction, or several problems with the shapes may be posed. For example, "What is two plus eight? That is the number of squares you will use in your construction." "What is three minus one? That is the number of triangles you will use."

Procedure

Have the children select the correct number of shapes that they will be using. Give each child the base for his construction. Demonstrate how to glue the pieces together. If too much glue is used, it will run down over the blocks. The child should paint the glue on with a stiff brush. He must wait for the glued pieces to dry, especially if he is dealing with a balance problem. The child can count to 30 while holding the pieces together before adding a second piece to the construction. No matter how fast or slow the count is, by the time the child gets to 30 the glue will be dry enough to hold the wood together. After the construction is completed, let it dry overnight. Finish the work by painting with tempera paint or nontoxic wood finish. Have a separate table covered with newspapers set aside for this final operation, and have the child use a smock or old shirt.

Adaptations

CHILDREN WITH MENTAL RETARDATION. Children enjoy building and having the chance to create different structures. They can begin with just a few wood pieces so they learn the process before getting involved in a large construction. Unless the group is older, it is suggested that the wood be painted. When painting, limit the colors used to one or two. This is done so that there will be a built-in harmony. (Too many colors can be distracting and can fragment the shapes in the sculpture.) Also, some children may lack the fine motor skills to cover each different shape with one color without getting that color on other parts of the sculpture. An alternative would be to paint or stain the wood pieces first and then after they are dried glue them together.

CHILDREN WITH LEARNING DISABILITIES. Just explore and build with the shapes first. Then, when a desired structure is discovered, glue it together. Right/left concepts can be stressed by having the children add more shapes on the right side, etc. If the group is particularly active, suggest that each child get started with two or three shapes. When these are glued, the child can go to the wood box for more.

CHILDREN WITH BEHAVIORAL DISORDERS/EMOTIONAL DISTURBANCE. In addition to all of the above considerations, some children may need to work in small groups. As a group activity, this lesson should come after the class has built with wood several times. They will then be familiar with all of the art processes and can concentrate on cooperative solutions. Suggest that in this problem no one talks. The group members must agree before a piece is glued, but no words should be spoken.

CHILDREN WITH PHYSICAL DISABILITIES. Explain that the glue must dry before adding another shape to the sculpture. Emphasize this, or let the children discover this drying factor on their own. Part of the sculpture can be built and glued one day and finished the next. Work in teams to maximize abilities.

CHILDREN WHO ARE DEAF OR HARD–OF–HEARING. Care of materials is essential in any art lesson. It will help to demonstrate using *too much* glue and then *just enough*. This will also reinforce these language concepts. Explain that if they use the wood finish, it should not get on clothes. Smocks or old shirts should be worn. Brushes should be washed thoroughly in soapy water *right* after use.

CHILDREN WITH VISUAL IMPAIRMENTS. Smaller wood shapes may be easier to use because the child can more easily gestalt the wood scupture idea. By working smaller, the child can also understand the total sculpture concept because examples can be held and explored easily with the hands. Have glue in a container that is very stable and does not easily tip. Have the box of wood shapes on the table near the child. Or circulate the box around the class several times to avoid traffic jams. This will allow each child to explore and to select the shapes that he wants on several occasions.

Evaluation

POTENTIAL OUTCOMES. The child has made a construction using five or more wood shapes. He has learned how to glue these shapes by using enough glue to hold them but not so much that the glue runs off the sides of the wood. The child has learned to wait for the glue to dry before adding upper parts to his work. The child has made his own decision as to how he will finish his construction. He has learned how to cover all surface areas with paint or wood finish. If he has used wood stain, he has learned how to clean it out of a brush.

CLOSURE. The children can share their work. Counting skills and shape recognition may be reinforced by counting the number of each kind of shape in each child's sculpture. A larger group construction can be planned, or several small constructions can be put together to make a larger one. Balance can be discussed.

PUZZLES: MATHEMATICS, PERCEPTION, AND ART

Purpose/Rationale

This activity builds on the mathematics skills of measuring and counting and on the perceptual skills of discriminating shape and perceiving figure-ground and part-to-whole relationships which are necessary for other academic skills (Buktenica, 1968). As the child expresses himself, he learns some sensitivity to composition as he realizes that his space (his puzzle) must have interest and detail in each area. If it does not, then the puzzle will be very difficult to assemble. Not only the process, but also the completed artistic statement will have importance in this activity. As such, children who deal mostly in concrete concepts will be highly motivated in this learning situation.

Motivation

The activity can be presented by showing commercially produced puzzles and by explaining that the class will be making their own. Have several examples of puzzles made by other children. Emphasize that the class is not to copy these examples but rather to think of topics on their own. Suggest some topics such as a subject already under discussion in the classroom.

Materials

Cardboard, thin and about 9 by 12 inches (*c.* 22 by 30 cm), and thicker cardboard that is 11 by 14 inches (*c.* 27 by 35 cm), plus some additional thick cardboard strips 1 inch (*c.* 2 cm) wide and 14 inches (*c.* 35 cm) long or longer
Old newspapers
Paper towels, some dampened for cleanup
Rulers
Scissors that will cut cardboard, or a paper cutter
Watercolor markers
White glue in small bottles or potpie tins with ½ inch (*c.* 1 cm) wide flat brushes

The kind of cardboard that is used on the back of school tablets works well as a source of thin cardboard. Discarded boxes are good sources for thicker cardboard. Check before using the paper cutter because cardboard can dull the blade.

Procedure

Have several puzzles in stages of partial completion, and use them to demonstrate the process. Determine the topic of the puzzle drawing beforehand. First, a black line is drawn around the edge of the thin cardboard that will be the puzzle. This black edge will be very helpful later when the child is trying to assemble his puzzle. Next, have the children draw their puzzle pictures.

Before the children cut out their puzzle pieces, make a puzzle frame (Fig. 7.10). This is optional, but it will provide a means of storing the puzzle and will greatly ease the assembly of the puzzle. Lay the uncut puzzle picture on top of a piece of scrap cardboard that is about two inches larger in dimensions than the drawing. Thus, if the puzzle picture were 9 inches by 12 inches, then the scrap cardboard would be 11 inches by 14 inches. Cardboard strips of varying lengths but of the same width can be provided for the frame edge. With these, the child can measure the appropriate length, cut them, and glue them onto the cardboard base. He will then have a cardboard frame (holder) for his puzzle.

Next, have the child cut his picture into pieces. Some sort of minimal number of pieces should be established. Approximately ten to fifteen pieces would be a good number for this size puzzle. The child divides the puzzle into parts and numbers them on the back. Cut the parts with scissors or a paper cutter. Finally, the child assembles his puzzle or tries his skill with his neighbor's puzzle (Fig. 7.11). The puzzle will take one-half hour to draw. One-half hour will be needed to make the frame, and about one-half hour will be needed to cut the pieces.

Adaptations

CHILDREN WITH MENTAL RETARDATION. In addition to limiting the number and type of shapes for the puzzle (described below), the child may need help in cutting out his puzzle pieces. This can be done by using a paper cutter instead of scissors. Cut the puzzle into fewer larger pieces.

CHILDREN WITH LEARNING DISABILITIES AND BEHAVIORAL DISORDERS. Limit the number of puzzle pieces to four or six initially. This will make the puzzle easier to assemble. The shapes of pieces should be limited to triangles or rectangles. Later, more complex puzzles can be made with many more pieces and shapes. Instead of drawing with markers, a variation might be making a puzzle from a crayon rubbing, paper collage, or a magazine photograph montage. (A montage is a picture created mainly from parts of magazine photographs.) This would appeal more to older children.

CHILDREN WITH PHYSICAL DISABILITIES. If the group is not able to draw using their hands, feet, or mouth, their puzzle pictures can be printed. This can be done by using simple found objects that are easy to grasp. It might be desirable to laminate or cover the puzzle picture with a spray plastic coating before cutting it into the pieces. A box lid or just a large L made from thicker cardboard may be used here instead of a puzzle holder. This will facilitate the assembling of the puzzle after it has been cut. Large puzzle shapes are recommended, as they are easier to manipulate. Help probably will be needed with cutting these out.

CHILDREN WHO ARE DEAF OR HARD-OF-HEARING. Encourage the group to make individual artistic statements. Scrutinize the activity for possible vocabulary building. Words such as *measure, limit, perimeter, assemble,* and *composition* could be stressed.

CHILDREN WITH VISUAL IMPAIRMENTS. Instead of using markers for the drawing, use a line of white glue. The child can trail glue from a squeeze bottle. Emphasize that the space needs to be filled. Four or six pieces may be a good number for the first puzzle attempt. The child can use a box lid for a puzzle holder instead of making a holder of his own. The puzzle cardboard should be cut to fit inside the box lid before any drawing is done.

Evaluation

POTENTIAL OUTCOMES. The child has learned what a puzzle is by making one. He has learned how to measure and make a frame for his puzzle drawing. His puzzle fits into this frame. All the space in the puzzle drawing has been filled with color or objects. He has divided his puzzle up into 10 or more parts. These parts are some sort of straight-edged geometric shape that others can identify. He has learned to assemble his puzzle with complete accuracy.

CLOSURE. Give each child a chance to show his work to the rest of the class. The children can trade their work, each child having another classmate assemble his puzzle. A larger, more complicated puzzle may be made by part or all of the class.

Puzzles can also be made from drawings or paintings that have already been done. Mount these on cardboard, and then cut the parts out. To focus on figure-ground relationships, have the child cut around one object in his drawing. The puzzle, minus the object, can be mounted on another piece of cardboard, with a recessed place left for the missing object. The same kind of puzzle may be made from art reproductions. Older students can sharpen their knowledge of artistic styles by trying to sort out two different types of styles characterizing two different famous artists.

REFERENCES

Buktenica, N. A. (1968). *Visual learning.* San Raphael, CA: Dimensions.

Carpenter, T. P., Carey, D. A., & Kouba, V. L. (1990). A problem-solving approach to the operations. In J. Payne (Ed.), *Mathematics for the young child* (pp. 111–132). Reston, VA: National Council of Teachers of Mathematics.

Crosswhite, F. J. (1990). National standards: A new dimension in professional leadership. *School Science and Mathematics, 90*(6), 454–466.

Hill, S. (Ed.). (1990). *Reshaping school mathematics.* Washington, DC: National Academy of Science.

Janson, H. K., & Cauman, S. (1971). *A basic history of art.* Englewood Cliffs, NJ: Prentice-Hall; New York: Harry N. Abrams.

National Council of Teachers of Mathematics. (1989). *Curriculum and evaluation standards for school mathematics.* Reston, VA: National Council of Teachers of Mathematics.

Neufeld, K. A. (1989). Body measurement. *Arithmetic Teacher, 36*(9), 12–15.

Payne, J. (1990). New directions in mathematics education. In J. Payne (Ed.), *Mathematics for the young child* (pp. 1–16). Reston, VA: National Council of Teachers of Mathematics.

Piper, D. (1984). *Looking at art.* New York: Random House.

Shaw, J. M. (Ed.). (1990). Focus issue; spatial sense. *Arithmetic Teacher, 37*(6), 1–35.

Trafton, P., & Bloom, S. (1990). Understanding and implementing the NCTM curriculum and evaluation standards for school mathematics in grades K–4. *School Science and Mathematics, 90*(6), 482–486.

Worth, J. (1990). Developing problem-solving abilities and attitudes. In J. Payne (Ed.), *Mathematics for the young child* (pp. 39–62). Reston, VA: National Council of Teachers of Mathematics.

Chapter 8

ART AND SCIENCE

Art and science are more related than one might think. An examination of the contents of specially developed curricula materials in science and basic elementary science texts reveals many aims and attitudes that are shared with art and many opportunities where art either can be, or already is, integrated. As with mathematics, science curricula emphasize active learning situations in which the child manipulates many objects. This emphasis is grounded in the research of Piaget (Piaget & Inhelder, 1956) on the ways that the child develops her cognitive abilities.

The child's active involvement in science learning can be enhanced in many ways through art activities. For example, in a science lesson or unit on growing plants, the child explores growth through actually planting seeds and constructs the container that will hold the plant in clay or decorates existing containers, cans, or cups. Thus, a personal artistic statement is a part of the science activity. Or in the process of studying wind concepts, the child gains deeper understandings of these concepts by constructing and flying pinwheels or kites. In making kites, the child designs the surface area using shapes and logos and colors that are artistic statements. These logos will help differentiate the kites when they are up in the air.

In 1986, Gainer and Child reported on a very successful high school art and biology project based on observation and illustration. This project, called Children's School of Science, is a six-week summer course in illustration and biology which, since its inception in 1977, has been running for over a decade of summers at Woods Hole, Massachusetts (Gainer & Child, 1986). Gainer and Child adapted the concept for children ages 5 to 11. Included in their science and illustration program were units requiring renderings of maps, insects, seashells, flowers and McClintock's 1983 maze genetic study.

These are a few examples of ways of integrating the two fields. Several other ways are presented in the following discussion of more specific science aims and attitudes. These examples are presented to spark readers to develop their own integrated art and science lessons.

BASIC SCIENTIFIC PROCESS SKILLS

There are basic skills in science that need to be acquired so that students can be prepared to experience science studies that are inquiry-centered. These are termed *process skills* and include the following: the ability to observe, to sort, to classify, to order serially, to operationally define, to communicate, and to predict (Jacobson & Bergman, 1987; Hadary & Cohen, 1978; Jacobson & Bergman, 1987).

Observation

This skill is essential to a large number of scientific investigations. Included in observation is a heightened ability to attend to details and to see both the broad picture as well as the minute details. This skill of observation is acquired by a study of the physical properties of objects and systems. Observation is best acquired in young students by engaging as many of their senses as possible. This means providing opportunities for children to look, taste, hear, smell and touch. Art media and activities provide a host of opportunities to assist children with their observational skills. Young children can be encouraged to observe the specific qualities of paint, clay and crayons. Additionally, any time the child is encouraged to portray a specific subject, specific questioning by the teacher can assist the child in observing details that she might want to include in her artwork. For example, the child may be asked to go home and study the place in which she lives. Asking the child to count the number of rooms, to describe the colors of outside walls, the kinds of trees on her street, etc., will facilitate observation. As noted earlier, observation and drawing were key ingredients in the Woods Hole, Massachusetts Children's School of Science.

Sorting

Sorting focuses on grouping objects according to some property. One of the simplest ways of sorting is in terms of a binary or yes/no system which is the basis for many scientific classification systems. Examples of objects that can be sorted in a binary system are: those that have a smell or do not give off odors, objects that are animate or inanimate, etc. For example, children could go on a nature walk and make a collection of all sorts of things found lying on the ground. Later in the classroom they can sort their treasures into different groupings such as: things that are rough or smooth, hard or soft. Then they can make nature collages based on these groupings. Nature collages are described in detail later in this chapter (Fig. 8.5 & 8.6).

Classification

This process skill centers on the arrangements of objects into one or more groups. Children who have collected all different kinds of leaves on their nature walk could develop groupings such as leaves that have needles and those that do not, leaves (and needles) that come in pairs and those that come in bunches, and leaves (and needles) that are smooth and those that are not. Later, they can make leaf prints or seed mosaics (Fig. 7.1) based on these different groupings.

Examples of art activities that lend themselves to classification are those dealing with geometric shapes already discussed in the art and mathematics chapter (Chap. 7). In these art learning situations, the child is asked to make distinctions between objects. The child must match items by looking and feeling for similarities. She can also be asked to decide which items are hard, soft, heavy, light, etc.

Serial Ordering

Serial ordering involves the ability to rank materials and objects based on the amount of a particular property which these items have. One thinks of this in terms of leaves, or rocks or natural-occurring phenomena, but serial ordering can also be practiced during art experiences. For example, brushes can be grouped and then ranked in terms of length of bristles, or width of bristles, or length of their handles. In studying color, older children can serially order various tints or shades of one color according to the amount of white or black that is added to the color. In working with clay, students can serially order clay projects on the extent to which they are dry or damp. In executing a seed mosaic, children can first make a progression of seeds from largest to smallest and then incorporate these differing sizes into the areas to be filled.

Operational Definitions

Language must be especially precise in science. In defining terms, one must be able to observe and identify the terms in some recognizable context. For example, yellow can be defined in terms of the color of a ripe banana. Orange can be identified as the color of a ripe pumpkin or the outcome of mixing equal parts of yellow tempera paint and red tempera paint.

Communication

In terms of science, conveying results of various science experiments and observations in clear, readily understood, written and spoken terms (terms that utilize operational definitions if appropriate) is essential. Unless there is good communication (based on good observation and record keeping), the results of an investigation cannot be validated or replicated (Cain & Evans, 1990; Jacobson & Bergman, 1987).

The importance of communication can be brought into an art experience in many ways. Drawing, painting, and model-building activities are important art activities that can also be important adjuncts to scientific observation and communication. Intermediate students who are learning about their environment, plant growth, or climate changes can record changes in these phenomena via drawings or a group mural.

In color mixing, students can be urged to carefully record variations of colors they are mixing so that others can achieve the same color. Tie-dying, using food coloring and paper towels, is another example of how good observation and record keeping can be important. A child may discover a particularly intricate and unusual color pattern on her fold-and-dye work. Others may want to achieve the same results so the steps involved must be carefully recorded and then communicated to others.

Prediction

In terms of science, prediction is the process of utilizing what information one has about a material or a phenomenon to predict something about that material or phenomena. For example, if a student knows that heat can change the physical form of some objects, then that student may be able to predict what will happen when heat is applied to a wax crayon — and what happens when it is withdrawn. The crayon will melt and change form, be sticky for awhile, then will cool and become hard and nonsticky. This melting action along with the transformation of the wax into a sticky substance is an essential component of producing crayon wax paper laminations, which are discussed later in this chapter. Finally, those children who do not know the basic concept that heat can change the form and property of a substance can learn this idea by doing the crayon wax paper laminations.

SCIENTIFIC ATTITUDES

Science educators stress certain attitudes which are necessary to a child's scientific literacy. These are *curiosity* (which is described by science educators as the utilization of more than one sense to explore objects), *inventiveness* (which is the unusual and constructive use of scientific equipment), *critical thinking* (which is described as basing ideas, conclusions, and thoughts on evidence), and *persistence* (described as "stick-to-it-tivity," i.e., persevering with an activity when others in the class have lost interest in the project), *skepticism* (which is a healthy questioning), and *humility* (which involves the ability to be willing to make mistakes and to accept uncertainty) (Attitudes in Science, 1972; Carin & Sund, 1990).

These attitudes are not the sole domain of the scientific world. They are necessary to artistic literacy as well. Every time a child picks up a brush or crayon and makes marks on a page, she is *inventing*. When the child is given a choice of materials and makes a decision to try the new material, the child is demonstrating artistic *curiosity*. When a child is willing to try a new combination of colors or materials and these do not generate her desired outcome yet she accepts this and tries other combinations, she is exhibiting both *humility* and *persistence*. When a child is given the opportunity to decide what she will do and exactly when her particular art activity is finished, she is displaying *critical thinking*. Moreover, when a child sets her own problem in art and completes this set task, she is being *persistent*.

The art projects described in this book are designed to foster these scientific attitudes. These scientific (and artistic) attitudes can be developed by providing a supportive environment that encourages the child to make decisions and to follow an art project to fruition and completion. Throughout the teaching/learning situation, careful questioning by the teacher or the therapist will greatly facilitate the development of scientific attitudes.

A more specific example of the ways these scientific attitudes can be enhanced is illustrated by the life-sized portrait/body trace (Fig. 8.1) (Anderson, 1978, 1992). This activity can be introduced so that the child is *curious* about her height and how this height would appear on the paper. By providing a choice of materials, i.e., cloth, paint, or a combination of these, the child is able to *invent* ways to solve the problem of dressing her figure. The choice of materials and the specific ways that the child decides to place these on her life-size figure necessitates many *critical decisions*. At times these decisions may not provide a desired outcome, and the child may accept this and try other combinations. She is thus also exhibiting *humility* and a willingness to try other solutions to the problem of dressing her figure. Also in the process of thinking and trying various combinations of media to dress her figure, she may also be accepting the possibility that some combinations may not work (thus exhibiting *humility* and being free to make mistakes). Additionally in exploring other combinations of materials and media, the child will be doing so in an inquisitive spirit (exhibiting *healthy skepticism*). Since the project requires an investment of time, *persistence* is encouraged on the part of the creator to complete the portrait.

DISCOVERY/INQUIRY/EXPLORATION

Science curricula writers emphasize the importance of *discovery, exploration* and *inquiry* in science learning. Exploration in elementary science is accomplished by providing the child with a variety of experiences with equipment and materials in the actual, real world (Carin & Sund, 1990; Hadary & Cohen, 1978; Jacobson & Bergman, 1987; Karplus & Lawson, 1974). In fact, the real world of the child and the objects that exist in it are her first science laboratory (Ennever & Harlen, 1971). The exploration of the child's own environs is preliminary to the development of abstracting abilities.

Moreover, science educators feel that as the child explores her world and the items in it, she begins to ask questions. If the child can ask questions, the belief is that she can begin to discover answers as well (Rogers & Voelker, 1972). There are three types of questions that children need to ask in scientific inquiry: "What" questions, such as what is sand, what is clay; "How" questions, such as how does a solid become a gas, how does a kettle make steam, how does clay become hard as a rock when it is fired; and "Why" questions, such as why do fields have a reddish glow at sunset, why can two colors become a third color (Carin & Sund, 1990).

In the field of art, the child deals directly with materials. These materials are familiar to her. One of the underlying philosophies of the art activities discussed in this book is that they must be created with familiar materials and media that are readily available in the classroom and/or the child's home.

The artistic process necessitates *inquiry* and *discovery.* This is readily apparent if a child is observed as she picks up a crayon or brush and explores the quality of lines or colors that emerge on her page. The learning situation is crucial in encouraging the child to explore and discover. Carefully posed problems or situations that require the child to ask questions are essential. The art activity leading to the discovery of the secondary colors discussed in the introduction to Chapter 7, the art and mathematics chapter, the kite making explained in Figure 8.2, and the crayon-wax paper laminations discussed earlier in this chapter (Fig. 8.4) are examples of discovery lessons.

There is a definite place for open-ended discovery and exploration in art. This is always necessary as the child learns about new materials and media. Art cannot be made without having a storehouse of knowledge about what is possible with media. Armed with this knowledge, the child is prepared to draw or paint or create in any medium which she has mastered. Creation and expression do not occur in a vacuum. The artistic processes are enhanced with a deeper knowledge of media. The only way a child can attain such knowledge is through exploration per se. Exploration can be the major aim of an art lesson.

In many cases, however, exploration is but one phase in the total artistic process. Stopping at exploration and failing to encourage the child to go beyond can foster erroneous concepts about art activities and art learnings. Art is more than exploration of media. Art is also the expression of an idea, a feeling, and an experience. The expression depends on the art abilities and skills of the child and her knowledge of the materials which can be used to accomplish this expression.

PLEASE NOTE: The next illustration section focuses on art and science activities. The reader is encouraged to examine the illustrations before reading further.

Figure 8.1. The life-size portrait can be an art activity that reinforces the scientific attitudes. Curiosity can be triggered by asking if the child knows how tall she is. The choices that are made about how to dress the figure require critical decision making. The child also must be inventive in how she dresses the figure. Her willingness in trying different solutions and willingness to fail as well as to succeed instills humility and sometimes healthy skepticism. Since the project is quite involved in terms of time, the artist must have persistence to complete the artwork. Here we see the artist and her completed portrait. The artist is nine years old and has cerebral palsy. From Frances Anderson's, *ART FOR ALL THE CHILDREN: Approaches to Art Therapy for Children with Disabilities* (Springfield, IL: Charles C Thomas, Publisher), 1992.

Figure 8.2. Making and flying kites can be an integrated art and science activity. First a wrapping paper pattern is made, and the child decorates it. This kite was painted by a six-year-old boy (who is hard-of-hearing). The next step in the kite activity is to assemble it and go out on a windy day and fly the creation. Often the best way of explaining something is to do it. What better means is there of communicating the concept of kite than to make and fly one? Wind concepts may also be tied into the activity.

Figure 8.3. Making stained-glass windows illustrates ways that media can be explored and discoveries made about light and color mixing. The "window" was made to actually fit over existing classroom windows so that part of the light would be blocked out and the rest softened. A nine-year-old girl with physical disabilities shaves crayon scraps with a hand-operated pencil sharpener for the window filling. A vegetable grater or a dull flatware knife can also be used to shave crayons. She is experimenting with different sizes of crayons and colors of tissue paper.

Figure 8.4. An eight-year-old girl with multiple disabilities shows the results of her exploration of overlapping tissue papers and melted crayons.

Figure 8.5. After going on a search for natural objects outside, the children sort their items into various categories and begin to construct a nature collage as this eight-year-old girl who is deaf is doing.

Figure 8.6. This nature collage was completed by a 14-year-old boy who is blind. He has repeated the bark and moss to build design unity (in addition to the unity provided by a collage comprised on one category of objects, i.e., nature forms).

Figure 8.7. Combining movement and role playing often makes an experience more meaningful. First each classmate chooses a different animal. Then the class discussed what the animal ate, where it lived, etc. Next the group role-played their animal choices on the playground as part of an art and science activity. After space is assigned to each child, a chalk drawing is started. Here, a zebra begins to emerge. The artist is a nine-year-old boy who is deaf.

Figure 8.8. After all the drawings are completed, the group goes on a "viewing" walk around the playground "gallery."

WINDOWS: THROUGH A GLASS BRIGHTLY

(Crayon Waxed Paper Laminations)

Purpose/Rationale

This activity focuses on a discovery/inquiry/exploration approach to an art lesson. This lesson centers on several basic science concepts also. The children are asked to explore ways in which sunlight can be blocked. This discovery may lead to a discussion of the differences in meaning between the words *transparent* and *semitransparent* and an inquiry into the nature of different types of paper (Figs. 8.3 & 8.4).

The children explore what occurs when heat is applied to crayons. Wax melts, and the colors of crayons can be mixed. They also learn that color can be mixed by the overlapping of colors of tissue paper and/or cellophane. Finally, measurement becomes important if an area is to be adequately covered.

Materials

Cellophane scraps in various colors	Ruler
Crayons, old broken ones, peeled	Scissors or vegetable grater or dull
Iron	knife
Masking tape	Tissue paper in various colors, sizes
Old newspapers	Wax paper
Paper clips	A window that needs covering

The cellophane can be omitted. Scraps of tissue paper can be used.

Motivation

A situation may exist in the classroom to prompt the solving of a specific problem. This actually happened in the classroom in which the windows pictured in this chapter were created. Too much light was pouring into the room, and there was a need to cut down on the amount. Blinds cut out too much light, so another solution was needed. Different types and thickness of papers were tried over the window. The activity as presented here was the solution.

A variation on this idea might be to make "sunglasses" instead of a window covering. Another means of exploration would be to have crayons and a warming tray available. The students can explore what happens when heat is applied to the crayons. In fact, this can be a separate lesson in itself, and exploration and discovery may go on for several days or weeks.

If the class is an intermediate group and fairly bright, they can get into a discussion of the differences between the words *transparent* and *opaque*. They can also study Egyptian encaustic painting. (Egyptians used tempera suspended in a wax medium for their early painting on wood. This painting was called encaustic.) Finally, the class can discover what happens when primary colors of tissue or cellophane are overlapped; the same kind of exploration can occur by using pieces of scrap stained glass.

Procedure

Whether the lesson is to focus primarily on exploration or its aim is to actually make window coverings, the process is exactly the same. If a specific area is to be covered, it must be measured. *Two* pieces of wax paper, each having these measurements, are required. If the area is not too large, the wax paper can be folded over to make the two pieces needed. A sandwich of wax paper is necessary. The "filling" of this sandwich is the pieces of tissue paper and other papers or other items that are fairly flat. The sandwich is held together with crayon pieces or shavings that are melted. The crayon can be shaved by using a vegetable shredder or by taking scissors and scraping old crayons.

It is recommended that children work on a surface covered with old newspapers. When the sandwich is complete, it is covered with another paper layer of newspaper. The whole double-decker sandwich (with an additional layer of old newspaper added to both the top and bottom of the sandwich) is then ironed with an iron set on a moderate setting. Some experimentation will be needed to determine the best setting for the iron and for how hard and long it will take to press the sandwich together. Before ironing, clip the sandwich together with paper clips to prevent slipping. This activity will take about one-half hour. If any of the children do some measuring, allow an additional 15 minutes.

Adaptations

CHILDREN WITH MENTAL RETARDATION. Language can be tied into this lesson. Key words might be *cover, overlap, mix,* and the color names. Red, blue, and yellow tissue paper should be included in the materials for this lesson so that secondary colors can be "discovered." Some children will be impatient to see their finished project and may not iron long enough. To facilitate the long time needed for ironing, have the child count to a specific number. For example, each child can count to 40 as she rotates the iron.

CHILDREN WITH LEARNING DISABILITIES. Shorten the activity for those children who have a short attention span. Just demonstrate the process and let the children get involved in the activity without too much questioning and waiting. With this kind of process, there is no *right* or *wrong* way to accomplish the final design. The composition can be very abstract or realistic.

CHILDREN WITH BEHAVIORAL DISORDERS/EMOTIONAL DISTURBANCE. In addition to the above, the child can crush the crayon pieces by putting them between newspapers and by using a hammer. After this, she can sprinkle these small pieces over the design she has created before the top wax paper is added.

CHILDREN WITH PHYSICAL DISABILITIES. It may be easier for these children to crush the crayon pieces. It is suggested that their designs be kept in the abstract realm to avoid frustrating children who do not have the motor control to create a realistic picture. Older children may enjoy looking at and discussing the work of Abstract Expressionist painters such as Jackson Pollock, Franz Kline, and Willem de Kooning in connection with this activity. (These painters, as the reader probably knows, created works that will look much like the outcomes of this activity.)

CHILDREN WHO ARE DEAF OR HARD–OF–HEARING. Vocabulary can be tied in with this activity. Examples of key words might be *press, iron, melt,* and *transparent.* Because the child will be actively using these words, the development of meanings for the words will be facilitated.

CHILDREN WITH VISUAL IMPAIRMENTS. The child who is blind may not fully comprehend the value of making a window covering for the room. For this child, drawing with crayon on paper taped over a warming tray or set into an electric frying pan may be an alternative. With such an activity, the child can sense the heat and explore what happens as she draws and the crayon melts. The paper used should be slightly smaller than the tray or pan.

Evaluation

POTENTIAL OUTCOMES. The child had made one or more stained glass windows. She has discovered that crayons melt when heat is applied to them. She has discovered that two primary colors overlapped produce a secondary color. Therefore, the child has discovered one new color. The child has explored what happens when light is partially blocked by semitransparent paper. She has explored these light effects by taking time to look at all the stained glass window pictures classmates have made. She has demonstrated her curiosity by wanting to try at least one additional combination of crayon pieces and cellophane colors in creating another stained glass picture.

CLOSURE. The class should spend time looking at the effects of each child's work displayed in the classroom windows. These window pictures can be studied at different times of the day and can evolve into a study of direct and indirect light. This light study may involve a study of stained glass. The students may also study paintings done by the Abstract Expressionist painters, which will look very similar.

NATURE COLLAGE

Purpose/Rationale

Perhaps an obvious tie-in between science and art is an activity involving a field trip into nature and the construction of a collage with the items collected (Figs. 8.5 & 8.6). The field trip offers numerous opportunities to study many objects and things (phenomena) in nature's own laboratory. Students can examine similarities and differences in natural objects such as leaves, grasses, weeds, trees, twigs, and bark. Such an excursion also can provide the occasion to make comparisons between living and nonliving creatures. Students can also get a feeling for the concept of environment.

Decisions about how much detail and how many scientific concepts are to be incorporated in the activity depend on the level and interest of the class. It may be helpful to have several discussions prior to and during the excursion. Students will be asked to make collections of a variety of objects. Categories may be set up prior to the trip, or they may be discovered afterwards when the students are back in the classroom with their collections. Some observations may be recorded in drawings made during the trip.

A WALK IN THE WOODS

Materials

Brushes about ½ inch (*c.* 1 cm) wide
Cardboard about 6 by 10 inches (*c.* 15 by 25 cm) or longer
Nature items such as leaves, bark, weeds, etc.
Old newspapers
Paint shirts or smocks
Paper towels
Playground or woods for nature collecting
Sacks or plastic bags for nature collection
Water in container to clean brushes
White glue in small potpie tins or other containers, one per child

Motivation

The field trip will provide much of the motivation. Having each child observing and searching for natural items (perhaps in some systematic way that has already been discussed) will insure active involvement in the outing. The children can be told that they will be doing several art experiences with their collections after the trip. Or what is prepared after the field trip can be kept a mystery.

Procedure

After the trip, place the students' collections in one pile and discuss ways of sorting, classifying, and describing what they have found. This can be done individually or by working in pairs or teams. A series of collages can be made according to some of the categories suggested by the class. A collage usually refers to a picture made entirely from different kinds and textures of papers. Here it is defined more broadly to mean a picture made with a variety of items that are "found" and arranged, as opposed to items drawn or completely created by the artist. Several examples of partially completed collages and a partial demonstration may help.

If the students have sustained interest, suggest that they plan their placements and experiment with these natural forms before actually gluing them down. This will enable a discussion of composition and ways that the space may be filled so that it is not wasted. The aim is to have items that are interesting to observe in each area of the page and a visual emphasis in one or two parts. This visual emphasis is created by using one or two larger nature items in the collage.

After design decisions are made, white glue is brushed on the cardboard surface and the natural objects are added. The collages should be left to dry overnight. Some students will discover that some items are too large to be included or are too heavy or bulky to be glued down. In this case, a discussion might emerge about weight and gravity and strength of glue. This is just one example of how discovery and experimentation may emerge from an activity. The nature walk will take about 45 minutes. The discussion afterwards may take up to another hour, depending on the interest and level of the class. The collage will take another one-half hour to make.

Adaptations

CHILDREN WITH MENTAL RETARDATION. Simple distinctions and words should be emphasized. It may be helpful initially to get the child to make distinctions among leaves, grass, and bark. Matching leaves that are similar or the same may also be an important discrimination activity. The collage may be as simple or as complex as the teacher wants to structure it.

CHILDREN WITH LEARNING DISABILITIES. Perhaps a more structured approach will be called for. If the class cannot go on a field trip, then bring natural objects and collectibles into the classroom. The composition discussion may be especially helpful if *left* and *right* and *top* and *bottom* are emphasized. The student may prefer constructing a more realistic picture using the natural objects. The relief quality of the collage will help the child separate the figure from the background.

CHILDREN WITH BEHAVIORAL DISORDERS/EMOTIONAL DISTURBANCE. The field trip may be stimulating to the more withdrawn child as she is given responsibility to make a personal collection. Set some rules and limits on what and how items are to be collected. In this way, respect for the environment is also taught. With a larger piece of cardboard, the students can work in small groups and make a mural or group picture. The children should be aware that patience is needed in gluing and that items must be left for several hours before they will adhere to the background. Tell students that some objects will not glue as easily as others. This may prevent some frustration.

CHILDREN WITH PHYSICAL DISABILITIES. Secure the cardboard with tape or clamps, and have the children brush on a good coating of glue. Items that are added to the cardboard can then be placed on the prepared surface. If the child desires to shift positions of these items, she can use a short stick to move them into the desired position. It may help to complete one section at a time and leave it to dry as described below in the adaptations for children with visual impairments.

CHILDREN WHO ARE DEAF OR HARD-OF-HEARING. In addition to the above, stress meanings of words such as *similar, different,* and *same.* Demonstrate some of the problems encountered in gluing heavy objects to the cardboard. This may lead to a discussion of what happens and why. It may stimulate scientific thinking and some spontaneous language as well. Different leaf names and tree names can also be discussed.

CHILDREN WITH VISUAL IMPAIRMENTS. More planning for the field trip may be needed. Perhaps begin by bringing in some natural objects first and by letting the child explore these *before* the field trip. Place the collected objects in a large box with low sides or in a tray. The child then may explore what is there and make her choices in this way. Larger cardboard background pieces are recommended. Secure these to the work area with clamps or tape.

Make the child aware that it takes some time for glued items to dry. It may help to have the child work from left to right in her collage so that she will not unglue or knock off items already glued. Or work in stages on the project and let each section dry before going on to the next.

Evaluation

POTENTIAL OUTCOMES. The child has made a collection of five or more nature objects. She has learned to sort these according to various categories (such as shapes, colors, textures, sizes, and forms). She has learned some of the names for these natural objects. She has made a collage with nature objects. She has used enough (but not too much) glue to hold all the items. She has learned to wait until the glue dries. The child has demonstrated her understanding of composition by filling the surface of the collage with a variety of shapes and sizes of items and by not leaving large empty areas.

CLOSURE. Each child should have a chance to share her work with the class. The different nature objects can be pointed out and discussed in terms of their names and how they are similar and different. The various ways each child has solved the problem of filling the available space may also be discussed. The emphasis should be on the positive aspects of each child's work. Display the collages on a shelf, or line them up along the chalk tray. For added color interest, construction paper can be glued to the chalkboard before the children begin their collages.

ANIMAL STUDY

Purpose/Rational

Investigating animals is a part of many elementary science curricula. In this sequence of art experiences, the children communicate what they know about a particular animal in terms of how the animal looks, how it moves, what sounds it makes, where it lives, what it eats, whom its foes are and with whom it lives peaceably, etc. The same type of art learning series may be developed for a number of other science topics.

The focus of the study is on actual animals in the real world. The teacher can extend this study to imagined animals if it seems appropriate and desirable for the class to delve into the fantasy world. Science concepts of food habitats, food chains, and environments could be a part of the learning.

ANIMALS ON THE PLAYGROUND

Materials

Chalk of various colors
Playground with blacktop or concrete
Permission to draw on the playground
Relatively warm, sunny day

Motivation

Prior to going outside, the class discusses and reviews animals they have been studying. Ask each child to select an animal. If she has trouble doing this, the child can pick one from a list of names on the chalkboard. Another alternative is to have a box of animal names from which each child may choose. After this selection is made, each child demonstrates how her animal walks, what sounds it makes, and discusses where the animal lives. Tell the class that they will go outside and dramatize their animal and then draw it in its habitat. Once outside, give each child a space on the playground to draw.

Procedure

When outside, start the children in a circle and, one by one or in pairs, have them act like the animals each has chosen. Then, in a line, lead them to their drawing areas. In some playgrounds, there are natural areas marked off already by the lines of a volleyball or basketball court. If these lines do not exist, mark off areas for each child. After each child has her area, have her draw her animal in its habitat (Fig. 8.7). At the end of the lesson, line up the class and go on an animal-looking expedition (Fig. 8.8). The activity should take about 15 minutes for the discussion and 40 minutes on the playground.

Adaptations

CHILDREN WITH MENTAL RETARDATION. If possible, do not have the same animal chosen by more than one child. Then the children will not be tempted to copy each other's work. If going out on the playground presents too many management problems, have the class draw on the chalkboard or on large sheets of brown wrapping paper. This type of acting and drawing activity will reinforce what the children already know about animals. Another approach may be to do this activity *as* the class is learning about animals.

CHILDREN WITH LEARNING DISABILITIES. Set specific limits in terms of how involved each student can become in acting as her animal. For example, the lion cannot really eat up everyone. *Left* and *right* dominance can be emphasized in part of the acting. For example, the raccoon can dig and eat with her *right* (or *left*) hand (paw). If the class cannot go outside or there is not a good blacktop on which to draw, have the class draw with colored chalk on the chalkboard.

CHILDREN WITH BEHAVIORAL DISORDERS/EMOTIONAL DISTURBANCE. In addition to the above adaptations for the learning disabled, establish more structure. Provide a carefully selected list of animals from which the child can choose. Include animals with cooperative characteristics and which are known to cohabitate well. A large group mural can also be made on the chalkboard or on the playground.

CHILDREN WITH PHYSICAL DISABILITIES. Tempera may be easier to manipulate than the chalk. Thicken the paintbrush handle as needed for grasping, or use a sponge instead. In making this decision, let each student experiment with the materials. The child can then decide which she prefers to use. If the child cannot be taken out of her wheelchair, have a piece of chalk (or a brush) attached to a stick so that she can reach the drawing surface.

CHILDREN WHO ARE DEAF OR HARD-OF-HEARING. Some pictures of various animals may spark the discussion. Because the children will be actively involved in creative dramatics and will be doing their drawing outside and away from these pictures, there will be less opportunity to copy.

CHILDREN WITH VISUAL IMPAIRMENTS. Each child will not need to pick a different animal because there will be less tendency to copy. A zoo visit or exploration with actual animals, such as gerbils in the classroom, will help transmit the concepts. Models of animals that are small enough to hold in both hands will help blind children "gestalt" what a specific animal is. Constructing clay animals in a prior art lesson will help establish animal concepts and prepare the children for this large outdoor drawing activity.

These children also need the experience of working and drawing on a large scale. The playground can be used for this with the following changes. Anchor large brown wrapping paper sheets using weights and tape. The children can then draw on this with large crayons. The rough texture of the blacktop will leave a texture on the paper. The children can feel and know where they have already drawn.

Evaluation

POTENTIAL OUTCOMES. The child has discussed animals and demonstrated her knowledge of one of them by dramatizing that animal (making appropriate gestures, actions, and sounds), so that others can identify the animal portrayed. She has drawn her chosen animal and has included appropriate habitat details.

CLOSURE. Some time may be spent looking at each child's playground drawing. Some specific facts about each animal can be reinforced as this is done. Animal study can be extended by having each child construct an animal mask and/or a paper costume of their chosen animal. A play can be written about animals by the children. (See examples of plays discussed in Chapter 6.) Immediately after the children produce the play for another class or group of children in the school, have the actors draw pictures of themselves in the play. Direct immediate experience is one of the most motivational activities for art.

REFERENCES

Anderson, F. E. (1978). *Art for all the children: A creative sourcebook for the impaired child.* Springfield, IL: Charles C Thomas.

Anderson, F. E. (1992). *Art for all the children: Approaches to art therapy for children with disabilities.* Springfield, IL: Charles C Thomas.

Attitudes in science. (1972). *SCIS/material objects evaluation supplement.* The Regents of the University of California.

Cain, S. E., & Evans, J. M. (1990). *Sciencing: An involvement approach to elementary science methods* (3rd ed.). Columbus, OH: Merrill.

Carin, A. A., & Sund, R. B. (1990). *Teaching science through discovery* (6th ed.). Columbus, OH: Merrill.

Ennever, L., & Harlen, W. (1971). *With objectives in mind: Science 5/13* (6th ed.). Bristol, England: Nuffield Foundation. Columbus, OH: Merrill.

Gainer, R. S., & Child, J. S. (1986). Scientific illustration for the elementary school. *Art education, 39*(6), 19–22.

Hadary, D. E., & Cohen, S. H. (1978). *Laboratory science and art for blind, deaf and emotionally disturbed children: A mainstreaming approach.* Baltimore, MD: University Park Press.

Jacobson, W. J., & Bergman, A. B. (1987). *Science for children: A book for teachers* (2nd ed.). Englewood Cliffs, NJ: Prentice-Hall.

Karplus, R., & Lawson, C. A. (1974). *A science curriculum improvement study, Teacher's handbook.* Berkeley, CA: University of California.

Piaget, J., & Inhelder, B. C. (1956). *A child's concept of space.* New York: Humanities Press.

Rogers, R. E., & Voelker, A. M. (1972). Programs for improving science instruction in the elementary school; Part I, ESS. In R. C. Good (Ed.), *Science children: Readings in elementary science education.* Dubuque, IA: William C. Brown.

Chapter 9

ART AND SOCIAL STUDIES

As with science, the emphasis in social studies is on an exploratory/ discovery methodology (Banks & Clegg, 1990; Sigel, 1969) and on an active-involved learning approach (Maxim, 1987; Spodek, 1969). Social studies curricula deal mostly with ideas, relationships, and the behaviors of individuals and of groups. This type of content does not directly lend itself to the concrete manipulation of materials. A child cannot as easily touch human behavior or point to it as he can touch a leaf or count wood scraps.

Does this mean that actual materials and objects cannot be used in social studies learning? Far from it. Concrete materials can be used as symbols and representations from which inferred ideas, concepts, and relationships in social studies emerge and are clarified (Eisner, 1981, 1968; Spodek, 1968). Since art can provide the necessary concrete materials so very essential to learning in social studies (Lavatelli, Moore, & Kaltsouns, 1972; Maxim, 1987), it has a crucial role to play in this part of the school curriculum.

Many children with disabilities have difficulty dealing with abstract ideas and concepts. Art can bridge the gap between the concrete and the abstract. Concepts about topics such as the family, shelter, the world of work, transportation, geography, and other cultures are but a few of the possible areas where art can facilitate idea clarification. Moreover, a multicultural curriculum naturally lends itself to being experienced through the visual arts.

Drawing activities can be central to many learning situations in social studies. For example, the child can draw his family as it engages in a variety of activities. This helps the child focus on what a family is and does, and on some of the relationships among family members. The class discussion about the family can be coupled with this drawing activity. Students may even role-play in exploring family roles (Hennings, Hennings, & Banich, 1989). This learning situation will have more direct meaning and be more motivating for the child because he has started from his personal experience and from a personal expression of that experience, rather than from commercially prepared materials or photographs.

If members of a class are too self-conscious or lack the drawing abilities to make a series of drawings that relate to social studies topics, a magazine collage or montage with key words and photographs can be made. The aim is to personally involve the child with art materials and with social studies concepts. Posters and bulletin boards are other obvious ways of integrating art and social studies.

When there is a nearly equal balance of art and social studies in the learning situation, knowledge of both subjects will be enhanced. The teacher should consider not only the art information to be emphasized but also the types of questions to ask for clarification of the social studies concepts (Banks & Clegg, 1990; Evans & Brueckner, 1990). Questions will take many forms including questions dealing with basic knowledge, comprehension, application, analysis, synthesis and evaluation (Bloom, 1956). For example, it is not sufficient to discuss transportation and then have students draw pictures of different types of transportation. That is a good beginning, but the questions asked after the art activity is completed are also very important. For example, why do people use buses? What advantages are there for having buses? What disadvantages or drawbacks are there to using buses? What kinds of behaviors are appropriate on buses? What forms of transportation were used before we had buses? Where can one go on a bus? What are the differences between school buses and city buses and cross-country buses? Does it make sense to use buses to conserve energy? Other questions will emerge in the course of the discussion.

Social studies also deals with groups and group behaviors (Maxim, 1987). Art can be a primary way of helping children learn about groups through numerous group art experiences, such as group murals and group sculpture, which are discussed in some detail in this chapter.

Critical thinking skills are an essential outcome of education. Social studies is an area that has as one of its goals instruction in many kinds of thinking skills including critical thinking (Beyer, 1988). When one becomes aware of the discipline of art, one can understand that in the process of many art experiences, the student is challenged to think critically. Decision-making opportunities also abound in the artistic process (Eisner, 1981; Gardner, 1973). In fact every time a child is given a choice of materials to use and a subject to paint or draw, he is given the opportunity to make decisions. When the child decides that he has finished an art endeavor, he also is exercising a judgment. A review of the potential outcomes of each art experience described in this book suggests opportunities for the teacher and the child to exercise critical thinking and judgment.

Multicultural issues play an ever-increasing role in our society. Art experiences are natural partners in providing experiences to help children understand and appreciate different cultural groups represented in the schools. Art can be a powerful connecting point in helping children experience, understand and appreciate different cultures (Lippard, 1990).

What follows are a number of examples in which art and social studies have been integrated. It is hoped that these examples will suggest other ways which social studies and art can be merged. In so doing, both subject areas will benefit, and *most importantly,* the child's learning in both areas will be enriched.

PLEASE NOTE: The following illustration section integrates social studies and art activities. Please examine the illustrations carefully before reading further.

Figure 9.1. Children with disabilities need many opportunities to play. However, because of their disabilities, they may not have as many occasions to play as nondisabled children. Having an opportunity to dress up and role play helps to clarify concepts about various roles. It is also fun. A nine-year-old boy who is deaf looks at himself dressed as a construction worker.

Figure 9.2. An eight-year-old girl who is deaf, dressed as an elegant lady and still regaled in her finery, draws herself.

Figure 9.3. An eight-year-old boy who is deaf shows the partially completed drawing of himself as a soldier. Notice that he even is adding glasses and the stripes of his shirt to his drawing.

Figure 9.4. Constructing a house can lead to making a number of design decisions and can also spark a discussion of the family. An eight-year-old girl who is deaf works on constructing her house from cardboard.

Figure 9.5. This is a completed house by a nine-year-old boy who is deaf. Note that he has added details such as cellophane windows, a doghouse and "smoke" coming from the chimney.

Figure 9.6. A very exciting way of learning about transportation is to make some vehicles. A group of children with disabilities are painting the bus which they have constructed from a furniture box. Note that the floor of the box has been taped up so that children will be able to ride and move in the bus when it is finished.

Figure 9.7. A child adds a parking lot and cars to this neighborhood model. The cars have been cut from thin scrap cardboard, and other rectangular pieces of cardboard have been slotted and added to make each car "stand up." The completed model is left in the classroom so the children can discuss traffic patterns, city planning, and other neighborhood concepts.

Figure 9.8. Murals may have many, many different themes. Holidays are a good topic. A mural can also be a way of building cooperation and cohesiveness in a class of children, some of whom are disabled, because each and every child can contribute in some way. The background paper has already been put up and this eight-year-old boy who is deaf has decided to use crayons to draw his Pilgrim. He is cutting his figure out so that it can be easily taped onto the background paper. It is easier to make separate items to put into the mural. The whole group can then discuss the best placement and composition of these items on the mural, and separate items can be rearranged if necessary.

Figure 9.9. This is a section of the completed Thanksgiving mural. Children from many different classes with varied disabilities have all contributed.

Figure 9.10. To better understand the Mexican culture, a group of children, some with disabilities, are making a piñata. The children are so involved in painting the activity that two have climbed on top of the table to work.

Figure 9.11. A blindfolded eight-year-old girl attempts to locate the piñata by touching it with a stick before she breaks in to get the "goodies" inside.

DRESSING UP: IT'S MORE THAN JUST PLAY*

Purpose/Rationale

Many persons, whatever their ages, enjoy dressing up or putting on a costume and pretending to be another person. Usually most children have many opportunities to do this because they can initiate such activities. Disabled children may not so readily have these opportunities, partly because they cannot play as easily on their own. When children are dressing up, they are doing much more than trying on clothes or hats or other props. They are trying on various roles and exploring them. Thus a child playing the role of a parent is testing how it feels to be a mother or a father. In other situations, the child may do the same with various occupations, exploring the work of a firefighter, a doctor, a nurse, a teacher, or a member of the police force (Figs. 9.1–9.3).

The child needs ample opportunity to do some role-playing in addition to wearing the various clothes and using the various props. In this way, roles can be clarified and social studies concepts can be formulated. This activity may be repeated with more of an emphasis on what persons from different cultures wear or an emphasis on the world of fantasy rather than on real persons and occupations. After this activity of dressing, role-playing, and discussing, it is important for the children to further clarify these experiences in some art expression.

Materials

Clothing, props, and various hats
Crayons or watercolor markers
Drawing paper or newsprint 12 by 18 inches (c. 45 by 60 cm)
Mirrors, including a full-length one

Often an SOS to a community-oriented radio station will result in contributions for this type of activity.

Motivation

In most instances, the clothing and props, such as hats, will be all the motivation needed. In other instances, discuss what some of the roles are. This can be done by asking what kinds of things mothers, fathers, and children do at home. If the lesson is to center on vocations, then questions about what police or construction workers do, etc., will help, as will having

*The author wishes to acknowledge Larry S. Barnfield as the source for this concept.

the children actually role-play these occupations. Spontaneous dramatic situations may also emerge.

Procedure

With the class still in their costumes and hats, have them examine how they look in the mirrors. The children will then draw themselves. They can use the mirror as a reference or draw themselves as they were in playing their various roles. Some questions may help in this situation. Dressing up should take about one-half hour to do. If desired, more time can be spent dramatizing the various roles. Allow another one-half hour for the class to draw something about their experience. The children might like to make life-sized body traces of themselves IN their costumes/dress-up clothes (see Fig. 8.1). If so, each child will need to lie down on large brown paper and be traced by a classmate or adult. They can be traced one at a time over the course of a week. Allow ample time for the children to paint or glue material scraps to their life-sized portraits (at least two additional hours of working time).

Adaptations

CHILDREN WITH MENTAL RETARDATION. In addition to the adaptations discussed below, it may help to keep the roles and characters in the real world. These roles (and the props available) should be of people to whom the child can relate and who are within his reference frame. Later, the activity can be expanded to include roles and persons that are more remote.

This activity would be a good adjunct to a field trip. For example, in studying occupations, the class can visit a dentist's office. Later, they can role-play with props and then draw themselves. To prevent classroom management problems, have only a few children at a time actually dress up and role-play. The rest of the class becomes the audience. While drawing, it is important to have each child remain in the props and clothes used.

CHILDREN WITH LEARNING DISABILITIES. It may be motivating for these children to make their drawings by using a variety of papers or cloth scraps. Several choices should be provided. In using cloth scraps, check to be certain that they are not too difficult to cut or tear.

CHILDREN WITH BEHAVIORAL DISORDERS/EMOTIONAL DISTURBANCE. A follow-up activity, after they have chosen real people/vocations and drawn themselves, would be to encourage the child to take on the role of an imaginary character or mythological person. This might facilitate the expression of scary feelings or emotions which ordinarily would not be expressed. For example, the child might choose a large cape and pretend to be Dracula.

Allowing the class to do this requires some organization and *sensitivity* on the part of the teacher and art therapist. Clear limits in terms of what is to be acted and for how long will provide needed structure for both the child and the teacher or art therapist.

This type of adaptation should be attempted only when the teacher knows the children very well. It will be helpful to try the activity *first* as part of a unit on less controversial topics such as community helpers. Consider how to handle potential traffic problems and possible conflicts as the child chooses his props. Perhaps letting each child go one at a time to a pile of props and make a choice will prevent traffic jams.

CHILDREN WITH PHYSICAL DISABILITIES. Children with physical disabilities may have had less of an opportunity to do this kind of activity. Their disabilities may have often prevented them from dressing up, so it is important that they have these experiences. For those children who are too involved, it may help to have them use starter sheets with heads and hats that represent the various occupations or whatever the theme of the activity is. The child may then complete the picture using markers.

CHILDREN WHO ARE DEAF OR HARD-OF-HEARING. Key questions and clarification of the roles which the child will be playing are most important. The activity lends itself to the development of new vocabulary. Words related to the various occupations and what is done on the job may be emphasized, and experience stories can be written after the activity.

CHILDREN WITH VISUAL IMPAIRMENTS. It may help to have this child use different-textured papers for his portrait. It may be more appropriate to have the child use a three-dimensional material such as clay and make several figures depicting the dressing-up experience.

Evaluation

POTENTIAL OUTCOMES. The child has discussed various roles of parents or community helpers. He has picked one occupation and dressed up using props for that role. The child has done some dramatization as that particular role (pretended to do whatever job the person does). He has made one or more drawings of himself as the person in the chosen role.

CLOSURE. The drawing can be displayed and the represented occupations discussed. The activity can be repeated with the children changing their choices. A large mural may be made in which the children in their chosen roles are the topic. The children can also make life-sized portraits of their chosen roles.

COME TO MY HOUSE AND VISIT!

Purpose/Rationale

Constructing cardboard houses can be tied into a variety of art and social studies concepts. From an art standpoint, solving the construction problems and making design choices in interior furnishing and in exterior colors are all valid art activities. Making a house can tie into a discussion of types of shelter in our society (as well as other cultures) and who designs and builds them. The activity may also be an extension of a discussion of families (Figs. 9.4 & 9.5).

Materials

Boxes, shoe and other small ones	Old newspapers
Brushes, ½ inch (*c.* 1 cm) wide and some ¼ inch (*c.* ½ cm) wide	Paint shirts or smocks
	Tempera paint
Cardboard scraps	Wallpaper books or rolls
Containers for water and paint	White glue in small bottles or small
Magazine pictures of house exteriors and interiors	potpie tins with ½ inch (*c.* 1 cm) wide brushes
Masking tape	Wood scraps

The local paint store will gladly donate outdated wallpaper rolls and books.

Motivation

Because this activity will be a part of a unit on a social studies topic such as the family or shelter, the students should already have a grasp of the key concepts of housing, shelter, family, etc., and will already be motivated. Magazine pictures may help the initial discussion of various types of houses. Each child will build a house from the materials available. It is advisable to have the child think about the type of house to be built before beginning.

Procedure

Partially demonstrate some ways of attaching the cardboard parts. Cardboard can be scored and bent to form two, three, or four walls. The fewer pieces attached, the easier the constructing will be. This requires some preplanning. Sides can also be taped together. It is best to tape the inside of the walls. Paint does not cover tape smoothly, so hiding the tape is a good solution. Hiding the tape inside the house also results in a better-crafted building. It may help to attach the walls to a cardboard base. Windows and doors can be cut out with a knife (if an adult is around to help). Or openings may be drawn on the cardboard instead of cut out.

If the house has a roof that lifts off, the inside can be finished with wallpaper and details of furniture made from wood scraps. The project can become as complicated as the interest and abilities of the class allow. The activity will take about one and one-half hours to complete, depending on how involved the interior designing becomes.

Adaptations

CHILDREN WITH MENTAL RETARDATION. This child may relate best to making a replica of the place where he now lives. Perhaps constructing a house from pieces of cardboard may be too frustrating for this child. In this case, begin with a large box. One side can be cut away to enable access to the inside. Then the child can divide up the interior space and can decorate the interior and exterior.

CHILDREN WITH LEARNING DISABILITIES. It may help to use several boxes instead of building with flat pieces of cardboard. This will be less time consuming. After the project is finished, use the houses for other activities. Children can go and visit one another in their houses, write stories about the houses, or arrange a neighborhood by using the houses and making a map.

CHILDREN WITH BEHAVIORAL DISORDERS/EMOTIONAL DISTURBANCE. Again the box approach may be preferred, especially if the class has a short attention span. This can be turned into a group project, with each child making one room for a house. If such is the case, then one or maybe two sides could be left off so that the different rooms can be attached.

CHILDREN WITH PHYSICAL DISABILITIES. The box should become the basic building unit. Larger boxes with one side removed are recommended. The children can work in pairs, with one child who has fuller use of his hands working with a more involved child. In this team arrangement, the child with limited fine motor abilities can still make design decisions.

CHILDREN WHO ARE DEAF OR HARD-OF-HEARING. With these children, visual props such as magazine pictures may help clarify concepts of houses. After they are shown, put the pictures out of sight so that the children will not be tempted to copy. Consider some of the key vocabulary words that can be incorporated into the activity. Some possible words are *fold, cut, tape, wallpaper, window, curtain, home, house, architect, construction, rooms,* and *family.* Emphasize that each child must plan a house that is unique and personalized, possibly using his own home as a model.

CHILDREN WITH VISUAL IMPAIRMENTS. Use an existing box for the house instead of constructing all the walls of the house. Wood pieces can become furniture. Several boxes can be used so that each box becomes a particular room. The boxes should be large. The child can make a series of these, and he can actually represent his room at home or at the school. In this way, the child gets a more complete grasp of the spatial relationships within each room and its furnishings.

Evaluation

POTENTIAL OUTCOMES. The child has discussed houses and constructed his own model from cardboard. He has learned how to make the parts by scoring or taping them to form a well-crafted building in which the masking tape is hidden from view. He has made his own choices about how to finish the outside and the inside. Each room has the fundamentally appropriate furnishings (kitchen appliances in the kitchen, beds in the bedroom, etc.). He has learned something about size and proportion by determining how small or large the furniture must be to fit into the rooms.

CLOSURE. Give each child an opportunity to take the class on a tour of his house. Furnishing can be discussed. The class can design a neighborhood by using the houses that they have made. Stores, businesses, and schools may be added, and city planning on a simple level may be incorporated. Try various kinds of street and house arrangements.

A BOX IS A BOX IS A BUS!

Purpose/Rationale

In teaching about transportation and modes of transport, one way of reinforcing concepts is to construct vehicles. In doing so, many important details of the vehicle can be examined. This particular art and social studies learning activity focuses on the construction of a bus from a large furniture box (Fig. 9.6). Upon completion, the class can actually play in the bus and take turns being the passengers and the driver. Issues of group transport are then discussed as well as traffic problems and safety issues. Many other types of vehicles (or other items) can be constructed from large boxes. This depends on the particular social studies topic under discussion. Because this is conceived as a group project, issues of working together must be discussed.

Materials

Boxes, large appliance or furniture kind
Brushes, ½ inch (*c.* 1 cm) and 1 inch (*c.* 2 cm) wide

Containers for water and paint
Matt knife, kitchen knife, or utility knife
Old newspapers
Paint shirts or smocks
Paper towels
Tempera paint

If asked, most appliance or furniture stores will save their large boxes for the class.

Motivation

Since the class has been studying transportation, they should already be familiar with the topic. The idea of actually making a large bus will no doubt be sufficient motivation. If the class does not usually come to school by bus, a field trip on a bus will enhance the motivation.

Procedure

Divide the class into groups of five or six, and designate a leader. Each group should decide who is to do what task. Consult with each group and see that equal division of labor has been made and that the plans are good ones. It will help to go outside and examine a school bus periodically as the project progresses so that the children have an actual frame of reference. When the parts of the bus such as windows and doors are designated, they can be cut out with a knife. The cutting should be done by an adult. The bus is constructed so that the bottom cardboard flaps are folded up and there is no "floor" to the box. The children can then move the bus along by walking inside it.

Next, the bus is painted. The tempera should be thick enough to cover the box with one coat. Details such as making bus tickets or a bus route in the school hall, complete with a traffic control or police officer, may also be planned. If the classroom is too small to accommodate the buses, they can be left in the hall or elsewhere. Check with the administration to be sure that the hall can be used as a parking lot and that no fire codes are being violated. This activity will take probably two to three hours to complete.

Adaptations

CHILDREN WITH MENTAL RETARDATION. A trip on a bus and several trips outside to examine the school's buses will be invaluable in conceptualizing the art activity. It may be best to have only one group working at a time. The teacher may have to be the leader, advisor, and facilitator in the group. Later, another group can make a different transportation vehicle. Having the whole traffic fleet constructed at the same time in the same room may cause too many traffic jams.

CHILDREN WITH LEARNING DISABILITIES. Class activities with the transportation vehicles could emphasize directions. A child, acting as a driver, can be given a map to follow. Also, place traffic directions such as NO LEFT TURN, RIGHT TURN ONLY, etc., along the route. Have the children acting as passengers check to see that the driver is obeying the law.

CHILDREN WITH BEHAVIORAL DISORDERS/EMOTIONAL DISTURBANCE. The teacher may have to assign work tasks for each group member. If the class is small enough, all can work on the same box. If there is a large class, then perhaps have several groups.

CHILDREN WITH PHYSICAL DISABILITIES. The tempera paint should be thick enough to cover the cardboard with one coat. Thin paint may drip, run, or fail to cover the area with one coat. Thicker paint will not drip or run as easily and therefore will not become frustrating. The door to the bus should be large enough so that all wheelchairs can enter without getting stuck. Be sure the brush handles are shortened so no one gets poked. Sponges can be used instead of brushes.

CHILDREN WHO ARE DEAF OR HARD–OF–HEARING. The children should have ample opportunity to use the buses they make in numerous other activities. The idea of a bus trip or going through rush hour in the bus should stimulate much spontaneous language.

CHILDREN WITH VISUAL IMPAIRMENTS. This activity would be of particular significance for the blind child, especially when one considers that a totally blind person will never have a chance to actually drive anywhere. The same basic driving activity described under the section adaptations for "Children with Learning Disabilities" can be utilized. The highway will have to be carefully laid out, and someone will have to give verbal directions. When the bus is being painted, the children will have to be well-covered, since paint may not always end up on the vehicle. Mark off sections to be painted with some kind of reference point, such as a strip of cardboard about an inch wide that is masking-taped to the box. Have the group work in pairs moving in the same direction. As soon as one section is finished, mark the next section to be painted. Establish a set place for the paint containers, and anchor or weight them to prevent tipping.

Evaluation

POTENTIAL OUTCOMES. The child has learned about one form of transportation by making a bus. He has cooperated in his group by working with the others on his assigned task. He has used tempera paint and brushes appropriately, thus demonstrating his mastery of painting skills. He has helped clean up without prompting from the teacher.

CLOSURE. Take the group on an imaginary trip. Tickets and maps can be made, and the group can take turns being the driver. Passengers can be picked up along the way, or stories can be written about the trip. Traffic rules might be discussed and signs made. Have the children take turns being the traffic officer. If the trip is made outside on the playground, a route can be drawn in with chalk. Afterwards have the children draw pictures of their trip and the places they visited.

NEIGHBORHOOD MODEL

Purpose/Rationale

This activity provides a concrete idea of a neighborhood and the basis for discussing the relationships between the people and the structures in that neighborhood. In doing this activity, the child can study directions and traffic patterns and can make a map from the completed model. When the model is completed, the child considers some ways of improving the neighborhood. The class might even get into environmental issues in urban planning and design. The study of urban planning can lead to a study of architectural styles in neighborhoods (Leward, 1988). Children can experiment with possibilities of changing parts of the neighborhoods by removing buildings and adding others. The class can go beyond this activity and create a whole city, if they wish.

Finally, the child learns how to use cardboard and small boxes to create buildings and details such as cars. He also learns about proportion. This activity may be a part of a series of art activities, beginning with making houses (homes) and large box vehicles and finally ending with the creation of the school and neighborhood.

Materials

Boxes, small ones such as shoe, cereal, film, and toothpaste. (Boxes should have a surface that tempera paint will cover. Check this by trying to cover a small part of the surface before giving the boxes to the children to use.)

Containers for water and paint
Masking tape
Matt knife or kitchen knife or utility knife
Old newspapers
Paint shirts or smocks
Paper towels

Brown wrapping paper to cover the base

Brushes, ½ inch (c. 1 cm) and ¼ inch (c. ½ cm) wide

Cardboard from large box flattened for a base

Pencils

Tempera paint

White glue in small bottles or small open containers with ¼ inch (c. ½ cm) wide brushes

Bicycle boxes or other large boxes with wide uncreased areas make the best bases when flattened out. Local stores will save these on request.

Motivation

A walk around the school neighborhood after a discussion of neighborhoods will help the class get started. Next, suggest that the class build a model of the neighborhood. Have the base ready. Make the base from several large pieces of scrap cardboard taped together and covered with the wrapping paper. A chalkboard list of items in the neighborhood that need to be included will help. The class may need to visit the neighborhood several times to clarify details.

Procedure

After the class has discussed the task, divide them into groups to work on specific sections of the model. Some direction about where buildings should go will help. Either pieces of cardboard, small boxes or wood scraps may be used for the buildings. If cardboard is used, pieces should be taped together on the inside with masking tape because paint does not cover the tape. To make sides of the buildings, cardboard pieces are scored and folded. Discuss proportion. This can be done by relating to buildings in the real neighborhood. For example, if one building is six stories high and another is three stories high, then the first is twice as high as the second. This two-to-one relationship can be transferred to the cardboard model by simply measuring with a ruler or by locating a box that is twice as high as another.

After the buildings are made and placed on the base, cars and other details can be made from cardboard scraps and added. The model is then painted. It will take one-half hour to plan the model and 90 minutes to construct and paint. Additional time will be needed for the field trip if the activity begins with a walk around the neighborhood.

Adaptations

CHILDREN WITH MENTAL RETARDATION. Begin with some examples (handmade or commercially constructed) of model houses and car models to convey the concept of model. It may be best to use assorted small boxes or wood scraps instead of trying to construct buildings from pieces of cardboard.

CHILDREN WITH LEARNING DISABILITIES. The children can make special note of the signs in the neighborhood. These signs can be an important part of the model and may help reinforce reading abilities.

CHILDREN WITH BEHAVIORAL DISORDERS/EMOTIONAL DISTURBANCE. Carefully choose the groups so that the members work well together. It may be best not to have everyone working at the same time on the project because there may be some traffic jams. If the class cannot work in small groups, assign a specific task to each child and have the class work independently on the model parts. Assemble these into one large class neighborhood map made from flattened cardboard.

CHILDREN WITH PHYSICAL DISABILITIES. Assorted boxes or wood scraps that are already in the shapes of buildings might be best to use. Cutting and taping cardboard pieces may be too frustrating for these children.

CHILDREN WHO ARE DEAF OR HARD–OF–HEARING. Location and direction words may be stressed after the class has constructed its models. They can write experience stories about their projects, thus tying in language and writing with the activity.

CHILDREN WITH VISUAL IMPAIRMENTS. Use different sizes of boxes. Several field trips will be needed for this group. It may help to make a model of the classroom first so that the group has a concept of a model. Initially, arrange the neighborhood on the base using the boxes or wood "buildings." This will give the child a grasp of the model and neighborhood concepts. After the boxes are painted, tape them to the base. The neighborhood model will help these children "learn" the neighborhood, thus increasing their mobility.

Evaluation

POTENTIAL OUTCOMES. The child has used skills he learned in the earlier house-construction activity to make a neighborhood model. He has learned the definition of model by making one. He has been able to cooperate in a group and has shared materials and tasks.

CLOSURE. Discuss the neighborhood, including things that happen during different times of the day. Mapping, traffic patterns, and other social studies concepts can be studied. Situations like rush-hour traffic could be role-played. Better ways of arranging the neighborhood (city planning) can be discussed and the model changed. Have the class write stories about the group endeavor and/or ways of improving the neighborhood.

HOLIDAYS: A LICENSE FOR MURALS

Purpose/Rationale

A class mural is an important ongoing activity that is always valid. Inspiration for a mural comes from a season, a story, or just the teacher's pragmatic need to change a bulletin board. A natural source for a mural is a holiday. A mural personalizes and clarifies the event that is portrayed. No matter how limited his ability, each member of a class can contribute to a mural.

Materials

Construction paper in assorted colors, about 9 by 12 inches (*c.* 22 by 30 cm) and some scraps
Cloth scraps that can be easily cut or torn
Masking tape
Old newspapers
Other paper scraps
Paper towels

Stapler
Straight pins
Watercolor markers
White glue in small bottles or in small potpie tins with ½ inch (*c.* 1 cm) wide brushes
Wall or large area covered in light blue, pink, or grey paper

Motivation

It may help to put up the background paper several days before the activity is even discussed. This should make the class curious and spark interest in the project. Pictures from reading books, library books, or a visual file will help spark the discussion about what is to go on the mural. In this case, the topic is Thanksgiving.

Procedure

Put the class names and a list of things to be included in the mural on the chalkboard. The class may choose the things they want to make, or topics can be assigned. Some of the items can be written on separate pieces of paper, and each child can pick one out of a hat. The class may work in small groups. The parts of the mural should be made separately and then pinned or taped on the background. In this way, items can be rearranged if need be.

If one group finishes earlier than others, they may pick another item from the hat; or ask them to look at the partially completed mural and make what is missing (provided no other group is making these missing parts).

Discuss the importance of making good use of space. A discussion of proportion can be made simply by using three sizes of the same item. When these are placed on the background, ask the class which size looks best on the background and in relation to other items already on the mural.

If possible, include people in the mural. Depending on the abilities of the children, each can make a person to go on the mural. The mural will take about three or four 45-minute periods to complete.

Adaptations

CHILDREN WITH MENTAL RETARDATION. Have several illustrations of Pilgrims and Native Americans to help the children understand how they looked. Partially demonstrate how to make figures and other items for the mural. Place these on the background paper to show the children how the mural might appear when it is completed. (Then remove these examples so the children will not copy them.) The abilities of the group need to be considered. Let the more able children make the more difficult project items—for example, the people. Tasks should be individually tailored to fit the skills represented in the class.

CHILDREN WITH LEARNING DISABILITIES. Have children pick the written mural words out of a hat. This will be a good means of motivating them to read. Cloth scraps and textured papers may also be used to make the mural parts. This activity will help the child distinguish figures from background.

CHILDREN WITH BEHAVIORAL DISORDERS/EMOTIONAL DISTURBANCE. It may be best to assign specific things for these children to make. Divide up the mural space so that there will be no misunderstanding about what goes where.

CHILDREN WITH PHYSICAL DISABILITIES. The children should be given specific assignments. In this way, those children who can draw will make the Pilgrims and Native Americans. A child who is especially limited in his fine motor skills can still tear paper for parts such as the tree leaves.

CHILDREN WHO ARE DEAF OR HARD-OF-HEARING. If a child needs clarification about how a Pilgrim looks, let him look at pictures or visuals. Encourage him to make his own version and not copy visual ideas from others. Some key vocabulary words associated with the Thanksgiving mural would be *Pilgrim, Native American, corn, turkey, dinner, pie, table, thanks,* and *woods.*

CHILDREN WITH VISUAL IMPAIRMENTS. Set the background paper low enough to enable the children to explore the whole area to be covered.

Masking tape should be used instead of pins to attach the parts to the background. Designate specific work areas.

Evaluation

POTENTIAL OUTCOMES. The child has worked as a part of a group creating a mural. He has made one or more objects relating to the theme. These are recognizable to the teacher, art therapist and/or to other classmates. He has demonstrated mastery of the media he used by using materials properly. He has been able to discuss the concept of composition and noted one or more empty spaces that could be filled with additional images.

CLOSURE. Some time should be spent looking at and discussing the whole mural and the items on it. Positive comments about the ways each child used materials will reinforce good work habits. Other classes or teachers or staff can be invited to see the finished masterpiece, and the class can spend some time looking at murals done by well-known artists. Some suggestions are works done by Ben Shahn and Diego Rivera.

MULTICULTURAL ART: PIÑATAS

Purpose/Rationale

This activity demonstrates ways of tying in art with a study of another culture, this time that of Mexico. It also provides an example of a papier-mâché activity. Papier-mâché, as most readers know, is a very inexpensive media that can be used to make a wide variety of three-dimensional objects. By actually making a real piñata, the children are able to fully comprehend what one is and how the children in Mexico feel when they break the piñata and get the goodies inside.

Materials

Balloons, large
Brushes, ½ inch (c. 1 cm) wide
Candy, individually wrapped
Coffee cans with lids
Masking tape
Old newspapers
Paint shirts or smocks

Paper towels
Tempera paint
Scissors
Wheat paste or a mixture of half
    white glue and half water or liquid
    starch

The hardware store can supply wheat paste. Mix it according to directions and add a few drops of disinfectant. This mixture can be kept for several days in covered coffee cans. The class can work directly from the cans. A substitute papier-maché mixture can be made with equal parts white glue and water. Another mixture for papier-maché is liquid starch. These wheat paste substitutes are more expensive but do not shrink nor mold as does wheat paste. Paper towels (that are plain—without any patterns) may be used instead of newspaper. Because they do not have a printed surface, paper towels are easier to paint. Usually only one coat of paint is needed to cover the towels. It will probably take two coats of paint to cover newspapers.

Motivation

A discussion of Mexican culture and the origins of piñatas and their use in celebrating Christmas and other holidays will be an important part of this multicultural art experience. Also, ways other cultures celebrate holidays will help the children understand cultural diversity.

The activity itself should be sufficiently motivating. Knowing that a piñata is to be made with lots of candy inside will certainly spark any class. Pictures of piñatas may be helpful.

Procedure

After the class is motivated, demonstrate the procedure. First, a balloon is blown up. A large class can use more than one balloon and work in groups. The balloon is set in a shallow recycled plastic container. Strips of newspapers about two inches wide are dipped in the wheat paste mixture.

If the newspapers get too saturated with the papier-maché mixture, it will be difficult to cover the balloon. Point this out by showing the class strips with too little, too much, and just enough of the mixture on them. If there is too much on a strip, it can be slid off by pulling the strip between two fingers. If the balloon seems to be getting too wet, then add dry strips. The newspaper strips should be overlapped and crisscrossed. Sometimes using the analogy of bandaging the balloon will work. The papier-machéd balloon should be allowed to dry after the first wrapping.

When the papier-machéd form is dry, turn the balloon form upside down and pop it. Fill it with candy and cover the hole with newspaper strips and papier-maché mixture. At this point, add facial features or other details to the form. This is done by adding a part of an egg carton or wads of newspaper for the eyes, ears, nose, etc. Tape these on and cover with papier-maché. After the third coat is dried on the face, the piñata is painted with tempera paint. Variations on this procedure can be done by adding appendages to the form "head" to make a person or an animal. After the piñata is finished, it is hung and broken. This activity will take about two hours of class time. It will be best to work in several blocks of time so that the papier-maché can dry between coats.

Adaptations

CHILDREN WITH MENTAL RETARDATION. A step-by-step procedure should be specified in demonstrating the papier-maché process. Also, specific class rules about cleanup and who is to do what will be needed. If the child cannot follow the procedures, then he may have to watch the others and not participate. Emphasize that the mixture is to go *only* on the newspapers. In painting, a limited number of colors is recommended so that the children will not get overwhelmed by too many choices.

CHILDREN WITH LEARNING DISABILITIES AND BEHAVIORAL DISORDERS/EMOTIONAL DISTURBANCE. To insure good working groups, all groups should be chosen by the teacher or art therapist. If a child is really averse to getting his hands in the papier-maché mixture, then do not push him. Have this child do other parts of the project such as tearing or cutting the newspapers. Set some ground rules before beginning so that the paste ends up in the right place.

CHILDREN WITH PHYSICAL DISABILITIES. Assistance and teamwork will be needed to get the balloons blown up. Even the most severely disabled child can participate by tearing the newspaper strips and sponging on paint. The balloon should be weighted down while being papier-machéd. Rocks can be put in the plastic tub and the balloon taped to it with masking tape. Tempera paint should be as thick as cream so it will cover and not run too much. Then the children will be better able to control the paint. Fewer colors will also prevent the possible chaos and frustration resulting when children try to use many colors which may all run together.

CHILDREN WHO ARE DEAF OR HARD-OF-HEARING. The children may need help in inflating the balloon(s). After the piñata party, stories can be written about the experience. The breaking of the piñata may be a topic for a drawing activity.

CHILDREN WITH VISUAL IMPAIRMENTS. Discuss the papier-maché process, and have several partially completed projects in various stages so that the child can examine each. Stress that getting one's hands in the paste is very much a part of the activity. Place a bell on the completed piñata to help those playing locate it.

Evaluation

POTENTIAL OUTCOMES. The child has learned how to papier-maché. He has demonstrated mastery of the papier-maché process by being able to use the correct amount of papier-maché mixture that goes on the newspaper strips and by carefully overlapping strips on the balloon. He has worked in a group and helped to make a piñata. He has learned more about Mexican culture in doing this and can explain how piñatas are made and how they are used. He has demonstrated he can cooperate in a group and share materials.

CLOSURE. The piñata should be hung up in the room for a day or two. Then a party can be planned around breaking the piñata. A plan should be designed so that each child has a turn at trying to break the piñata. Some rules should be set up so that when the piñata does break, no one is hurt getting to the candy. Perhaps the candy can be equally divided afterwards so that each child will get his fair share.

REFERENCES

Banks, J. A., & Clegg, A. (1990). *Teaching strategies for the social sciences.* White Plains, NY: Longman.

Beyer, B. K. (1988). *Developing a thinking skills program.* Boston: Allyn & Bacon.

Bloom, B. (1956). *Taxonomy of educational objectives — handbook I: Cognitive domain.* New York: Logmans.

Eisner, E. (1981). The role of the arts in cognition and curriculum. *Phi Delta Kappa, (1)63,* 48–52.

Evans, J. M., & Brueckner, M. M. (1990). *Elementary social studies teaching for today and tomorrow.* Boston: Allyn & Bacon.

Gardner, H. (1973). *The arts and human development.* New York: John Wiley & Sons.

Hennings, D. C., Hennings, G., & Banich, S. F. (1989). *Today's elementary social studies* (2nd ed.). New York: Harper and Row.

Lavatelli, C. S., Moore, W. J., & Kaltsouns, T. (1972). *Elementary school curriculum.* New York: Holt, Rinehart and Winston.

Leward, K. (1988). Neighborhood discovery: An opportunity for improved visions. *School Arts, 88*(4), 28–29.

Lippard, L. R. (1990). *Mixed blessings: New art in a multicultural America.* New York: Pantheon.

Maxim, G. W. (1987). *Social studies and the elementary school child* (3rd ed.). Columbus, OH: Merrill Publishing.

Sigel, I. E. (1969). A teaching strategy derived from some Piagetian concepts. In W. L. Herman, Jr. (Ed.), *Current research in elementary school social studies.* New York: Macmillan.

Spodek, B. (1968). The role of materials in teaching social studies to young children. Unpublished manuscript, University of Illinois, Champaign/Urbana, IL.

Spodek, B. (1969). Developing social studies concepts in the kindergarten. In W. L. Herman, Jr. (Ed.), *Current research in elementary school social studies* (pp. 59–70). New York: Macmillan.

Chapter 10

ART MATERIALS AND WHERE TO FIND THEM

Look at a pile of discarded building materials, a stack of flattened cardboard boxes, a container of cloth scraps, or a bundle of old newspapers. Is there anything more to see in this assortment of trash? Absolutely, if the observer is thinking art. All those items are potential art materials. They are all free and can all be recycled into art. Therefore, the building materials can become wood sculpture; the cardboard and cloth, free-standing life-size figures; the newspapers, valuable art-proofing media. It is this kind of art perception and flexibility that is necessary if there is to be any substantial art program, given the shoestring budgets that are a reality today in schools and agencies.

Ferreting art materials requires an entrepreneur's wisdom, energy, and selectivity. Recycling these materials into art necessitates a touch of the Master Artist. Using discarded materials can easily result in a hodgepodge of junk art unless some care is exerted to transform the discard so completely that no one recognizes its original form or source. Therefore, an ice cream carton mask is so transfigured by paint and paper that anyone seeing the mask would never suspect its origins. A cardboard model of a town is so executed that the buildings *are* buildings and not a chaotic mix of film and toothpaste boxes. Those boxes have been so disguised that they can only be perceived as the bricks and mortar of a town.

In recycling materials, it also helps to rely on their own harmony and relatedness. Therefore, boxes belong with other boxes, papers with other papers, and nature objects with other nature objects. These innate common-alities can then be incorporated into art activities which may *only* use different kinds of recycled boxes, different kinds of wood scraps, or different kinds of scrap papers.

To help trigger the entrepreneur and her scrounging instincts further, the sections that follow briefly enumerate local school, agency and commu-nity resources. A short list of mail-order suppliers is provided. A discussion of safety issues and hazards in art programs and art materials for children with disabilities is also included. Finally, an art survival kit is described to insure that all the very special children have art.

232

LOCAL RESOURCES

There are many, many local resources for art materials. Each community has its own unique character and thus differs in possible opportunities for various art items. Before doing any purchasing, investigate and explore all other potential free local sources. Realize also that recycling and scrounging materials requires storage space. The artroom may not have such space, so other areas must be located.

A list of possible sources for all items discussed in the art activities in this book has been compiled. It is presented in three areas: School Sources, Community Resources, and Mail-Order Suppliers. Such a list can only be a beginning. Hopefully, it will trigger thought toward other potential places where art materials can be obtained.

A CALL FOR HELP

Before purchasing or scrounging any items on the three lists, put out an SOS to local church groups and on the local radio station. Ask for those items that cannot be easily located or are expensive to buy, as well as the following:

Buttons	Needle and thread
Cloth scraps	Paint shirts and smocks
Costumes and props such as	Socks
different types of hats	Yarn and yarn scraps
Mirrors, especially a large one	

Collaborate with other teachers and/or staff and enlarge the list to include their requests. Organize a pickup point and storage areas. Some boxes will be needed for sorting your collection.

SCHOOL AND AGENCY SOURCES

The school or agency at which one works can be a fertile field for art media. Once sensitized to the needs of the art program, the staff can become key factors in obtaining art materials. Probably the most valuable persons are the custodial staff and the kitchen personnel. School and agency sources have been broken down into four parts: the custodian and his closet, the main office, the school kitchen, and other departments.

The Custodian and His Closet

Bleach	Paper towels
Boxes	Pliers

Buckets
Cardboard
Disinfectant
Hammers
Nails

Razor blades, single edge
Soap, liquid and bar
Sponges
Synthetic foam packing pieces
Toilet paper cardboard rolls

The custodian may also be the source of many discarded items that can be recycled.

The Main Office

Brown wrapping paper
Carbon paper
Cardboard, especially thin grey
   tablet backs
Chalk
Discarded computer paper
Ditto paper
File folders
Index cards
Hole puncher

Paper clips, including large ones
Paper cutter
Pencils
Rubber bands
Rulers
Scissors
Stapler
String
Synthetic foam packing pieces
Tape, cellophane and masking

There may be other potential materials. A secretary can be a powerful ally in scrounging and recycling office discards for the art program.

The School or Agency Kitchen

Aluminum, foil in rolls and pie tins
Bleach
Boxes in various sizes
Buckets
Cardboard
Coffee cans and lids
Containers: tin cans, dishpans, etc.
Cookie sheets
Disinfectant
Egg cartons
Electric frying pan
Flour
Food coloring
Ice cream cartons, round 3, 5 or 10
   gallon (*c.* 10, 20, or 40 liter size)
Jars, including gallon size (4 l) size
   for mixing tempera paint

Meat trays, beadboard type
Mixing bowls
Muffin tins
Paper sacks in all sizes
Paper towels
Paper towel cardboard rolls
Pasta
Plastic bags, small and large garbage
   size
Plastic bottles
Pie tins
Salt
Soap, liquid and bar
Seeds
Tin cans
Tubs
Vegetable shredder

Knives, flatware and sharp pointed ones

Warming tray

Wax paper

Take a tour of the kitchen. There may be other things that can be used. If the school or agency kitchen does not have a particular item, someone else's kitchen can provide it. If kitchen resources are exhausted, the grocery store can supply the item, probably at a price. (But don't hesitate to ask for free contributions first!)

Other School/Agency Departments

Athletic Department
Used 16 mm film

Home Economics Department
Bleach
Cloth scraps
Fabric cement
Dye
Iron
Needles and thread
Scissors
Yarn

Playground
Drawing surface
Nature objects: bark, leaves, tree branches, seeds, stones, and weeds

Industrial Arts Department
Hammers
Metal nuts, washers, etc.
Nails
Pliers
Sand
Sandpaper
Sawdust
Sheet metal
Tubing
Wood scraps
Wood shavings

COMMUNITY RECYCLING RESOURCES

Local merchants are often very willing to donate items for the art program. The following list includes materials that are usually discarded by local businesses but that can be saved and recycled into art.

Commercial Recycling Sources

Appliance, Bicycle, and Furniture Stores

Cardboard, large and small boxes
Carpet scraps
Cloth scraps
Metal nuts and washers
Outdated pattern books
Synthetic foam packing pieces

Make personal contact with store owners. They may have other potential art items and will save these for the art program on a regular basis.

Camera Store

Slide mounts
Used film

Probably slide mounts will have to be purchased.

Businesses with Computer Operations

Paper computer tape
Used computer printout paper

The computer paper will be clean on one side. The paper can be used for most drawing activities.

Lumberyard, Hardware, or Paint Store

Carpet scraps
Cloth scraps
Metal screen roll ends and scraps
Paint in discontinued lots
Wallboard scraps
Wallpaper, outdated sample books
Wallpaper rolls, discontinued and outdated
Wood scraps

Ask at the store for other discarded items that can be recycled for the art program.

Newspaper Publishing Company

Ends of newsprint rolls
Other papers

Newsprint at the very end of the roll cannot be printed and is usually discarded. This newsprint and other paper scraps are good sources for drawing paper.

Print Firms and Photocopy Stores

Boxes
Scrap Papers

Many kinds of novel paper scraps can be scrounged for use in any art activities requiring construction paper and assorted paper scraps.

Restaurants and Food Chains

Beadboard meat trays
Boxes
Cardboard circles from pizza restaurants
Containers for water and paint
Ice cream cartons, round 3, 5 or 10 gallon (*c.* 10 liter, 20 liter, or 40 liter) size

LOCAL SOURCES FOR PURCHASING ART ITEMS

Some art materials just cannot be scrounged and have to be purchased. A list of local sources for such items follows. In some instances, these firms may donate art materials. Ask!

Art Materials Locally Available

Lumberyard, Hardware Store, or Paint Store

Brushes	Nails
C-clamps	Sand
Carpet tacks	Pliers
Hammers	Wheat paste
Matt knife or utility knife	Wood stain (water base)
Metal nuts and washers	

Variety, or Discount Store

Brushes	Markers, watercolor and permanent
Bulldog metal clips	(alcohol base)*
Burlap	Needle and thread
Cellophane	Newsprint
Chalk	Pattern books
Clay, oil base	Pipe cleaners
Cloth	Shoe polish
Clothespins, pinch kind	String for wrap
Clothing dye	Tissue paper
Construction paper	Tempera paint
Crayons	White glue
Drawing paper	Wooden spoons
Fabric cement	Yarn
Felt	

---

*Permanent markers may be toxic. Check with the manufacturer or write the Arts and Crafts Materials Institute (715 Boylston St., Boston, MA 02116) for a list of nontoxic art materials by brand name.

Ask for outdated pattern books. They are a good source for starter sheets. The tempera paint, drawing paper, construction paper, and newsprint may not come in large enough quantities to be economically purchased for the whole art program. The school district central warehouse or a mail-order supplier may be a better source.

Local Art or Hobby Store

Brayers
Glazes
Rug backing
Rug hooking machine or needle
Water base (earth) clay
Water base printer's ink

Generally, these items are cheaper when ordered through a mail-order arts and crafts supplier. Check with an art supervisor or ceramics artist before ordering glazes, because some glazes contain lead and other harmful chemicals. Check with experts and with the manufacturer to be sure the glazes are not hazardous. (See discussion later in this chapter on health hazards and art materials.)

Mail-Order Suppliers

Sometimes it is desirable to mail-order supplies. In ordering, it helps to team up with other art therapists and/or teachers because quantity orders are cheaper. For example, papers are cheapest in large sizes. However, a paper cutter will be needed to cut paper to usable sizes. A storage area will be necessary to store large items including papers that come in 18 by 24 inch sizes.

It is always sensible to window shop and compare catalog prices. A list of some major suppliers follows. They will send free catalogs on request. Many items may be available through the school district's central warehouse. Check there first before ordering through the mail.

In ordering, remember to include freight charges. Many suppliers feature their own generic brands for many items. These items may be comparable in quality and cheaper in cost than brand names. However, do not always assume the generic brands will consistently be comparable in quality. If one cannot field test generic brands, then consult with local art specialists, art supervisors, or art teachers who can provide more specific consumer advice.

Address List of Mail Order Suppliers

General Suppliers

Dick Blick
P.O. Box 1267
Galesburg, IL 61401

Creative Materials, Inc.
5377 Michigan Ave.
Rosemont, IL 60018

DLM Teaching Resources
One DLM Park
Allen, TX 75002
 (Supplier For Easy Grip and Double-
 Handled Scissors)

Nasco Arts and Crafts
901 Janesville Ave.
Fort Atkinson, WI 53538-0901

OR

Nasco West
1524 Princeton Avenue
Modesto CA 95352-3837

Pyramid Artist Materials
6510 North 54th Street
Tampa, FL 33610

Triarco Arts and Crafts
Delco Craft Division
1001 Troy Court
Troy, MI 48084
 (Triarco has several regional locations:
 ask for nearest one)

Arts and Activities Magazine
150 N. Central Park Ave.
Skokie, IL 60076
 (Includes a comprehensive list of
 suppliers annually, usually in its
 February issue)

Clay Supplies

American Art Clay, Inc.
47717 West 16th Street
Indianapolis, IN 46222

Sax Arts and Crafts
P. O. Box 2002
Milwaukee, WI 53201

Hobbie Craft Division
Westwood Ceramic Supply Co.
14400 Lomitas Avenue
City of Industry, CA 91744

Leather Suppliers

Tandy Leather Company
2221 Stevenson Drive
P. O. Box 16
Springfield, IL 62703

Printing Supplies

Hunt Manufacturing Company
1405 Locust Street
Philadelphia, PA 19101

Weaving

Belding Lily Company
Shelby, NC 28150

J. L. Hammett Company
10 Hammett Place
Braintree, MA 02184

THE ART SURVIVAL KIT

How are art materials ordered? How does one plan and order materials
for a whole year? Where does one start? What is absolutely essential? To
answer these questions, especially for the beginning art teacher or art
therapist who has little idea about how many and what kind of art supplies

are essential for a yearlong art program, the art survival kit has been compiled.

The kit is just that, a survival kit. It represents a bare-bones list of materials which will be necessary to an art program's survival. The kit is not absolute, and the art therapist or art teacher may amend some parts of it for special needs of a particular client, class or group. The kit is built around the needs of a group of twelve primary special education children over a school year. If a larger group needs the survival kit, then multiply the amounts by the appropriate factor. For a smaller group, divide by the appropriate factor.

Before doing any ordering of art supplies, consider what, if any, are provided by parents and/or the school district agency. Often crayons and scissors will not have to come out of the art budget. Also consider what can be recycled and scrounged locally and what can be provided through the school district's central warehouse.

If ordering is to be done in large amounts or with another teacher or art therapist, be sure there is sufficient storage space for the supplies. Also consider the trade-off between saving money by ordering dry paint and dry clay and the time necessary to add water and mix these materials. Also, dry paint colors tend to be less intense and harder to mix. Unless one has a ceramics studio or similar area, it will be very hard to mix water with the dry clay. Dry clay and tempera are comprised of very fine dust that can cause breathing problems if they are not mixed in a well-ventilated room. Premixed clay and tempera in cakes or liquid form are preferred because they do not pose potential hazards to adults and children with respiratory problems.

It might make sense to only order part of the materials and wait for class or group reactions and needs before spending all the monies. It may also help to have a discretionary fund for some special art items. In this way, much more flexibility and spontaneity will be incorporated into the art program because an immediate need for an art item can be met.

In determining the specific amounts of materials outlined in the art survival kit, a "guesstimate" was made based on several factors. There may be other factors in operation which teachers or art therapists might wish to consider. This is a purely individual matter. Here is the formula for this "guesstimate" of art materials and supplies needed.

Based on 180 school days and 50 minutes per week for art, there are 36 art days (art once a week). About two-thirds of these art days are spent on two-dimensional artwork requiring paper (24 days). Allow five pieces of paper (9 by 12 inches) per child per art class ($4 \times 12 \times 24 = 1152$). The result is 1152 pieces of paper and insures enough for use at other times in each week. Remember that paper can be ordered in larger sizes and cut into smaller ones. One fourth of the amount (288 pieces, 9 by 12 inches) should be construction paper and the rest various drawing papers.

The other amounts were determined based on personal research and other sources (Hoover, 1961; Salome, n.d.). Above all, it must be underscored that these are *suggested* amounts and the individual's own experience with a particular child, class, or group will be the ultimate judge.

Finally, in presenting the art survival kit, it must be noted that materials for some art activities discussed in this book have been eliminated because the kit is for basic *survival*. If the art teacher or art therapist is truly resourceful and fortunate in having a larger budget, then activities such as slide- and film-making, meat tray printing, rug hooking, hand tying, dyeing activities, and creating with papier-maché can also be included (Anderson, 1978, 1992). The kit is summarized in two charts: a purchase list and a scrounge list. Before presenting the art survival kit, issues related to quality, safety and health hazards in the art program need to be addressed.

SAFETY, QUALITY ISSUES AND HEALTH HAZARDS

Safety Issues

For over 50 years the Art and Craft Materials Institute, Inc. has underwritten a program to identify children's art materials that are nontoxic. The program bases its research on independent testing, information from toxicologists and published scientific data. To be labeled with the Institute's Approved Product Seal (AP) the art product "must not contain any substance in sufficient quantities to be harmful, even if ingested" (Binney and Smith, 1987, p. 2).

A product that is labeled AP and "meets or exceeds minimum quality standards, if applicable, receives the CP or Certified Product Seal" (Binney and Smith, p. 2). The CP and AP labels on a product also mean that the product meets the criteria for "labeling of chronic health hazards. If toxic, a product will be properly labeled for the specific risk and protection during use" (Binney and Smith, p. 2).

The Labeling of Hazardous Art Materials Act of 1990

The Labeling of Hazardous Art Materials Act (LHAMA) became federal law in November, 1990. Under the provisions of this legislation, a qualified toxicologist must evaluate all craft and art materials sold in the United States. All art and craft media and materials must be labeled with the correct health warnings and instructions of safe use. Additionally, all art materials with potential for chronic hazards (cancer, eye irritants and other health problems of an immediate nature) must be labeled in accordance with ASTM D-4236 which is a chronic hazard label standard for art materials. Art materials and products that have the threat of potential health hazards are also required to include the following information on their labels.

- A conformance statement to ASTM D-436, whenever practicable.
- A signal word, such as Warning or Caution.
- A listing of the ingredients in the product that might be hazardous.
- A listing of how the product may hurt you if not used properly. (May cause lung cancer, may cause harm to the developing fetus, etc.)
- Instructions on how to use the product properly and safely. (Do not eat, drink or smoke; use a respirator; wear gloves; etc.)
- An appropriate U.S. telephone number, this will usually be the telephone number of the manufacturer or importer.
- A statement that the product is inappropriate for use by children. (Doyle, 1993, p. 20)

Labels on art products will have one of the following if they comply with the LHAMA: *AP NONTOXIC,* Certified by the Art & Craft Materials Institute (Conforms to ASTM D-4236); *CP NONTOXIC,* Certified by the Art & Craft Materials Institute (meets performance standard and conforms to ASTM D-4235); and *HEALTH LABEL,* Certified by the Art & Craft Materials Institute (conforms to ASTM D-4235).

Thus to be certain of safety in art materials and products, it will be essential to check all items for one of these three labels. If the product is not labeled, then it will be crucial to check with the manufacturer to be sure the product is in compliance with LHAMA legislation.

Quality Issues

In considering which crayons, tempera, markers and brushes to order, there are some characteristics that contribute to the quality of these art products. Crayons should be evaluated on intense full color. Crayons should provide good coverage without streaking, uneven buildup or sloughing of the layers of color. Crayons should not break easily.

Markers should also have clean, intense and full color. They should cover evenly without dragging, squeaking or scratching. There should be no color bleeding or spreading on the paper. Also, markers should have the capacity to be revitalized should their caps be left off for some period of time. To revitalize a marker, dip the tip in warm water for a few seconds. A good marker has a conical-shaped nib that enables one to make both fine lines and broad strokes. A conical-shaped nib also permits the child to hold it in any way to make marks. A wedge-shaped nib requires that the marker be held at a particular angle to produce marks. The ink should easily wash off the hand for the marker to be a truly washable marker.

Liquid tempera should have an intense clean color and colors should mix well. The paint should not streak, should look opaque when applied and should have a solid matte finish when dried. There should be minimal separation between the water and pigment when containers are first opened. Clear plastic containers with flip-top lids will permit easy dispensing of paint and easy choice of colors. The paint should flow off the brush without dripping. The paint should not rub off or flake when it dries on the paper. The paint should cover well and should also be easy to clean off of tabletops and hands.

Brushes also vary widely and should be checked for quality in the bristles and in the coating on their handles. The bristles should hold their shape and not splay out or split in use. Handles should be covered with a finish that permits ease of cleaning. The ferrules should be sturdy and not fall off the handle with hard use. The bristles should load the paint without dripping. The laydown of paint should be even and the line easy to control (Binney & Smith, 1987).

Papers can vary a great deal. Colors of construction papers should not fade with age and should fold easily (not crack along the folded edge). Manila drawing paper should hold the paint well and should not crack and tear easily with age or when folded. Drawing paper should also hold paint easily without buckling. White drawing paper can also be used as construction paper. Generally, the higher the weight of the paper, the better the quality and the greater the cost.

HEALTH HAZARDS OF ART MATERIALS
FOR CHILDREN WITH DISABILITIES*

In 1987 the Center for Safety in the Arts published a set of guidelines for art therapists and teachers to consider in working with children with disabilities (McCann, 1987). These guidelines will be summarized here.

High-risk factors include the following: children who are deaf or hard-of-hearing who work in wood shops and other situations where there is a lot of noise; children with epilepsy who may become exposed to paint thinners, lacquer thinners or turpentine; children with mental retardation and other problems that limit their ability to understand and follow safety directions and labels with warnings; children with physical and neurological disabilities who have problems and difficulty in running machinery that is hazardous;

---

*This section is from F.E. Anderson, *Art for All the Children: Approaches to Art Therapy for Children with Disabilities* (Springfield, IL: Charles C Thomas, 1992) pp. 301–310.

children with respiratory problems including asthmatics who may be exposed to molds, dusts and spray mists; and finally children who are on medications that may interact with solvents or that may impair judgment relative to operating hazardous equipment.

Chemical Hazards

Exposure over a long time to organic solvents (turpentine, paint thinners, lacquer thinners), asbestos, silica, cadmium and lead may cause immediate or long-term illness. This exposure can happen through ingestion, inhalation or skin contact and absorption. Chemical hazards can affect the skin, eyes, lungs, heart, nervous system, liver, kidneys and the reproductive system.

Physical Hazards

Included in the category of physical hazards are: noise, infrared and ultraviolet radiation, vibration and heat stress. For example, noise exposure has resulted in many wood designers and woodworking teachers (and sometimes students) developing hearing loss. Children with hearing impairments can have added damage to their ears and hearing when exposed to high noise levels.

Safety Hazards

Safety hazards include working with unsafe hand and power tools, and unsafe electrical equipment. Burns can result from exposure to hot surfaces and equipment. Excessive repetitive motions can result in damage to musculoskeletal and neuromuscular systems in the body.

Biological Hazards

Biological hazards include a wide variety of viral (including AIDS), bacterial, fungal, and mold and mildew infections and allergies. These infections can result from unsterilized tools held in the mouth (or failure to sterilize art tools that children put into their mouths), mold-contaminated clay or acrylic paints that have been diluted. These biological agents if inhaled, ingested or absorbed via skin cuts can result in allergies and infections.

RISKS THAT CHILDREN WITH SPECIFIC
DISABILITIES MAY ENCOUNTER

CHILDREN WITH MENTAL RETARDATION. Due to short attention spans, poor motor control and problems in grasping some concepts associated with chemical hazards, and the tendency to put tools and hands and fingers in the mouth, these children are at risk for a variety of safety and health hazards in the art room. It is recommended that only art materials that are nontoxic for children be used. Sharp tools and machinery that could cause burns and cuts should not be used by these children, or used only under close adult supervision. Children need to be evaluated on a case-by-case basis to insure they have learned proper use of art tools and machinery. Additionally, there is a greater tendency for children with mental retardation to carry the Hepatitus B virus. This virus can be transmitted via moist or wet art materials such as tempera paint and clay. Children should be medically checked to insure they are not carrying the virus. If they are, then they should not use wet art materials. Finally, therapists and teachers should know what medications children are taking to prevent hazards that may occur due to side effects of medications and risk factors that increase under the influence of medications.

CHILDREN WITH LEARNING DISABILITIES. Children may have poor coordination which can result in injuries as the result of handling art tools (especially sharp tools). These children may have difficulty understanding specific steps in written or spoken directions. Directions need to be repeated using as many communication channels as possible. To insure children understand directions, they should both repeat the directions and demonstrate the steps in a mock run-through. Children should be monitored to be sure they understand directions.

CHILDREN WITH BEHAVIORAL DISORDERS AND EMOTIONAL DISTURBANCE. Children who have the potential to act out, be aggressive and violent both to themselves and to others, can be at risk for causing hazards in the art room. Some of these children may totally reject rules and regulations on the proper use of tools, chemicals, and dangerous machinery. Inhalant abuse, commonly called glue sniffing and huffing, is a potential area of danger. Inhaling Liquid Paper and rubber cement are examples of materials that contain substances that can cause nerve and brain damage (and addiction). Many children with behavioral disorders and emotional disturbance are on psychotropic drugs and medications that can impair judgment. Medications can also interact with inhaled substances and cause serious side effects. Art teachers and art therapists should know exactly what medications their students are taking and should know the side effects of taking these medications. Art therapists and teachers should also know the substances in art media that can cause serious hazardous interactions with these medications. Organic solvents are especially potentially hazardous to children who are taking tranquilizers and similar medications. Close supervision of children is recommended around machinery and sharp tools. Children may need to be evaluated on a case-by-case basis to determine suitability and safety (to them and to other children) of placements in classes where there are dangerous machinery and tools.

CHILDREN WITH NEUROLOGICAL IMPAIRMENTS. Central nervous system impairments can result in some of the following symptoms: spasticity, loss or diminished motor control and balance, weakness, fatigue and loss of balance. Peripheral nervous system damage may result in paralysis, numbness, pain, loss of reflexes and fine motor control. The resulting problems include motor difficulties (lessened muscular strength and endurance and/or spasticity), sensory difficulties, coordination (difficulty with eye-hand coordination, inaccurate sense of position), balance and behavioral problems (emotional swings, lack of alertness and judgment, hyperactivity). Organic solvents, lead, manganese, mercury and toxic art media can seriously damage already damaged nervous systems. Children should not be exposed to organic solvents and neurotoxins (except in small amounts in well-ventilated areas that include ventilation hoods). Use volunteers or physically-able students to operate machinery or tools. Monitor students with impaired sense of touch to insure they do not burn or cut themselves. Monitor children with weak muscles and limited muscular endurance to insure their physical limitations are not exceeded (be particularly sensitive to the weight of art tools and dangers of repeated motions). Also, be sensitive to children who tire easily, and provide limits to prevent fatigue. Check to insure children are not on medications that can impair judgment or can have dangerous interactions with art materials.

CHILDREN WITH PHYSICAL DISABILITIES. These children have difficulty in mobility, motor coordination and control, and problems in balance. They may have problems using tools safely and operating machinery. Falls and spills while handling art materials may occur. Nonbreakable containers should be substituted for glass containers. Medications may also affect perception. Ease of accessibility to art materials and tools for children in wheelchairs and in braces is recommended. Dangerous tools and machinery need to be inaccessible. Aides and volunteers can provide additional margins of safety. Children who use their feet or mouths to manipulate art media may be at risk for ingesting or absorbing art media, so care needs to be taken to use nontoxic media. Also, art tools that are used in the mouth need to be washed and sterilized between use.

CHILDREN WHO ARE DEAF OR HARD–OF–HEARING. Contrary to some myths, it is inadvisable to expose children with hearing impairments to excessive noise because additional damage to hearing may result. Deafness can be a serious hazard because audible warning signals are one way of warning people about danger. Children should be tested by specialists to determine if further exposure to noise could cause further damage. Protective gear including earmuffs and plugs may need to be worn around noisy equipment. Ear molds and hearing aids with vented ear pieces that are not fitted properly can transmit additional noise, so the fit of these devices should be checked periodically. Visual warning signals may need to be utilized in addition to auditory signals to alert children with hearing impairments of danger including fire alarms. Safety procedures and safety precautions must be clearly articulated, verbally explained and written so that learners with hearing impairments understand all safety regulations.

CHILDREN WITH VISUAL IMPAIRMENTS. Special precautions need to be taken to protect the children's eyes from chemical splashes, flying objects and infrared and ultraviolet radiation. Moreover, because some learners with residual vision may work at exceptionally close distances to art media and materials, there is greater danger that toxic substances can be absorbed and inhaled. Some solvents and art materials can cause further damage to eyes. If learners work at very close proximity to art media, fatigue may result and then they may be less alert to other potential dangers and more prone to accidents. Teaming volunteers and learners who have no vision problems with children who have visual impairments may be a good way of preventing possible hazards. Protective eye gear is strongly recommended (not only for students with visual impairments but for all students). Prescription lens goggles can be made. Good ventilation will be a priority for students with visual impairments who must work at very close range to potentially hazardous art materials.

Other General Guidelines

1. Students should not be allowed to use potentially dangerous machinery or tools if they are taking medications that affect the central nervous system, causing symptoms such as drowsiness, loss of coordination, dizziness, and slow reaction times.
2. Students taking pain medications should be monitored to ensure that the medication is not masking warning signals.
3. Students taking medications known to interact with the central nervous system should not be exposed to organic solvents, unless the solvents are used in a local exhaust hood. For example, oil painting and use of permanent markers or rubber cement in the open room could be particularly hazardous.
4. Students taking medications which might interact with alcohol or other chemicals or cause photosensitization should have their art

program evaluated to ensure that they will not be at excess risk for injury or illness.

5. Students taking any medication should be closely monitored by medical personnel to see if chemicals found in art materials might be causing an adverse reaction with the medication (McCann, 1987, p. 5).

OTHER PRECAUTIONS TO INSURE SAFETY IN THE ART ROOM: A HAZARD-FREE ENVIRONMENT AND ART PROGRAM

For children under the age of 12 years, only nontoxic art materials should be used. A list of these materials can be obtained by writing the Center for Safety in the Arts, New York, New York 10038. The list does not account in every case for long-term effects but only immediate hazards. The Arts and Crafts Materials Institute (715 Boylston St., Boston, MA 02116) does provide a list of chronic hazards for products. A form called the Material Safety Data Sheet (MSDS) can be requested from manufacturers of art materials. The MSDS should provide a list of ingredients, their industrial standards, data on health hazards, fire hazard information and "common chemicals with which it may react dangerously, and more" (Peltz and Rossol, 1984). Children with mental retardation who are chronologically older than 12 years should also use only nontoxic art materials.

Good ventilation is essential for any art room. Special ventilation is required when glazes are used and when a kiln is installed in a school or agency.

A plan for handling emergency medical situations should be in place. The plan should be updated on a regular basis.

If hazardous art materials are purchased and used in grades K–6, there may be cause for litigation (Fanning & Neville, n.d.). Additionally, if the art room is poorly ventilated and has other potentially hazardous situations such as tables that are not the right height for wheelchairs, space that inhibits mobility, etc., there also may be cause for litigation (Qualley, 1986). These factors may provide important justification for the teacher's school or the therapist's agency to provide a hazard-free art room and art materials and machinery (Fanning & Neville, n.d.) (Anderson, 1992, pp. 302–310).

THE ART SURVIVAL KIT: PURCHASE LIST
Based on Needs of Primary Class of 12 Children for Entire Year
(Metric equivalents are indicated in parentheses.)

It is *crucial* that all art materials be nontoxic. Materials will have their nontoxicity stated on the label. If there is no such statement, check with the manufacturer for their Materials Safety

Data Sheet (MSDS) or write The Art and Craft Materials Institute, Inc. (715 Boylston Street, Boston, MA 02116) for a list of products bearing the Certified Products Seal or the Approved Product Seal of nontoxicity.

Item	*Amount*	*Comment*	*Source*
Brushes	16, ½ inch (*c.* 1 cm), flat with short handles. 4, ¼ inch (*c.* ½ cm) wide. No. 6 watercolor can also be used.	There is no need to invest in expensive brushes. They wear out too quickly. Handles can be cut off if too long. Hold back a few for later in the year.	Local discount stores
Clay	50 pounds (*c.* 11 kg) of water base (earth) clay.	Check school for kiln. If using kiln, need to order 4 pints (*c.* 1840 g) of glaze. Check with art supervisor on recommended type.	School district local central warehouse or mail-order house may stock.
	Or 20 pounds (*c.* 9 kg) flour and 20 pounds (*c.* 9 kg) salt, mix to make flour clay.	Cannot be used for making wind chimes or liquid-holding containers. Mixing can take time.	School kitchen may provide, or local grocery store.
Construction Paper	2 packages of 50 sheets each in assorted colors, and 1 to 2 packages all 1 color (green, red, black, orange) 12 by 18 inches (*c.* 30 by 45 cm).	Can be cut in half for smaller sheets. If paper cutter is available, can order in larger sizes and save some money. Cheapest source will probably be central warehouse or mail-order house.	School district central warehouse, or mail-order house, or local variety and/or art store.
Crayons	1 box per child of 8 assorted colors, plus 4 extra boxes for refills.	Older children can use thinner crayons. Some classes may bring their own.	Same.

Drawing	4 packages of 50 sheets each, 12 by 18 inches (*c.* 30 by 45 cm). Cream manila or white paper, 60 pound (*c.* 27 kg) weight.	Can be cut in half for smaller projects. If paper cutter is available, order in larger sizes and save money. Drawing paper is also used for painting. Cheapest source will probably be central warehouse or mail-order house.	Same.
Glue	½ gallon (*c.* 2 1), white, nontoxic.	Can share with another teacher and buy 1 gallon of glue (*c.* 4 1)	Same. Local hardware stores also supply white glue.
	Or 12, 1¾ oz. (*c.* 49 g) containers for the children, and 3 larger 16 oz. (*c.* 450 g) containers.	Smaller containers can be refilled from larger ones.	
Markers	24 sets of 10 assorted colors; 2 or 3 sets of 15 assorted colors. 3 sets scented markers	Best to have 2 sets per child. (Save 1 dozen for second half of year.) Share larger sets. Use scented sets occasionally.	Local discount store, school district central warehouse or mail-order supplier.
Masking Tape	3 rolls, ¾ inch (*c.* 1.5 cm) wide, 60 yard (60 m) roll.	Need for displaying artwork, taping papers to work surface, etc.	Local discount stores often cheapest. School districts may provide as part of office supplies.
Newsprint	100 sheets of 12 by 18 inch (*c.* 30 by 45 cm).	Local newspaper may donate. Computer printout paper can be substituted. Local	School district central warehouse, mail-order house

		firms will donate used printout paper. Newsprint used for many drawing and some printing activities.	or local art store.
Scissors	12 pair, 4 inch (*c.* 10 cm), blunt; 2 pair pointed; 1 pair large desk type; 1 pair easy grip. Order 1 or 2 pair of left-hand scissors.	May need to order left-handed pairs. May need 4-holed training scissors. Some children provide their own.	School district central warehouse, mail-order house or local variety or discount store.
Tempera Paint	Dry 1 pound (450 g) cans. 2 each: red, blue, yellow. 1 each: black, white, orange, green, violet (purple), brown.	Dry paint is cheaper but must be mixed and stored. (Mix with liquid soap for easier cleaning.) Often the dry tempera colors are not as intense in color. If ordering liquid, increase amounts by 1.	School district central warehouse or mail-order house. Local discount stores may have in smaller-amounts.
Wrapping Paper	1 roll, 36 inch (*c.* 30 m) wide.	Can share with other classes. Often front office has wrapping paper. Scrap cardboard can be substituted in many of the activities. Makes a good large painting surface. White is more expensive than brown.	School district central warehouse or mail-order house.

THE ART SURVIVAL KIT: SCROUNGE LIST
**Based on Needs of Primary Class of 12 Children for Entire Year.
Before scrounging anything be sure there is storage space for the
items.**

Item	Comment
Cardboard	Can be used as a painting surface and for all kinds of construction.
Cloth Scraps	Test to be sure children can cut or tear.
Containers	Need potpie tins, butter tubs, tin cans, coffee cans for water, glue, paint, etc.
Knife	A sharp kitchen knife or single-edge razor blade needed to cut cardboard.
Mixing Bowls and Spoons	Needed for clay mixing. Probably can be borrowed.
Old Newspapers	Necessary to artproof work areas.
Paint Shirts or Smocks	Necessary for most art sessions. Each child should have his own.
Paper	Ditto paper, computer printout paper; other types might be scrounged.
Paper Towels	School or agency may provide.
Pencils	School or agency provides or child brings.
Plastic Bags	Drycleaning bags can be used. Smaller bags can be recycled. The school lunchroom or local grocery store may donate.
Sacks	School kitchen, local grocery stores can provide. Children themselves can collect and donate all sizes of paper sacks.
Soap	School or agency provides.
Sponges	Custodian may provide.
Stapler	School or agency office supplies.
Straight Pins	School or agency office supplies.
Water	Either via sink or via 2 or 3 buckets (1 for dirty water and brushes).
Wood Scraps	Lumberyard, construction sites provide free.

Note: Amounts have not been specified in the scrounge list. These would depend on the individual lesson planned, materials immediately available, the needs of the teacher and the children, and available storage space.

REFERENCES

Anderson, F. E. (1978). *Art for all the children: A creative sourcebook for the impaired child.* Springfield, IL: Charles C Thomas.

Anderson, F. E. (1992). *Art for all the children: Approaches to art therapy for children with disabilities.* Springfield, IL: Charles C Thomas.

Binney and Smith Co. (1987). *Selection, testing and specifications guide. Criteria for purchasing school art supplies.* Easton, PA: Binney and Smith International.

Doyle, L. (1993). LHAMA—What's it all about? *NAEA News,* August, Reston, VA: National Art Education Association.

Fanning, D. M., & Neville, M. J. (n.d.). *Does the new art material labeling law affect you?* Boston, MA: Art and Craft Materials Institute.

Hoover, F. L. (1961). *Art activities for the very young.* Worchester, MA: Davis.

McCann, M. (1987). *Teaching art safely to the disabled.* New York: Center for Safety in the Arts.

Peltz, P., & Rossol, M. (1984). *Children's art supplies can be toxic.* New York: Center for Occupational Hazards.

Salome, R. A. (n.d.). Suggested amounts of several basic materials for elementary art. Unpublished manuscript, Illinois State University, Normal, IL.

Qually, C. A. (1986). *Safety in the artroom.* Worcester, MA: Davis.

AUTHOR INDEX

A

Altschuler, R., 48, 53
Anderson, Frances E., 3, 8, 9, 11, 15, 23, 25,
　28, 30, 31, 40, 41, 48, 50, 52, 53, 55, 56,
　60, 71, 72, 78, 80, 81, 82, 83, 85, 86, 87,
　88, 89, 90, 91, 97, 98, 99, 100, 101, 102,
　103, 121, 129, 130, 145, 157, 158, 166, 189,
　192, 205, 241, 243, 248, 252
Anderson, J., 96, 99
Anderson, Tom, 119, 120, 122, 123
Arles, 108
Ash, L., 99, 101, 129

B

Banich, S.F., 206, 231
Banks, J.A., 206, 207, 231
Barbe, 112
Barnfield, Larry S., 69, 103, 129, 215
Barnfield, S., 87
Bergman, A.B., 186, 188, 190, 205
Beyer, B.K., 207, 231
Blandy, D., 3, 25, 84, 99
Bloom, B., 207, 231
Bloom, S., 160, 184
Bowen, M., 112, 113, 114, 115, 116, 117, 118,
　121, 125, 129, 130
Brancusi, Constantin, 110, 173
Brittain, L., 26, 27, 30, 34, 38, 39, 44, 46, 47,
　48, 49, 54, 86, 100, 101, 111, 131
Brommer, Gerald, 108, 130
Broudy, H.S., 107, 108, 130
Brueckner, M.M., 207, 231
Bruemmer, S.S., 140, 153, 158
Bruininks, R.H., 4, 25, 92, 96, 99
Buktenica, N.A., 177, 180, 183

C

Cain, S.E., 188, 205
Calder, Alexander, 110, 111, 177
Caldwell, H., 101, 105, 130
Callan, E., 59, 63, 64, 65, 68, 72, 83
Campbell, D.T., 90, 100
Canter, D.S., 82, 83
Cardinale, R., 121, 129, 130
Carey, D.A., 160, 183
Carin, A.A., 189, 190, 205
Carpenter, T.P., 160, 183
Catchings, Y.P., 101, 130
Cauman, S., 110, 131, 170, 173, 183
Cezanne, Paul, 170, 172, 173
Chapman, Laura, 51, 52, 53, 86, 99, 108, 126,
　127, 130
Child, J.S., 185, 205
Clegg, A., 206, 207, 231
Cohen, S.H., 186, 190, 205
Colchado, J., 80, 97, 99, 129
Cowen, J., 131
Craven, 125
Crosswhite, F.J., 159, 183

D

De Chira, E., 102, 130
Degge, R., 49, 54
de Kooning, Willem, 110, 198
de la Cruz, R., 102, 130
Doyle, L., 242, 253
Duke, L., 107, 130
Dunn, P., 30, 53

E

Effland, A., 92, 100
Eisner, E., 100, 108, 130, 206, 207, 231

SUBJECT INDEX

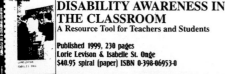